PAUL CLAUDEL

THE MAN
AND THE MYSTIC

PAUL CLAUDEL

THE MAN
AND THE MYSTIC

BY

LOUIS CHAIGNE

Translated from the French
by Pierre de Fontnouvelle

APPLETON-CENTURY-CROFTS, INC.
New York

TO
JACQUES DURON

PAUL CLAUDEL

THE MAN
AND THE MYSTIC

PROLOGUE

AN ASSESSMENT

We who had loved and admired him were gathered reverently around our old master, in the drawing room of his boulevard Lannes apartment, for a last homage, a parting salute. Paul Claudel rested on a low bed, cloaked in the majesty of death. Words are poor things at best, and we found them totally inadequate now. Only silence seemed worthy of the gratitude in our minds and our hearts at the thought of the great debt we owed him.

In Claudel we had known a man both disciplined and free. He was a pioneer, always open to progress, refusing to be bound or immobilized by the past. Each morning found him eager to behold, and show us, the gifts of the new day. At the same time, however, he remained on guard against the vain flights of fancy indulged in by so many pathfinders, and had inherited an earthy sense of reality from his peasant forebears.

He had traveled so extensively and acquired such a deep understanding of foreign civilizations and literatures that his broadness of outlook could be matched only by a handful of contemporary thinkers. This octogenarian had remained incredibly young in spirit. This nonconformist had proved abundantly that common sense should not be confused with mediocrity.

From *Tête d'Or* to *Le Soulier de satin*, with other masterpieces such as *L'Otage* and *L'Annonce faite à Marie,* he has left us a long poem made up of elements which are often biographical; where legitimate love or guilty passion are never renounced passively, but where, on the contrary, renunciation becomes a creative force developing its noble virtues in the spirit of the Beatitudes. Beethoven's *Appassionata* and *Ninth Symphony* introduce the same emotional climate, the same epic mood, transposed into music. But Claudel's greatness also shines forth in *Cinq grandes Odes,* which range with consummate ease from the esoteric to the familiar; or in *La Cantate à trois voix,* which sings of nature in all its glory but where, nevertheless, mere hedonism is tempered through an exalted sense of the supernatural.

Admittedly, this vast literary production has its flaws, some glaring or difficult to explain; enough in fact to keep generations of critics happily busy. We may feel quite confident, however, that an artistic achievement of such magnitude, scope, power, originality and beauty will stand the test of time.

Even if Claudel had not been a writer his faith would have been enough to command the admiration—indeed the envy—of the believers among us. This faith was the result and the reward of a long and agonizing struggle, the fruit of blood and sweat. After the sudden spiritual illumination experienced on Christmas Evening of the year 1886, he had to fight that *bataille d'homme* which Rimbaud wrote about, before yielding to his liberator. For many of us he will have been a *délégué à la lumière,* a messenger of light and of unutterable joy. His peaceful and happy death, which completes his Biblical and Christian side, bears witness to this contribution which, *sub specie aeternitatis,* surpasses all those he made to literature and art.

Such greatness is most uncommon, and the world is left the poorer for his death. Did Claudel's life close an era or, on the contrary, usher in this new century whose *Processional* he ordered in the unforgettable poem written from Shanhait-kwan in 1907? How could the answer remain in doubt when we sense, in his joyous and emphatic stanzas, the very substance of slowly nurtured beginnings?

When I first "discovered" Claudel he was fifty years old. In an issue of the *Mercure de France* François Porché drew a comparison between Péguy—whom I already admired, but might never have read had it not been for his heroic death and for the articles which Barrès devoted to him—Francis Jammes and the author of *Cinq grandes Odes*. If my memory serves me well, Porché wrote that Péguy's works reminded him of vespers in a parish church; Jammes' of devotions to Mary in a country chapel; and Claudel's of High Mass on Easter Sunday in St. Peter's, the most imposing basilica of Christendom. These are apt and striking comparisons.

The first of Claudel's pages which came to my attention immediately fascinated me through their stimulating originality, and even more so through the depth of Christian feeling which they embodied. Although rather startled by the unusual literary form—at once archaic and daringly new—I was deeply conscious of having entered an astonishing and stirring world of inexhaustible resources and attractions. All my senses were seized, nourished and transported with delight. I breathed in the pure air of the summits. I drank a generous wine with a slightly bitter and earthy tang. I beheld broad and luminous landscapes. I touched rough and primitive things, unamenable to adornment or paring. All my perceptions and feelings were heightened. Although love was not unknown to me, I had never experienced this expansion of being, this power, this violence. One particular paragraph delighted me in a special way and stood out from the rest, for it summed up my reasons for living, it provided an answer to this fundamental and persistent question: "Why has God created me, why has He brought me into the world?" An

answer already given by Catechism of course, but in terms
not always able to withstand the tempestuous probings of
adolescence:

> . . . the miserable circumstances in which we live, however,
> leave us with the feeling that something in us—and precisely
> the best and deepest in us, perhaps—remains unexpressed: it
> is this need, this great latent yearning which can be fulfilled
> neither by ordinary ethics nor by ordinary art. . . . Amid
> all our vain preoccupations we are pursued by the feeling of
> emptiness which accompanies inactivity, unless we embrace
> the Cross, which stretches us to our fullest dimensions.[1]

From love to the Cross, and from the Cross to Resurrection and fulfillment: such is the direction and progression of
Claudel's Catholicism. No different, to be sure, from the
orthodox view, but expressed in strikingly personal terms.
(It seems noteworthy and highly significant that the same
word, Passion, designates both the ardor of human love and
Christ's total sacrifice for the salvation of all men, even and
particularly the humblest.) . . . At last I found something
like a new vision of the world and of life.

On arriving in Paris I inquired after everything which in
any way concerned this truly inspired author. My first pilgrimage took me to the house where he had lived on the quai
d'Anjou on the île St. Louis, where I was later to meet his
mother and his sister Louise. In the cathedral of Notre-Dame
I found the spot where Grace turned this prisoner of darkness into a free man. My greatest wish was to meet him in
person. But he was then ambassador to Japan and seldom
returned to France. One day, however, I read in a newspaper
that he was soon to arrive in Paris for a short visit.

I saw him for the first time at the opening meeting of the
Catholic Theatrical Union, held in the hall of the Geographi-

---

[1] In an interview given to *Le Temps*, June 28, 1914, during the first
few performances of *L'Otage*.

cal Society, on the boulevard Saint-Germain. On the dais,
next to the Cardinal Archbishop of Paris, sat Georges Le Roy
of the Comédie française (who, much later, was to play the
part of the Pope in *Le Père humilié*), Henri Lavedan and
Paul Claudel. I was surprised that by far the most distinguished writer present was not called upon to speak: he
remained completely silent throughout the meeting, and no
one saw fit to consult him. But I noticed a gesture which to
me seemed perfectly in character. The impassioned and im-
petuous Le Roy, moved by some kind of inner fire, suddenly
launched into a flight of glowing oratory and dropped his
handkerchief. . . . Very deliberately, Claudel grasped it full
in his hand, rather than gingerly retrieving it with delicate
finger tips, and placed it in plain view on the green baize
table top.

A few days later Gaétan Bernoville invited me to a small
party given in honor of the poet. As I arrived and was about
to ring the doorbell I saw, next to me on the landing, a man
wearing a gray fedora and a yellowish raincoat, and immediately recognized Claudel. He entered very calmly, with a
kind of graceless composure, left his hat and coat, and was
shown into the salon with the placidity and good-natured
simplicity of a traveler who finds himself everywhere at ease,
and yet everywhere a stranger.

What did I hear him speak of that evening? I remember
that Henri Brémond was discussed: Claudel expressed regret
that the author of the monumental *Histoire du sentiment
religieux* had turned to less fruitful research in pure poetry.
In the course of the evening he also declared that Japan interested him enormously. Turning to his own theatrical works,
he complained of instances where some of the lines or scenes
had been cut from his plays by an overzealous producer
("Let them do as they wish, when I am dead"), and deplored
that Paris theatergoers were submitted to the tyranny of the
last evening subway ("In Bayreuth one is allowed all the

time necessary to follow the full development of Wagnerian dramas"). By his own admission, his knowledge of modern literature was fragmentary; judging from the samples he had read, however, it appeared to him sadly lacking in imagination ("Always the same stories of fornication and adultery, as though nothing else were of interest").

We proceeded to the dining room. Claudel stood by the mantelpiece, allowing himself to be questioned by anyone so inclined, and answered as though reciting a lesson learned in advance. I admired the poet's noble brow, rounded like a Romanesque arch, and his eyes, strangely motionless in the effort of concentration. I wondered at the curve of his mouth, quick to express disdain, greedy and sensuous perhaps, but appearing to scorn overdelicate savors. His opinions and assertions were phrased without grace or shading, in an almost mechanical voice, strongly marked with the accent of his native Champagne. He literally chewed his words, biting and tasting them as though they were a food, extracting all their flavor and pungency.

On another occasion I heard a conversation between him and a well-known bibliophile. As often happens, the introduction had been so perfunctory that neither realized with whom he was conversing. The lover of books was asked by his host whether he owned a special edition of any of the author's works, and answered that he felt it would have been the worst possible investment. Claudel didn't turn a hair, but merely removed his heavy tortoise-shell spectacles, polished them and put them on again, faced his detractor serenely, and said, "And yet, sir, I understand from Gal-li-mard [he emphasized each syllable] that a copy of the original edition of *Le Partage de midi* reached a price of [there followed a very large sum, which I have forgotten]." The host turned to the bibliophile, "It is Monsieur Paul Claudel to whom I had the pleasure of introducing you a few moments ago." The unwitting blunderer all but fell to the poet's feet. "Please

excuse me, Monsieur l'Ambassadeur. . . . In saying that such
books are a poor investment . . . I was only speaking relatively. Of course I know that, among your works, some . . ."
And the poor man floundered in his attempted explanation,
like Vauban with Louis XIV, after declaring that the king's
madrigal was a mediocre bit of versification. . . .

When he first allowed me to visit him Claudel lived at 80
rue de Passy, in a house which has since been razed and
whose site is now occupied by Franck, a fashionable tailor. I
was then twenty-five years old. He received me in a large
study where I noticed several Japanese curios, and a very fine
print of Piranesian proportions representing Roman ruins. As
I spoke of our time, of its iniquities and vulgarity, he pointed
out that the period of his youth was no better and that
he could not remember without a shudder of distaste the
eighteen-eighties, when Zola and his naturalists reigned supreme. When I mentioned his admirable correspondence with
Jacques Rivière, which had just been published and had left
me deeply moved, he told me that throughout his life he had
very often written to unbelievers or troubled Christians, and
that his advice had often benefited others than those for
whom it was originally intended. And he added, "If I have
sometimes been able to be of assistance it is because there
have been priests in my family. During the Revolution one
of my ancestors even hid a servant of God in her home, which
gave me the idea of *L'Otage*."

Sometime later I met Claudel's mother and his sister
Louise at the house on the quai d' Anjou, thanks to Dr. de
Massary—who was to die while still quite young. The apartment lacked that "humility" mentioned by Francis Jammes
in his memoirs, where poetic license at times pushes factual
truth into the background—unless we postulate that poetry
is the only kind of truth. I found a charming grandmother
of the old school, gracious and unaffected, with a definite
likeness to her son. When she stirred the fire I was reminded

of the scene in *L'Annonce faite à Marie* where Anne Vercors is conversing with his wife.

She had this to say about her son's plays: "*L'Otage* is beautiful, but in *L'Annonce* there is holiness." Louise Claudel (Madame de Massary, the doctor's mother) was equally affable and helpful. The devoted admiration she felt for her brother was clearly apparent, and she spoke at great length about him, although admitting that in childhood and youth she and the other members of the family did not understand him, and that his behavior nearly always struck them as unpredictable.

In 1927 I was invited by Dr. de Massary to visit Villeneuve-sur-Fère, Claudel's birthplace. I was the second pilgrim to be received there by the poet's nephew (the first had been a German writer). He drove to meet me at the Fère-en-Tardenois railway station, showed me the fifteenth- and sixteenth-century church with its fine stained-glass window by Maurice Denis; then took me to a strange place called Géyn, which reminded me of Violaine's desolate retreat when she became a leper. We finally reached the village built on the brow of a hill, a wind-swept height where the spirit blows and inspires hatred or love.

During another trip to Champagne, Claudel's mother invited me to dinner. The old house had changed somewhat since the poet's childhood, when he had found in it both terror and joy, but it was still full of his memories. The garden still held the tree he liked to climb, and in the branches of which he would dream of circling the globe or would conjure up a vocation of "gatherer of the earth." A little later, after returning from Japan and before leaving for his new assignment in Washington, the ambassador was to give me bad news of his mother; and at the same time recall this vocation. "It is infinitely sad," he commented, "to see someone so dear gradually lose possession of her faculties."

Pierre Lasserre's name came up in the course of our conversation, and Claudel let himself go, complaining bitterly that this critic seemed to be completely lacking in good faith since he persisted in judging him exclusively on the basis of his earlier plays. "It is true that *Tête d'Or* contains and prefigures all my later works, but nevertheless, *L'Annonce* and *L'Otage* add or develop many new elements." Claudel emphasized the idea that his entire literary production forms a balanced totality, and integrated whole, and said how thankful he was to have "closed the loop" and fulfilled the dreams which he had formed as a child and adolescent, in the garden of Villeneuve where I had followed his footsteps a short time before this conversation.

Before his retirement, and on the occasion of one of his trips to France, I had the privilege of another long meeting with Claudel on May 17, 1930. He complained of his innumerable incidental professional obligations—dinners, receptions, speeches—as distinct from his actual diplomatic activities. "It is the cross [of this career] and must be accepted. A priest once said to me, 'To fulfill the duties of one's estate, that is everything.' It was the same for Christ," added the writer. "Imagination is our greatest enemy. We must not be like the musician who is called upon to play the French horn, but who prefers the trombone, and keeps looking at his neighbor's score instead of concentrating on his own."

He then summed up the essence of Catholic life: Holy Mass, a daily quarter or half hour of prayer, of conversation with God ("even today, thou wilt be with Me in Paradise"), love of solitude and silence—which does not preclude concern for one's fellow men—namely, retirement into the cell spoken of in *The Imitation of Christ* (Book One, Chapter XX, Verse 5): "Thou wilt find in thy cell what thou wilt too often lose abroad." In a certain large foreign city he often approached various multimillionaires: "Many of them were likable, but they all gave the impression of being prodigiously bored with life." He spoke of beauty, of that "beauty on earth" extolled by his friend Ramuz: "It offers thanks in our stead, like a nightingale singing in a bush; we must bow humbly before it; such beauty was not made for our pleasure, but as a homage to God, Who created it." And he recalled the example—already given in one of his books—of a certain Brother Pacifique who wished to play the violin with two pieces of wood and who, although he had no bow, brought forth beauty in his own way. "I finally understood," he concluded, "that we must enter into the harmony of creation, counting ourselves as nothing; we have been placed on earth to write a story of God's choosing; our own story is of no interest."

I also remember seeing Claudel, shortly before the second World War, in the rue Jean Goujon; he had barely recovered from an illness and was deeply affected by the sudden death of his grandson. After the war I paid him another visit, at the rue Anatole-de-la-Forge, and found him rather angry at certain writers who, in the course of their café meetings, wanted to reform the Church, although the fact that they themselves did not fully and consistently practice their religion should have inspired them with more diffidence and less temerity ("For the slightest reason, if for instance they do not like the priest's face, they stop going to mass; their acts of generosity are mostly cerebral, mere 'intellectual exercises'; at least, the conventional and orthodox Catholics whom they despise and excoriate have left tangible good works behind them, and have given the Church nuns and priests.").

I will not dwell on several other occasions when I met Claudel very briefly, in the whirl of Parisian life. The last time I saw him was at the rue de Valois for the presentation of an important literary award. Age and deafness isolated him; he sat on a wide sofa in Olympian dignity. Upon leaving the building he realized that he had forgotten his hat, sent someone up for it, and briskly walked some distance to his car, chatting happily with his chauffeur as though they were old friends.

Such, then were my contacts with Claudel, and they form only a slender testimony. It would have been enlightening to witness him diligently following his daily schedule.

Paradoxically, everything was regulated, everything followed a set pattern and timetable, as far as possible, in the life of this supremely imaginative individualist. He arose at six, and was as punctual as the sun itself (during his last ten years, he allowed himself one extra hour in bed). After dressing, he would go to the nearest church and hear mass, which opened each of his days until he approached the age of eighty, when it became difficult for him to move about. Those who have read *La Messe là-bas* know the high value he set upon these daily conversations with a God every day younger. He returned home and ate a large breakfast with his family, after which he worked in his study until about eleven. At Brangues he would then putter around the park, shears in hand, snipping and pruning; not like a gardener attentive to the requirements of the hour or season, but in the manner of one whose mental processes are helped and stimulated by this manual exercise. By twelve he was back at his desk, and remained there until lunch was announced.

The main family meal, served at midday, never took place without him. His sturdy appetite was an encouragement to all. He would first inquire about the menu, then would express his satisfaction or disapproval after each course. His mother had been an excellent cook, and he had inherited from her an appreciation for well-prepared and tasty food. On one occasion he extolled "simple, traditional and sublime" cooking. For his last meal, on Shrove Tuesday, he enjoyed *andouillettes* and pancakes, hardly the fare of an invalid, or even of an old man. Diets were unknown to him, and he bore a grudge against his doctor, who had warned him not to use salt too freely. "If one can neither salt one's food nor pray," he said to his son Pierre, "life loses all its flavor." He could eat anything. At Brangues his favorite wine was Beaujolais. But he was far from scorning the bottles of Malaga which François Mauriac used to send him, nor the carefully selected cases of Sauterne which he occasionally received from his old friend Gabriel de Roton, who owned excellent vineyards. At the end of his dinner Claudel would drink a small glass of marc-brandy.

There was a strange, enigmatic, mysterious side to this uncommunicative, disciplined and withdrawn genius who had very few real friends. What a contrast between this secret self and the other facet of his personality which sometimes made him gay, facetious, brilliant and sociable if not gregarious! All depended on the kind of people he was with. If he did not feel in sympathy with them he would utter not a single word, and stubbornly refused to make the slightest effort to be amiable, or even polite. He would be swayed neither by social convention, nor by the rules of decorum, nor by the expediency of creating a favorable impression. His family vainly tried to influence him and reason with him; in this respect he never changed and never improved. This may be explained by his origins, his peasant stock, the "complex" he apparently developed toward his elder sisters, and also, perhaps, by deeply ingrained habits acquired in the course of a lonely childhood and during the exile of his various diplomatic missions. One day as I conveyed to him an invitation from some friends who had a genuine liking for him, he answered, "I am willing to accept, but I hate to be stared at like an animal in a zoo." He had an intense dislike for society, and in addition he defended fiercely—almost religiously—an inner life which, as a young man, he had at one time planned to devote entirely to God.

Just as joy is the dominant mood of his literary works, it

should be emphasized that cheerfulness was the main characteristic of his personality. He detested sadness like an enemy, like an alien presence. Whenever his family received bad news of any kind, whenever the home atmosphere became heavy with grief or trouble, he would take everyone to see a motion picture, which he generally abhorred. He knew how to appreciate a good joke, and it grieved him that the comic element in his plays, best seen in *Protée* and *L'Ours et la Lune*, was not generally understood by the critics or the public. He was a born mimic and his humorous impersonations were a delight to behold. Until the end of his life he enjoyed singing, and had a rich repertoire of old French folk songs[2] to which he added melodies and words of his own composition. He had a good ear for music, and could carry a tune perfectly, although his voice was perhaps a trifle harsh.

He appeared gruff and surly, and sometimes really was. But he could be kind, and knew how to show great tact, delicacy, consideration and thoughtfulness. Although proud, he was not without humility.

After proving an excellent father he practiced the art of being a grandfather, without affectation or self-consciousness. He loved children, especially little ones; watched them tirelessly, sat them on his lap, told them stories, and played happily with them. At Brangues he would often be seen on his way to the farm or vegetable garden, leading one of his grandchildren by the hand. During the last few years of his life he liked to mingle with children in the parks of Paris; they grew to know him, and he became a familiar figure to them. Within his family he greeted each new birth with joy, and would improvise a little poem for the occasion, as he did for christenings, anniversaries and first communions. Just as he favored smaller children, he seemed to show a preference for little girls.

[2] *Contacts et circonstances*, p. 172.

In the highest sense of the word, Claudel was an educator.[3] A singularly rich pedagogical treatise could be drawn from his works. His literary activities and diplomatic duties did not allow him much time to guide and supervise his children's schooling and general training, so that he left this important task to his wife. He always showed an active interest in these matters, however, and was particularly concerned with the religious upbringing of his sons and daughters. For many years the whole family would pray together every evening. He admired the traditional catechism taught in his youth, from handbooks written in the eighteen-twenties, or during other periods when the Church played a vital part in French life. He would answer his children's questions concerning the creed clearly and simply. When they failed to understand, he asked them to believe unquestioningly, explaining that religion implies mystery, and that faith is the test which every Christian has to meet. "Blessed are they that have not seen, and yet have believed."

Paul Claudel, whose early vocation to the priesthood was thwarted, might well have wished one of his children to enter God's service. If he entertained such a thought he never suggested it to anyone, however. In fact, young people who felt a call to the church sometimes came to him for advice, and he would caution against their own imagination those who seemed impulsive or impressionable, or those whose decisions might have been influenced by their families and friends.

He had always been an enthusiastic and tireless hiker, and walking formed an important part of his daily pattern. Nature in all its manifestations was a subject of endless fascination to him; he was eager to see it at firsthand, to immerse himself in it. In his youth he occasionally went on very long tramps lasting eight or ten hours, over several mountain passes in a single day. As the years went by he gradually

[3] *Conversations dans le Loir-et-Cher,* pp. 189-190.

reduced these expeditions to two hours, then to one. He also liked to split logs and help in the felling of trees, "to grasp nature by the hair in an invigorating struggle."

After lunch Claudel used to take a nap, after which he tackled the voluminous mail which daily reached his desk. He immediately answered all letters. Sometimes his replies were long, sometimes short, and occasionally they showed a certain informality (I know of an important personage who was deeply offended, and not totally without reason, at receiving a few kindly words of answer written on the very letter which he had sent the poet), but all were punctual and to the point. Requests for spiritual advice always received priority.

At five in the afternoon he would go to church again, and would spend an hour in daily adoration, an hour of presence: "I bring nothing and ask for nothing." He worshiped a Black Virgin, his "unfailing advisor." It was to him a subject of indignation that churches did not always remain open. "If, as some people unreasonably maintain, churches were meant only for praying, would they be closed exactly at the time they are most needed? The baker and the grocer would not put up their shutters just when housewives do their market- ing. But when do the faithful—and unbelievers, too—need God? Is it not at the end of the day when offices and factories close down; when the meaning of these words becomes so abundantly clear to us: 'Come to me, all you who are ex- hausted by work, and I will ease your burden?' Well, let them come! They will find everything locked, the main door and the side entrance." (*Seigneur, apprenez-nous à prier*, p. 45.)

Upon returning to the château, Claudel took a bath, changed into a specially tailored silk reading jacket, and sat down to the game of solitaire which for many years had been a part of his daily routine. After having dinner with his family he would read a few pages of a novel, then retire— never later than ten.

He was deeply interested in world events, and avidly studied several newspapers; all the more as he knew most large foreign countries and was familiar with their problems. In fact, he used to read much more than he admitted. An ill-informed reporter once wrote that Claudel did not like books. I asked him about this, and he protested, "On the contrary, I read a great deal." He enjoyed novels, especially English novels. He did not have a very high opinion of modern French literature which, he felt, all too often wallows in eroticism and pornography, and preferred to return to the French classics. He reread all Balzac in 1950, and all Racine in 1954. He even reconsidered certain harsh judgments made during his youth—on Goethe for instance—and particularly on Racine, whose seat he was to occupy at the Académie française, and whose works he came to admire deeply. Lives of saints always interested him, even when poorly written. He devoured periodicals and magazines, keeping informed of everything: painting, music, architecture, and especially science in whose progress he saw a ringing confirmation of his own intuitions, expressed in *L'Art poétique*.

During the period when he was fighting to recover his faith, Claudel often turned to Pascal, Dante, Newman, Bossuet's treatises, the translations of Hello, Catherine Emmerich, the great catechism of Hauterive—"filled and brimming with invaluable precepts—" and many other works and authors. He vastly enjoyed Chesterton who was in a sense his English counterpart, and Nathaniel Hawthorne. Jules Verne fascinated him. But there is little point in continuing this catalogue for he had read practically all important books and many others besides.

This poet preferred men of action and businessmen, and actually did not associate with many artists and dreamers, whom he sometimes looked upon with suspicion. His friends were nearly all "builders": Father Robert (of the Foreign Missions), Philippe Berthelot, Emile Francqui. What ap-

pealed to him in Herriot was not only a remarkable literary culture, but also his achievements in the economic
field and, in particular, the Lyons Fair. Brazil and the
United States were two diplomatic assignments cut to the
measure of a man in whom poetic vision merely sharpened
and heightened unusual native powers of observation and
analysis. In Brazil he was to meet an outstanding personality,
the jurist Ruy Barboza, who became Finance Minister in
1889 at the age of forty, and died in 1923.

These are a few selected and typical episodes of Paul
Claudel's long and astonishingly varied life. As the story
unfolds, other events and other facets of his personality will
gradually come to light.

I

PROVINCIAL TOWNS
AND VILLAGES

AS A CHILD PAUL CLAUDEL[1] ALWAYS RETURNED AT VACATION
time to the horizons of his early years, either at La Bresse,
in the Vosges—his father's birthplace—or at Villeneuve-sur-
Fère, in the Tardenois district,[2] where his mother was born.
Both places were central and umbilical to his childhood
and youth. Predestined to long trips, ocean voyages and explorations of distant continents, he received the benefit of
these deep roots. Every summer, until he set out for faraway
lands, these familiar settings witnessed the leisurely flow
of his life as a schoolboy and student. The rest of the year
was spent in various small provincial towns where his father,
Louis-Prosper Claudel, performed with resigned punctuality
and calculating prudence the monotonous duties of a minor
civil servant. Paul was of peasant stock, and his upbringing
was partly rural. But he was also to remember the austere
example of a bureaucracy pervaded with the musty smell of
old documents, notarized records and dusty real-estate
ledgers.

The road from Fère-en-Tardenois to Villeneuve climbs
through woods and meadows, through fields of wheat and
sugar beet, with occasional glimpses over wide stretches of

[1] The name Claudel seems to be derived from *claudus,* the Latin for
claudicant, or lame.
[2] A small district of prerevolutionary France covering parts of the
present departments of the Aisne and the Marne.

plain. It suddenly reaches the first houses of the village, and soon runs into a surprisingly large square with a tree-planted market place, two old wells, an unpretentious cenotaph, a town hall flanked by a tower, and, overlooking the cemetery, an old church whose leaning steeple has now been straightened and renovated. Near the church, facing each other, stand the two houses where a great destiny began. Paul Claudel was born on August 6, 1868, in the rectory— at a time when it was secularized and occupied by Dr. Athanase Cerveaux, his grandfather—"on a Sunday when the sun was shining brightly, just as the bells were pealing for high mass."[3] Opposite the rectory may be seen the patriarchal home into which the good doctor moved a year later, with his whole family. Gradually improved, renovated and modernized, it was to remain family property.

What can have been the thoughts of young Paul when he returned to his native Champagne and to the village of his birth from the small towns where his father Louis-Prosper was in charge of the registry office, and later served as registrar of mortgages? Shy, unsociable and uncommunicative by nature, he took no part in the pleasures of those around him, and enjoyed mostly the primitive elements and natural presences—both vegetable and animal—directly within his reach in this opulent but melancholy countryside. He did not scorn other beings, but from an early age he felt that no one understood him; and his sister Louise told us, without hiding her affectionate admiration, that his usual behavior disconcerted all those around him.

He dearly loved, and even worshiped, his kind grandfather; a figure who might have stepped out of a Balzac novel, and who enjoyed great authority in the district. A colorful type of country doctor, selfless and devoted, jovial and amusing. A Catholic of blunt and simple faith after the manner of Veuillot, he inspired respect through both his

---

[3] *Lettres à Gabriel Frizeau* (Gallimard), p. 51.

physical stature and a rare combination of professional and moral qualities.

In the Claudel-Cerveaux clan he was the main depository of authority. As for the future poet's father, family albums show him to have had ill-favored and unprepossessing features. Under a superficial guilelessness he appears as a prudent civil servant, careful not to jeopardize his future, escaping from his ledgers into bold, bizarre and fruitless daydreams and inventions. Completely lacking in charm, occasionally sarcastic, given to violent fits of rage, he was misanthropic by nature. He hated society and loathed strangers, and the atmosphere he brought into his home was more often stormy than peaceful. Although a former pupil of the Jesuits, he was hostile to the church, but had remained a deist. Discreetly opposed to the Empire, he could best be described as a cautious rebel. Unfortunately for his family, he unburdened himself only in the privacy of his home. And yet he understood his son, as a writer, much better than one might have expected. The letters he sent Paul about his literary works are surprising for the quality and pertinence of their judgments; some of his evaluations might have been signed by a literary critic.[4] It would be a serious mistake to confine him within the narrow purview of his professional activities. But this profession was to exert a definite influence on the frame of mind and way of life of the future diplomat:

> I could say that I became a poet through the grace or the caprice of some whimsical fairy, but that I was born a bureaucrat. My cradle, like Baudelaire's, was set not against a bookcase, but against a registry desk. . . . What the tang of brine and tar are to a sailor's son, that of official records was to me, and that secret fermentation rising from stacked papers.[5]

It is easier for me to speak of Claudel's mother, for I had met her on two occasions. After thirty years the dominant

---

[4] Cf. *Cahiers Paul Claudel*, No. 1, 1959.
[5] *La Table Ronde,* special issue devoted to Paul Claudel.

impression I retain of her is that of a humble and retiring
woman of marked peasant manner, much like Elisabeth in
L'Annonce faite à Marie, with certain traits which made her
resemble Colette's La Sido. I remember her stirring the fire
from her seat at the table and throwing morsels to her cat. I
can still hear her speaking of her son's works, which were
not entirely unfamiliar to her: "*L'Otage* is beautiful, but
L'Annonce is more beautiful still, for there is holiness in
it."

Her life was scored with trials and tragedy. While serving
in the army a brother of hers drowned himself in the Marne
at the age of twenty-three, in a fit of despondency. Camille's
mother could not escape being a *mater dolorosa.* And this
son Paul, of whom she could be proud, was also the child of
her tears. There was nothing in her of a Monique or a
Madame Acarie. Under the middle-class appearance of a civil
servant's wife, she was a peasant and nothing but a
peasant, knowing that every life is a cross. And yet among
her ancestors there were aristocrats as well as commoners.
The blood of both Coufontaine and Turelure flowed in her
veins. Pride of lineage, taste for service, and attachment to
honor mingled in her with a certain vulgarity of instincts,
worship of money and material possessions, resourcefulness,
lack of undue scruples, and a certain rustic, stolid and joyous
wholesomeness. Her own grandfather, a Thierry, had served
as village regent and later became a wood merchant; he
married a Mlle. de Vertus, who was descended from Louis
d'Orléans, brother of King Louis VI. One of Thierry's uncles,
a kind of desperado and a prodigal son, had rebelled against
the King, and his misdeeds had endangered the fortune im-
properly acquired during the revolutionary times. (H. Guillemin, *Revue de Paris,* April 1955, p. 23.)

Louis-Prosper and Louise first had a son, who was born in
1863 and lived only about two weeks. Their home was then
brightened by the birth of two daughters, preceding that of
the future poet. Camille, the elder of the two, was a radiantly

beautiful and physically precocious child; but she was also willful and hot-tempered, and soon entered into the family discussions through violent and unpredictable outbursts. Louise, the younger of the two girls and the least intellectual of the Claudel children, was to all intents and purposes a freethinker; under a surface traditionalism she harbored strong traces of Voltairian ideas. Irritable and high-strung, she was less domineering and more consistent than her sister. It would be tempting to draw a parallel between Camille and Mara on the one hand, and Louise and Violaine on the other. But this would distort the truth. Yet Paul was to recall, to a certain extent, oppositions and contrasts he had noted in his sisters, when he wrote *La Jeune fille Violaine*, the first draft of *L'Annonce*. Soon Camille was to devote her time to sculpture, Louise to music, and Paul to poetry. Too many diverse talents under one roof, with the inevitable consequence of diffculties and tragedies unthinkable in families not visited by genius!

Daily clashes and endlessly renewed quarrels made up the prevailing atmosphere of Villeneuve during the vacations. With more wit than truth, Paul Claudel blamed the "harsh wind of Villeneuve," which he sometimes hated, but in which he sometimes also liked to recognize a symbol of the breath of the Spirit. But he experienced keenly and painfully the lack of any real tenderness in his mother who could not even bring herself to embrace her own children. And before his sisters, who were "older and much shrewder" than he (to quote his own words), he was defenseless, awkward, and constantly forced by a kind of complex to yield and give way.

He felt intensely the sadness of this village, so often dark and rainy, but was grateful for the abundance of images and discoveries which its horizons offered him. He owed much to his long peregrinations, as a child and an adolescent, along the ageless forest roads where the entire history of

France has left its imprint and its signs. Later when he became an enthusiastic reader of English literature, he risked a comparison between Villeneuve and the extraordinary and spellbinding setting of Emily Brontë's *Wuthering Heights*.

Villeneuve [he wrote] is a harsh and austere place, a land of deeply ploughed fields and dark forests. With none of the usual gaiety of Champagne or of the charm of all those large vine-growing villages dozing in the warm sun, tucked into a comfortable curve of the Marne. It rains a great deal there, and when this happens it rains heavily, violently—I was about to say passionately. A cruel wind blows, the weathercock on the steeple gyrates ceaselessly and the weather vane of our modest house never stops squeaking. I can still hear that wet cry mingled with the splash of the gutter overflowing into the water barrel, while in an unused room I read, or rather devoured, with a huge interest which our classical literature had never in the least been able to inspire in me, *La vie des Saints,* by Alban Butler. Those who have not experienced the sadness, and who do not suspect the mixture of bitterness, compunction and inner satisfaction (I was going to say saturation), with which a Christian awaits the day of the Last Judgment, need only visit Villeneuve on the night of All Souls' Day, when a bell tirelessly tolls the knell, amid the torrents of an icy rain.

But there are even more distant memories: that of our old servant Victoire [Victoire Brunet] who, while tending her cow and opening fresh nuts for us with her sickle, told us, in a language studded with quaint local idioms, stories of olden times when the Duc de Coigny—whose name became famous through a sensational trial held under the reign of King Louis-Philippe—owned La Tournelle [an estate now belonging to Philippe de Massary, a grand-nephew of Paul Claudel]; the tale of the pilgrimage to Liesse, which in my imagination took on the importance of the travels of Marco Polo; the chronicle of the local families and their feuds, as bitter and ugly as those which inspired Dante and Saint-Simon. All this etched itself deeply into my memory. And there were also the personal explorations which I conducted toward the horizon. For Villeneuve, built on a kind of headland, commands four horizons—all as thrilling in my eyes, as rich in inspiration and legends as those of the Edda. There is the horizon to the east, the melancholy region of sheep runs and chalk hills darkened by all the movements of an enormous cloud mass in constant process of migration, formation and disintegration. There is the gloomy horizon to the south, the forest of La Tournelle with the fountain of La Sibylle in the foreground (just recently, I learned that in Old French, *sibylle* meant spinster). There is the horizon to the north, the beginning of that great plain sweeping endlessly to the sea, clothed alternately in plowed fields and crops, dotted with a multitude of melodiously named villages: Saponay, Cramaille, le Grand-Rozoy, Arcy-Sainte-Restitue. Without mentioning, farther away toward Soissons, Violaine and Coeuvres [so that some of the unusual names given by Claudel to his protagonists are actually borrowed straight from his native district]. In that direction I felt the call of the great invisible cathedrals—Laon, Rheims, Soissons. In the foreground were the old farmhouses of Combernon and Belle-Fontaine [Combernon was used as a place name in *L'Annonce faite à Marie*]. And finally there is the horizon to the west, as one discovers it from the old gables of Chinchy, standing on a headland: the knoll of Géyn, all heather and white sand, with its fantastic rock formations; and then the valley of the Ourcq, the water gap toward Paris, toward the world, the sea, the future![6]

Landscapes and nature were the great recourse of this lonely boy who sometimes muttered and stormed, in his harsh and heavily articulated voice, but who more often retired into prolonged silence. Their soothing influence had a powerful effect on him. Nor did he seek out these beneficent presences only to forget men and evade an ever-threatening opposition or hostility. He was already burdened with trials, struggles and difficulties. Ringing deep within himself, he

[6] *Contacts et circonstances*, Gallimard, pp. 24-26.

could not help but hear the imperious calls of life, at least during the time when the child was changing into the young man. Goethe's sound and pertinent advice to a despondent friend could have been applied to the future writer: "[I assured him] that one could recover from a painful moral state, from a morbid melancholia, only through the contemplation of nature and a sincere interest in the outside world. I pointed out to him that even the most general form of relationship with nature, such as the activity of a gardener or farmer, of a hunter or miner, draws man out of himself."

As a child Claudel still lacked the maturity—although his was precocious—to become fully aware of this gift of nature, but there is no doubt that this great blessing came to him at an early age. Indistinct and insistent longings made him seek something more, however. He had not been created and brought into the world to be satisfied with one place, one landscape, one province. Like all great souls, his yearning knew no bounds. Superior men build their familiar universe with all the elements visibly accessible to them and with everything which they invisibly sense or foresee.

A large and bushy apple tree grew in the garden at Villeneuve. It was probably in that tree that young Paul liked to climb, so as to meditate on the four directions of the wide world around him. One day he told me that, as a child, he had made the wish—which fate had later fulfilled—of circling the globe and *closing the loop.* An often-quoted page of lasting beauty, drawn from *Connaissance de l'Est,* allows us to share in this secret contemplation:

I can still see myself on the highest fork of the old tree, cradled in the wind, a child swinging among the apples. From this high point, like a god on his stalk—a spectator of the theater of the world—with deep contemplation I study the relief and the conformation of the earth, and the disposition of slopes and planes. With eyes as fixed as those of a crow I scrutinize the countryside stretching under my perch. My gaze follows the road which twice reappears on the crest of hills and finally vanishes into the forest. Nothing is lost on me: the direction of drifting smoke, the quality of light and shadow, the progress of work in the fields, yonder carriage advancing on the road, the shots of the hunters. No need for a newspaper in which I read but the past. I have only to climb on this branch to see, over the wall, the whole present unfolding before me. The moon rises; I turn my face toward it and am bathed in its light, high among the fruit. I remain perfectly still and from time to time an apple falls from the tree like a ripe and heavy thought.[7]

No, this young boy who escapes from his schoolbooks and from the depressing aura of his father's files and ledgers to taste the pleasures of the country cannot be content to remain within the walls of a garden. Everything calls him elsewhere. He needs both concentration and dispersion, solitude and participation in universal life. Designated by God, predestined to bear witness, he requires this recollection in a garden through childish ritual; or later through secret self-communion. And yet, at the same time, he must go farther afield to prepare for the ecumenical mission entrusted to him.

He had neither bicycle nor car at his disposal. As a free man, a "fierce individualist," he does not seem to have regretted the latter, which was not yet prevalent at the time, and he deplored servitude to the railway. But he praised the bicycle long before the *Tour de France* and the exploits of Lapize, Alavoine and Georget; and even more the motorcycle, which was better suited to his temperament. He wrote that with a motorcycle:

Instead of worming our way into nature we throw ourselves upon it, we seize it not only with our eyes, nose, mouth and face, but with our entire body—even the bone structure coming into play—with skin, stomach and lungs! Nature becomes ours, and no sooner have we rushed into it and

[7] *Mercure de France* printing, pp. 116-117.

swallowed all those horizons hurtling at once toward us, than
it is definitively and triumphantly thrown back over our
shoulder, dissolving like that cloud of dust—like that trail
of pungent blue vapor—which we leave as a trace of our
passing. [And a motorcycle appeals to him because it is]
Pure freedom, directly adjustable to our limbs, whose power
it does not replace, but multiplies.[8]

Be that as it may, he was quite satisfied with walking. This
was his favorite form of exercise, "those long jaunts, cane in
hand, through suburbs and along straight interminable highways, before reaching some arbitrary embarkation point
from which to launch into dreams and the future." Walking
allowed him to contemplate, in more detail and depth, the
various places he visited. Reading Claudel's works composed
long after these childhood years, *L'Otage* or *L'Annonce,* for
instance, one realizes what they owe to the boy's patient
exploring of the Villeneuve countryside. Throughout his life,
as a matter of fact, Claudel kept the habit of the long daily
walks which were in harmony with his wish to penetrate to
the very core of the created world. Possessed with a passion
for the universe, he was anxious every morning to see everything which the new day had to offer.

Maurice Barrès, with whom he had a few contacts, and
who considered devoting a study to Claudel, coined a famous
declaration of purpose: "The earth and the dead." To this
motto by the author of *Les déracinés,* Claudel opposed his
own device: "The sea and the living." Actually these two
programs are not incompatible, but complementary. To the
child exploring the world around Villeneuve, the earth and the
dead were just as important as the presence of the living and
the call of the sea. The tragic quality of his storm-swept
native district, so rich in threatening and obsessive omens
and symbols, was no doubt to a large extent at the root of
his dramatic creativity.

[8] *Contacts et circonstances,* p. 215.

Le Repos du septième jour always reminds me of the small cemetery near which the Claudel family lived. To reach the church one has to pass through its gate and walk along its paths. A few graves command attention. This moving epitaph can be seen on that of the poet's great-grandparents, who died in 1833 and 1837: "Goudelancourt, near Liesse in Picardy, was their birthplace. Both died full of hope and faith, in the arms of their children. Let us pray for the dead." There are also the graves of his maternal grandfather, Doctor Théodore-Athanase Cerveaux; of a Cerveaux grand-uncle, who was Pastor of Villeneuve; of the poet's father and mother and of his sister Louise. Claudel once explained to me that his religious vocation (which was unfulfilled through obedience to his spiritual advisers, but nevertheless remained a potent influence throughout his life) arose from the fact that one of his forebears had, at great danger to herself, hidden a priest in her home during the Revolutionary Terror. She had vowed to consecrate her own son to God if the priest escaped his persecutors. This family episode, I feel, inspired Claudel to write *L'Otage*.

The old church of Villeneuve, into which the child so often entered, in no way resembled the rustic temple of Milly, dear to Lamartine; nor that "low-arched" sanctuary lovingly described by Hugo; nor "the church clad in leaves" where Jammes prayed, wept and allowed himself to be taken by the hand. The single nave receives too much light from the twelfth-century bays, and no fine stained glass remains, except for a fragment dating from the Renaissance. The choir is decorated with carved wood paneling of indifferent artistic merit, representing the apostles. A naive St. George on horseback lifts a pitiless weapon against a fabulous beast. A St. Sebastian framed by votive offerings recalls that this was once a land of archers. Young Paul often came here to pray during his childhood; much later when faith, as though by miracle, was returned to him; and later still at irregular intervals in the course of his eventful and peripatetic life. A life whose unity, at such times, may have seemed restored, but which was destined to be broken and torn anew.

In 1870 Paul Claudel's father was transferred from Ville-neuve to Bar-le-Duc where he was to occupy a similar administrative position. He reached the former capital of the duchy of Bar during the early part of August. France had been at war with Prussia since July 19 and fighting was taking place near by. On September 2, Napoleon III was defeated and surrendered at Sedan.

As a child, it seems that Paul Claudel liked this provincial town of quiet beauty and unobtrusive charm. The poplar-planted banks of the Ornain River invite strollers to dream and meditate. In the upper part of the city a belvedere affords a wide view over the valley crowded with houses, old mansions and monuments.

Louis-Prosper Claudel took over the office and living quarters of his predecessor, a man named Clément, at 26 rue de la Banque, since renamed boulevard Poincaré. In 1873 he moved to 27 rue du Cygne, a street unrecognizable today due to the devastation wrought by the First World War.

Young Paul was sent to a school run by the Sisters of the Christian Doctrine, at 36bis of the same rue du Cygne. Later he was to remember Sister Brigitte who taught him Sacred History, with the help of crudely colored but highly effective pictures. The eyes of this "amazed child" stared at Abraham ready to sacrifice his son, at Jacob's dream and Eliezer's voyage, then at the story of Joseph and the New Testament:

> With what simplicity and reverence I made acquaintance with Our Lord, His Mother and His Apostles, and gazed upon a large picture of Jesus: it was noonday and He stood near a well like that of our garden in Villeneuve, conversing with a Samaritan! What sadness, what a sorry contrast, to leave those blessed scenes and—far from Bethel where God's

word rings—to enter the tangled paths, the horrible and muddy trails of profane history![9]

Claudel would never forget the solemnity or picturesque quality of the religious processions which he followed, banner in hand. In the fall of 1875 young Paul entered the town lycée as a day-pupil in the second division (first section of the primary education grades). His teacher was named Lasseaux. The atmosphere of this school was described with a certain animosity by Louis Bertrand—the famous member of the Académie française and author of a remarkable book on St. Augustine—who passed through its portals three years later as a boarder:

> Through a side door we entered the small courtyard which preceded the lycée. This little square is delightful, with its clumps of linden and chestnut trees left over from a former pasture! And the lycée, then fresh and new, had a most engaging appearance. It was modest, without architectural pretention, but so young, so tidy, so charming! All this should have pleased other eyes than mine.[10]

Another student at the same lycée was in the top classical form as Paul Claudel started his first year there. He belonged to a great family of the Bar-le-Duc *bourgeoisie,* and was to become a major historical figure. His name was Raymond Poincaré. Born in the Lower City, at 35 rue des Tanneurs, now rue Nève, he must have been proud, on his way to the school (which was situated between the railway tracks and a branch of the Ornain), to read on the street signs the name of Landry Gillon, his great-grandfather. He excelled in composing Latin verse, and was soon to bring credit to his lycée by receiving an honorable mention in Latin translation at the *Concours Général,* a yearly competition between the top students of the upper forms in all French schools.

As for young Claudel, he was still only at the very first and

[9] *Les Aventures de Sophie,* Gallimard, pp. 54-55.
[10] *La nouvelle éducation sentimentale,* Fayard, p. 5.

arduous stage of scholarship. In the honor list of the 1876 Prize Giving, however, his name appeared twelve times. His perseverance at work, stimulated by the exhortations of a demanding father, did not completely divert him from extracurricular preoccupations and pursuits which already revealed the awakening of the poet in him. Deliberation, circumspection and cautious wisdom were exuded by this ducal and industrial town of Lorraine where knitted goods plants and jam factories did not make the inhabitants forget the glories of the past, inscribed on so many stones. But Paul Claudel's inner ear was attuned to other solicitations. Bar boasts no less than three waterways: the two branches of its river, and the Marne-Rhine canal which forms the boundary of the town on the north and the east. Of an evening, the child would walk by the water and hear, "behind the fir trees, deep in the forest yonder," the call of the hunting horn—"that harsh sobbing, the past with us, what is no more and what has never been."[11]

In the church of Saint-Etienne he must have seen the famous skeleton by Ligier Richier, once part of the Prince of Orange's tomb. A realistic piece of sculpture, a nightmarish vision which the child may have remembered when his grandfather's death brought him to the brink of despair.[12]

On August 22, 1876, Louis-Prosper Claudel was appointed registrar of mortgages in another small town, Nogent-sur-Seine, only a hundred kilometers away from Paris. Nogent, which has three thousand inhabitants (against Bar's fifteen thousand), is supported by its food industries. Works of two sculptors may be seen there, and both were to play a part in the life of the Claudel family. One is Paul Dubois who was to die in 1905, and the other Alfred Boucher who lived until 1934. The latter had the merit of discovering the exceptional

---

[11] *Figures et paraboles*, pp. 165-166.
[12] I owe part of my information on Claudel's years in Bar-le-Duc to Msgr. Aimond, the well-known local historian.

talent of Camille Claudel, who was thirteen when her family met the sculptor. She had already started to model clay. He gave her lessons and was happy to note that she followed his instructions with the passionate interest which she devoted to all her pursuits.

The registrar's house was on the rue Saint-Epoingt and had a small garden, much to Paul's delight for it afforded him opportunities to retire into his own private thoughts. There could be no question of sending the eleven-year-old boy to continue his studies in Paris, and the local schools appear to have been inadequate. It was decided that he and his sisters would be privately tutored, and a journalist named Collin was chosen. Young Paul became very attached to him: "He was intelligent, discriminating and quick, slightly unconventional, and a staunch Republican; he read to us *Le Roman de Renart, La Chanson de Roland,* and Victor Hugo's *Les quatre-vingt-treize.* We were very fond of him. I owe him my faultless spelling."[13] It was probably around this time that his father, as a special treat, took him to the *Comédie Française* where Mounet-Sully and Sarah Bernhardt were playing in *Hernani.* It should be added that Claudel was also indebted to Collin for a solid foundation in Latin, and that his tutor developed in him a taste for Aristophanes to such an extent that his father, finding him one day with the complete works of that poet (from which Collin usually selected carefully expurgated extracts), took the volumes from the boy, who —in his opinion—was too young to read them.

On September 10, 1879, after three years in Nogent, Louis-Prosper Claudel was transferred to Wassy-sur-Blaise, in the Haute-Marne. This new assignment removed the family farther from Paris, which is more than two hundred kilometers distant, but at least Wassy boasted a good secondary school, and the Claudels were able to settle in a spacious and

[13] Cf. Henri Guillemin, "Claudel jusqu'à sa 'conversion,'" *Revue de Paris,* April 1955, p. 25.

pleasant state-owned house. Paul took to this small town, sadly famous for being the scene of a massacre which triggered the Wars of Religion (this occurred on March 1, 1562, in a barn situated on the rue du Prêche). He studied well there, in small classes, and attended catechism in a venerable Romanesque and Gothic church containing a fine carved-wood burial scene. This is where his First Communion took place, on May 23, 1880, and he noted that a noble prayer to Jupiter—written by Cleanthes, a Greek poet of the third century B.C.—sustained his fervor better than the nonliturgical sections of his prayer book. It was, he wrote much later, "a good First Communion; the crowning point and the end of my religious practices, as for most young boys."[14]

After having described Villeneuve, to which Paul Claudel belonged through the maternal side of his family, we must turn in thought to La Bresse, in the Vosges, where the poet's paternal relatives still lived. It is a pleasant summer and ski resort, at an altitude of about eighteen hundred feet above sea level, in the shadow of the towering mountains, not far from Gérardmer and its lake. Only the church and cemetery survived the war. The Claudel children used to spend part of their summer vacations in La Bresse (when they were not at Villeneuve), and would swim in the Lac des Corbeaux. Their father felt happier and more at home there than anywhere else. He had many relatives in the area, among them paper-makers, foresters and descendants of tax collectors. This meant numerous visits, glasses of good wine, joyous meals and endless conversations. Paul enjoyed these outings and the friendly relations with neighbors, which were made all the easier by his father's knowledge of the local dialect. He would go to Bocelles, a hamlet near Bruyères, to see his god-mother Marie Claudel who was only eight years older than

---

[14] "Ma conversion," *Contacts et circonstances* (Gallimard); and *Memoires improvisés*, transcribed by J. Amrouche.

himself. How proud she had been to hold the infant over the baptismal font, even though no one could have foreseen his brilliant destiny!

Claudel's roots were in the Vosges and in Champagne, both in northeastern France. He was to feed on the variety of his family background to prepare that conquest of the universe which is less of an illusion for a poet than for a soldier.

2

THE PARISIAN STUDENT

DURING THE YEAR 1881 AN IMPORTANT EVENT MARKED THE life of young Claudel. His grandfather, Athanase Cerveaux, died on September 5, in Villeneuve. From Wassy-sur-Blaise, where her husband performed his administrative duties, Madame Claudel, accompanied by Paul, had gone to the old doctor's bedside. It was with deep feelings of aversion, and even terror, that the boy witnessed "hour by hour" and "day by day" the slow and frightful death struggle of his beloved grandfather, who was gradually consumed by an incurable cancer. He later blamed his parents for not taking pity on his tender years, and for forcing on him the sight of such a tragic end. They must have been either strangely unperceptive or pressed by material necessities, not to have spared him this ordeal. At the age of thirteen it threw him into a kind of desperate panic, shaking his emotions and temperament to the core.

This was the forerunner of a dark succession of events; a grim introduction to the bitterness of human existence. One day he would associate the scar left by this great sorrow with *La joie de vivre*, a novel by Emile Zola which appeared in 1884 and brought him the sudden awareness of a real loathing for life: "Around us, and from one horizon to the other, it is the vision of death, everything has lost significance and interest, stupidly on the way to cassation, ourselves inwardly eaten away by a relentless enemy."[1]

[1] *Paul Claudel interroge l'Apocalypse* (Gallimard), pp. 112-113.

But his father looked to the future of the three children with confident optimism. Camille showed a definite talent for sculpture: she would be an artist and would become famous. Louise was an accomplished pianist: she would win renown as a musician. And Paul was a responsible lad and a good student: he seemed cut out for the Ecole Normale Supérieure. Perhaps he would one day hold—why not?—a professorship at the Sorbonne. These fine plans and prospects required years of intensive preparation which could properly be carried out only in Paris. He would send his whole family there, after trying to obtain a new assignment which would bring him closer to the capital. His efforts were successful, and in June 1883 he was appointed to Rambouillet.

When this appointment appeared in the Official Gazette Madame Claudel and the children had already been living in Paris for a year. The father's dreams and careful plans had been accompanied, or perhaps even preceded, by the strenuously active ambitions of his daughter Camille. Convinced of her own genius, she was quite capable of bending her mother, sister and brother to her will, brushing aside all objections and overcoming all obstacles. Paul admired her extravagantly. He also stood in awe of her, which may be explained, in part, by the memory of the many gibes and smacks she had inflicted upon him. It seems that he lost his religious faith at about the time when Camille arrived in Paris, shortly preceding the rest of her family; this faith, incidentally, had never been very strong in her or in the Claudel parents. Their first apartment was on the boulevard du Montparnasse, but they soon left it and moved to the rue Notre-Dame-des-Champs. Every Sunday the father came to Paris, briefly partook of family life, and returned to Rambouillet very early Monday morning.

Young Paul-Louis was deeply affected by the breakup of the family circle. In October 1882, he entered the lycée Louis-le-Grand which, at 123 rue Saint-Jacques, carries on the traditions and reputation of the collège de Clermont, made famous by the Jesuit Fathers. This was a completely new atmosphere for him, and he felt painfully out of his element. After leaving the fourth form in a provincial school, here he was, suddenly placed in the sixth form of a large Paris lycée. The headmaster was a certain Mr. Gidel, and his teachers for the most important subjects were called Bernage, Gaspard and Mangin. Bernage was a distinguished humanist; one of his daughters, Berthe, was later to play, through her novels, the role of spiritual director to countless young girls. Gaspard lacked eloquence and breadth of intellect, but was a superb stylist and a meticulous master; he wore out his health and his eyes correcting the assignments of his pupils. Mangin almost literally compelled Claudel to become interested in the natural sciences.

Among Claudel's fellow students some belonged to prominent families, and others were to make names for themselves as he did. There was Roman Rolland, who became his friend; Johannes Wehrlé, who later entered the priesthood; Fortunat Strowski, with his blue eyes and feline countenance, who was destined to high academic positions and honors; Paul Jonnart, a future Governor General of Algeria and member of the academy; Chavannes, who later turned to Sinology; Jean Guiraud, soon to launch into a threefold career as professor, historian, and journalist; and Gabriel de Roton, a clever draftsman who drew sketches of Claudel during this period (later in life they were to share a common interest in Greek vases and in Homer).

Young Claudel worked and studied furiously, but his soul was plunged in bitterness. During those years the prevailing intellectual climate was bleak and harsh. The Republic of the Dukes had ended. Gambetta, mysteriously wounded, was about to disappear from the scene. Jules Ferry had pushed through his educational legislation. Together, Renan and Taine reigned supreme, and in official circles were both surrounded with a respectful deference which was to keep the title of "Monsieur" before their names even long after their deaths. Bourget was just starting to defy the literary trend set by his elders, and to write a series of perceptive and penetrating psychological essays. Vallès and Bloy, those impenitent rebels, rose in open revolt against their time and charged their belligerent writings with verbal dynamite.

One suspects that the atmosphere in the Claudel household must have been stormier than ever, with Camille pressing her vociferous demands for greater independence, and her father demanding quick results from his children in return for the sacrifices he had made in moving his family to Paris. To top it all, the poor boy had lost his faith. One day at Villeneuve, Camille had waved a copy of Renan's *La vie de Jésus* in front of her family and cried out, "As far as religion is concerned, everything we have been taught is nonsense; here is the proof." The tyrannical authority she enjoyed was such that her outburst made a deep impression. The few beliefs which may have remained deep within Paul's soul were destroyed by the teachings he received at Louis-le-Grand. In a Paris lycée at that time it was impossible for a student to acknowledge even the slightest degree of faith. Everything was uniformly and completely black.

"Gambetta is dead. The year opens with this clap of thunder," wrote Ludovic Halévy in his *Carnets* on January 1, 1883. This was his judgment of the late statesman: "He was no longer anything, neither conservative nor radical; he was Gambetta." Paul Claudel was among the two or three thousand students who, on January 6, marched in or watched the stately funeral procession slowly moving from the Place de la Concorde and the rue de Rivoli to the Pantheon, to honor the god of the lower middle classes. The sight may have dazzled the young provincial by its pomp, but was not such as to give him a high opinion of official ceremonies of this type.

The spectacle offered nothing which might really have drawn him out of his disconsolate thoughts.

At the end of the 1882-1883 academic year, young Claudel failed to pass the baccalaureate. This failure smarted all the more since the age requirements had been waived in his favor: he was hardly fifteen at the time of the examination! He suffered beyond words to see that all his efforts in the course of that year of ordeal had been in vain. And it was deeply humiliating for him to have to face his irate father, who was most outspoken in his displeasure and disappointment, and who held up to him the consistent scholarly achievements of a certain Théodore Colardeau, Paul's most brilliant fellow student.[2] The elder Claudel refused to be mollified by the fact that his son had won Prize Giving laurels which were not to be sneezed at: a first prize in modern French oratory, barely wrested from Colardeau; and a first honorable mention in classical recitation, a "subject" in which Romain Rolland obtained only a fifth mention. (Who would have guessed, at the time, that he was writing a first Aristophanic play entitled *L'Endormie,* which was to be the initial draft of *Protée?*)

The awards were made in the lycée Louis-le-Grand itself, on August 7, at eleven in the morning. The descriptive program carried this pompous heading: "Solemn Prize Giving, under the chairmanship of Monsieur Renan, member of the

[2] Théodore Colardeau came out first in the competitive examination of the Ecole Normale Supérieure. His thesis on Epictetus shows him to have been a specialist highly familiar with Stoicism, as well as an eminent Hellenist. He became Professor of Philosophy at the University of Grenoble. He suffered a severe paralytic stroke and lost the power of speech, while retaining unimpaired intellectual faculties. As in a Greek tragedy, a kind of fatality weighed on his family. One of his daughters, in a fit of despondency, threw herself into the river Meuse at Mézières. Obsessed by her death, a son also committed suicide. Another daughter carried the spirit of sacrifice to the highest point; after the death of her father, who was rescued from atheism by his friend and colleague Jacques Chevalier, she entered a Belgian Benedictine convent.

Academie française, administrator of the College de France, assisted by Monsieur Perrens, Inspector of the Academy of Paris, representing the President of the Council, Minister of Public Education and Fine Arts."

Mr. Gidel, the headmaster, hiding an unexpansive kindness under a grave and icy countenance, had for the occasion abandoned the little black cap which, according to Léon Daudet, made him look like a disgruntled surgeon. Renan, small, plump and smiling, was of course very much the center of attraction. He was considered as something of a god by his admirers, and graciously allowed them to pay homage to him.

When everyone was seated Mr. Jacob, the professor of rhetoric, delivered the opening address. He congratulated Renan on the language "of which he holds the secret; substantial and warm like the painting of the masters, harmonious and intricate like the melody of beautiful poetry," and thanked him "for having diverted this day from his meditations and devoted it to this academic celebration." He hailed the Louis-le-Grand students, "hope of a people with a memory." He quoted La Bruyère, Joubert and Lacordaire, and ended with this plea, which was no doubt warmly applauded: "Remain students; tomorrow, when the country needs you, it will find men."

Then Renan stood up. One can imagine the almost religious silence which fell over the audience. We may assume that young Paul Claudel was particularly moved. Attentive as usual to the smallest details, he no doubt reverently received and pondered every single word spoken by the admired master.

> Young students, [said Renan] you will see the twentieth century. This is, I admit, a privilege I envy you. You will see unexpected things. You will hear what is said of us. You will know what will have proved fragile or lasting in our dreams. When that time comes I beg of you not to be too

harsh. This poor nineteenth century, which will be so abused, will not have been without its good features, sincere minds, generous hearts and heroes of duty. Succeeding generations are generally unfair to the past. You are the nursery of future talent. Sitting there among you I fancy seeing the critic who, around 1910 or 1920, will call the nineteenth century to account. I can imagine the article he will write (allow me to give my imagination free rein): 'What a sign of the times, for instance! How could one flout more completely all the healthy conceptions of what is suitable! In 1883 someone had the strange idea of selecting, to preside over the presentation of awards at the lycée Louis-le-Grand, a man who, although harmless, was the very last one who should have been chosen at a time when it was imperative to strengthen authority, to show firmness and warmly to achieve the *convicium sæculi!* He dispensed good advice, but what lack of vigor! What an absence of anger against his time!' That is what the twentieth-century conservative critic will say. After all, perhaps he will not be entirely mistaken.

Twenty-four years later, composing his *Magnificat* while in China, Claudel wrote these lines, which express a bitter resentment against Renan and a few others:

Abide with me, O Lord, for night is coming. Do not forsake me!

Do not leave me with Voltaire, and Renan, and Michelet and Hugo, and all the other infamous!

Their souls are with the dead dogs, and their books have been thrown in the dung-pit.

They are dead, and even after death their names are poison and decay.

These were harsh words and will sometimes be held against Claudel for their lack of Christian charity. They reveal an outburst of emotion brought on by the thought of an author who made him, and many others, lose the greatest of all blessings. He could not forgive Renan for never mentioning Jesus' clear and repeated assertion that He was the Son of

God. Claudel sees in this deliberate oversight a major imposture, a monumental deception compounding the responsibility of a master who drew thousands of human beings into darkness, and very nearly made him sink into the night. He eventually forgave Hugo, who inspired him with some beautiful pages, in the strictly esthetic sense. But he never absolved Renan, who proved prophetic in sensing that one of his listeners would deal harshly with him some day. As a matter of fact, Claudel is not the only one to have denounced Renan's influence and that of his time. Léon Daudet spoke of the "stupid nineteenth century," and was grateful to Renan only for having composed *Réforme intellectuelle et morale,* which provided grist for his nationalist mill.

Claudel's philosophy professor was Auguste Burdeau (1851-1894), a native of Lyons, who served Barrès as a prototype for Bouteiller, one of the protagonists in *Les déracinés.* Burdeau was a great admirer and advocate of the categorical imperative, which—according to Daudet and Camille Mauclair—gave rise to "violent altercations" between himself and Claudel. Outside the subject of Kant, however, Paul felt great affection and esteem for his master, who was very much of a spiritualist as well as a seeker after perfection. He told me one day that Barrès had slandered him; actually, *Les déracinés* had only fictionalized him.[3] These lines by Burdeau bear witness to the nobility of his thinking:

> I firmly believe [he wrote to a friend on August 7, 1892] that we turn our backs on truth in taking as the only purpose of our efforts an increase in man's material well-being. We forget that the true lever of the world and the most certain cause of all happiness are sacrifice and the joy of self-sacrifice. . . . Although an admirer of the Greek philosophers, and particularly of Socrates, I think that Christ uttered the noblest words ever heard by human ears: "The

[3] At the end of his life Barrès was to mitigate the severity of his judgments. See the last of his *Notebooks* (Plon).

kingdom of the earth and of heaven belongs to the one who knows the way of love and self-sacrifice."[4]

Burdeau's teachings were to bear fruit in his pupil. At the same time, young Claudel drew profitable and enlightening comparisons between Goethe, Leconte de Lisle and Flaubert, on the one hand, and Baudelaire and Dante on the other. (In Compiègne, he was to become an avid reader of the great Italian poet.)

Claudel passed his second baccalaureate examination in July, 1885. A month earlier he had witnessed Victor Hugo's funeral, a deeply impressive and unforgettable sight to the young poet. He stood for three hours on the boulevard Saint-Germain to watch the procession, which was described with feverish intensity by Léon Daudet and Maurice Barrès.

The thought of another death—his own—loomed on the youth's horizon. Driven to desperation by the entirely materialistic ideas dispensed at that time in schools and universities and by the depressing moral atmosphere of the period, he finally came to the point of considering suicide. One day he actually put a gun to his head. But his vital instinct prevailed. Divine Grace, in which the young man no longer believed, kept watch over his exceptional destiny.

Almost in spite of himself, circumstances and his own curiosity made him a true Parisian.

I was [he said] a prisoner of this Tyre and of this Babylon. I wandered deep within the dark bowels of the city, expecting to read on the street signs, instead of rue Saint-Jacques and rue du Faubourg-Poissonnière, the names of Hell Street and Despair Square. I paced with horror the frightful districts of Charonne and Belleville, of the gas tanks and slaughterhouses. . . . Every Sunday I walked down the rue Mouffetard and back again, a yard at a time, and those

[4] Quoted by Victor Bindel in *Claudel* (Vrin), pp. 155-156.

districts of the Bièvre, redolent of beer and tanneries, were for me a cup of bitterness.[5]

He was pervaded with the poetry of Paris in its darkest and grimmest overtones; with the spirit of its most wretched and miserable streets, which had also penetrated the thoughts of Balzac, Eugène Sue, Huysmans and Zola. He very frequently sought escape from this gloom in the Bibliothèque Nationale, conducting tireless explorations through the labyrinths of universal literature.

[5] *Paul Claudel interroge l'Apocalypse*, p. 127.

3

AN "EXTRAORDINARY MOMENT"

FOR CLAUDEL 1886 WAS TO BE A YEAR OF ENLIGHTENMENT, struggle, victory and spiritual recovery. By degrees the young man, this "unfortunate child," was to advance toward that "extraordinary moment" of that Christmas afternoon when he was touched by Grace and when he believed.

Were outside circumstances really quite as bleak as they appeared to this adolescent groping toward the light? The political scene was occupied by Charles de Saulces de Freycinet, an exquisitely mannered, fastidious and retiring old gentleman. A graduate of the Ecole Polytechnique, an engineer and an administrator, with more amiability than will power and more intelligence than energy; a busy and timid little "white mouse." He was later to be replaced as premier by René Goblet, a radical and a Jacobin with no taste for compromise or half-measures. The Freycinet cabinet included the celebrated General Boulanger, who had not yet invented Boulangism. The army was plotting for the return of the monarchy, and a sumptuous reception given by the Comte de Paris in the palatial hôtel Galliéra had been seized upon by the government as an opportunity to exile the royal pretender and his male progeny. There were signs of disintegration in the *materialistic prison*. Henri Bergson was gaining prominence. Paul Bourget was to disown Taine, and Barrès would soon turn against Renan. Huysmans' mystical conversion had started. The Russian novel, introduced by

Eugène Melchior de Vogüé, was received with eager curiosity by the younger literati of the day.

The end of spring marked the opening of a new phase in Claudel's life. He bought an issue of *La Vogue*, a periodical whose editor was the poet Félix Fénéon, and read the first few pages of Arthur Rimbaud's *Les Illuminations*. These ardent verses, burning with a powerful imagery and expressing a strange rapture, struck Claudel like a kind of spiritual thunderbolt and shook him to the core, in both soul and body; bringing about a complete collapse of everything he had been taught in his family life or at school—of everything he had learned so far.

At the end of the summer, on August 30, he wrote his first poem. He was probably in Villeneuve at the time. I have seen this deeply moving draft, in which the distinctive handwriting of his whole adult life can already be recognized. Entitled *Pour la messe des hommes, dernier sacrifice d'amour*, it is a religious poem, which is hardly surprising, although the young poet had lost (or believed he had lost) his faith:

> Harken, children and men, here I am,
> As on the first day, for Hope and for Love,
> I, the incarnate Son of God the Father, so
> That you may see humanity shine forth in Him.
>
> . . . O you, weeping with sorrow and gladness,
> Wounded and joyous, weep toward Me.
> O My dear simple hearts, I love you. Faith
> Will give you Wine and Fire to travel in my Path.

This was another kind of illumination, more specific and more direct than Rimbaud's, born of meditation in the leaf-clad church which he called his "cathedral in the fields."

The September issue of *La Vogue* brought Claudel *Une saison en enfer*, Rimbaud's latest work. This proved to be a capital encounter, an essential discovery. Others would have followed the rebel, the soldier of fortune thirsting after new conquests, even in his incoherence and deadly aberrations. Part of Rimbaud's spiritual posterity drifted, or rather sank, into delirium and anarchy. Not so Claudel, who immediately knew how to distinguish the positive contribution of this "uncivilized mystic," of this "lost spring welling forth again from a saturated soil."

Some of Rimbaud's dazzling lines flashed through Claudel's dark night: "We do not belong to the world. . . . True life is absent. . . . Through the spirit one goes to God. . . . I greedily await God. . . . Happiness! Its tooth, deathly sweet, warned me at cockcrow—*ad matutinum*, at the *Christus venit* —in the most dismal cities . . ." Later Claudel was to write: "For the first time, these books opened a crack in my materialistic prison and gave me a vivid and almost physical sense of the supernatural." This shock, this traumatic experience was to be a determining factor in Claudel's return to God, now close at hand.

He went from church to church, impelled by his utter solitude, not (it is true) as a devout young man really seeking God, but as one curious about new esthetic emotions and experiences: "I was starting to write and it seemed to me that in Catholic rites, considered in a spirit of higher dilettanteism, I would find an appropriate stimulus and material for a few decadent exercises." This state of mind was widespread at that time. A kind of spurious "mystical" revival occurred, based on estheticism and crystallized around Voguë, Henri Bérenger and a few others.

On Christmas, which fell on a Saturday, Claudel attended High Mass in the cathedral of Notre-Dame of Paris. He derived only "moderate" pleasure from the ceremony. These solemn occasions are usually graced by the presence of the Cardinal-Archbishop and enhanced by the attendant liturgical pomp. This particular mass was probably presided over by Monseigner Richard, who had become Archbishop of Paris only a few months before, and was to be created Car-

dinal a little later. The service was accompanied by the choir
of the young pupils of the famous St. Nicolas-du-Chardonnet
seminary, founded in the seventeenth century by Bourdoise,
one of the reformers of the French clergy. But the coming
and going of the crowd, which in that holiday season included
many tourists, hinders prayer and recollection. Claudel com-
plains of having been "elbowed and jostled by the crowd."

He returned to Notre-Dame for vespers. "It was the
gloomiest winter day, and the darkest rainy afternoon over
Paris."[1] He heard the Psalms, and particularly the *Magnificat* (surprisingly enough, he later wrote that he had not
immediately recognized the Blessed Virgin's song of thanks-
giving, which he had so often heard during his childhood and
the early part of his adolescence). He "stood near the second
pillar at the entrance of the chancel, to the right, on the side
of the sacristy." This is the emplacement of a famous four-
teenth-century statue representing Our Lady and the Child
Jesus.

> Then occurred the event which dominates my entire life
> [wrote Claudel]. In an instant, my heart was touched and
> I believed. I believed with such a strength of adherence, with
> such an uplifting of my entire being, with such powerful
> conviction, with such a certainty leaving no room for any
> kind of doubt, that since then all the books, all the argu-
> ments, all the incidents and accidents of a busy life have
> been unable to shake my faith; nor indeed to affect it in any
> way. I had suddenly experienced the excruciating conscious-
> ness of the Innocence, of the eternal childhood of God—an
> ineffable revelation. In trying, as I have often done, to re-
> member the minutes which followed that extraordinary mo-
> ment, I can identify the following steps or elements (these,
> however, formed but one flash of lightning, a single weapon
> used by Divine Providence to reach and finally open wide
> the heart of a poor desperate child): "How happy are those
> who believe!—If only it were true! And yet?—It *is* true!

[1] *Visages radieux*, p. 24.

God exists, He is there. He is someone, He is a being as personal as I am!—He loves me, He calls me." Tears and sobs had come, and the tender hymn of the *Adeste* only added to my emotion.

A most gentle emotion, yet with which was mingled a feeling of terror and almost of horror! For my philosophical convictions were intact. God had disdainfully left them standing. I saw nothing to be changed in them. The Catholic religion still seemed to me the same collection of absurd anecdotes; its priests and faithful inspired in me the same aversion, which reached the proportions of hatred and loathing. The edifice of my opinions and knowledge remained upright, and I saw no fault in it. What had happened was simply that I had emerged from this edifice. ("Ma conversion," in *Contacts et circonstances*, Gallimard, pp. 11 ff.)

From these lines it is clear that the previous illuminations and shocks had resulted in disappointing aftermaths, and that Claudel, who this time was more decisively shaken, had not yet reached a full and complete surrender. Later he was surprised to learn that, on the very same day, a young and unknown Lisieux Carmelite—Thérèse Martin—received an outstanding divine favor which she herself considered as a *conversion*, although she had always remained faithful to God. The night of Friday 24 to Saturday 25 of December was called by her a "luminous night." Suffering from an extreme sensitivity which frequently made her "shed profuse and bitter tears," she saw no way of overcoming this weakness:

All reasonings were in vain and I could not manage to correct this nasty fault. How could I entertain the sweet thought of entering the Carmel when I was still in the *swaddling clothes of infancy* . . . ? The good Lord had to work a minor miracle to make me *grow up* in an instant, and this He did on that unforgettable Christmas day, during that luminous *night* which irradiates the delights of the Holy Trinity. Jesus, the gentle *little* Jesus born but one hour before, transmuted the night of my soul into a great stream of light . . . during that *night* when He accepted *weakness* and sorrow through love for me. He made me *strong* and brave. He invested me with His weapons. From that blessed night onward, none of my battles ended in defeat, but on the contrary I advanced from victory to victory, and started forward with giant strides, so to speak! The source of my tears ran dry, and since then flowed but rarely and with difficulty, which bears out what I had been told: "You weep so much in your childhood that you will have no tears left to shed."

It was on December 25, 1886, that I received the grace of emerging from childhood, or in a word the grace of my full conversion.[2]

As for Claudel, he described in several of his writings the circumstances of the great personal event which had occurred on Christmas day of the year 1886. The main testimony is given in "Ma conversion," which appeared for the first time in *La Revue de la Jeunesse,* a Dominican publication whose editor was Father Barge.[3] This account may be compared only to the revelation given by St. Augustine in the *Confessions,* of his own answer to a similar divine call; or to some sections of Pascal's *Le mystère de Jésus;* some of Newman's more personal pages; or to a few chapters of Louis Veuillot's *Parfums de Rome.* Claudel wrote "Ma conversion" under the prompting of his spiritual director, but also as a witness who feels he owes a debt to truth; and as a man who considers himself a respondent for his brothers and a representative of his generation and even of future generations. The pillar of Notre-Dame where Claudel's illumination took place has become a kind of shrine which draws pilgrims from near and far. Toward 1930, the German philosopher Peter Wust,[4] on his first visit to Paris, made a point of meditating by that memorable column.

[2] *Manuscrits autobiographiques de Ste. Thérèse de l'Enfant Jésus,* Lisieux Carmel, fol. 44 and 45.
[3] *Revue de la Jeunesse,* Oct. 10, 1913.
[4] 1884-1940. Author of a remarkable treatise: *Uncertainty and Risk.*

Was Claudel really converted at that time? It would be more accurate to say that he acquired the mental attitude required for conversion. He was visited by God. He possessed faith, but good works seemed difficult to him. Many obstacles still stood in his way. Four years of struggle, of progress followed by setbacks, were to ensue. "It was the great crisis of my existence," he said, "this spiritual agony of which Rimbaud wrote that it was 'a combat as fierce as the battle of men.' Dreadful night! Clotted blood smokes on my face."

It was not an abstraction which he met, nor a new emotion he discovered within himself. Suddenly he stood before something alive; before a being; before the Being. He could not honestly and sincerely bow to the new demands gradually revealed to him. He could not yet accomplish the Christian act of will which joins practice to faith. One must not forget the undisciplined and rebellious nature of this student who, through many of his tendencies, was perfectly capable of behaving like a complete pagan; nor should one overlook how hard it must have been, particularly during that period in history, for a young man of eighteen to accept those requirements of Christianity which he was later to call—in a letter (written on March 3, 1907) to his younger friend Jacques Rivière—"so many things difficult to believe in, humiliating to practice; such a pitiless humbling of our small opinions and of our small person." Intellectual objections impeded his progress. He felt caught in the divine net, or rather seized by the hand of an imperious Father. He was at once delighted and disturbed, gratified and overwhelmed. He was determined not to lose again the newly recovered blessing of God's love; and yet stubbornly refused to give up the unruly and pagan part of himself, for it seemed to him that he could not forsake it without losing his freedom.

During this difficult period, the great educator and mentor of his soul was the cathedral. On December 10, 1945, he wrote to the Director of the Notre-Dame Choir School:

I have only one thing to say in answer to your kind invitation. For seven years, from 1886 to 1893 (date of a departure from which I am not sure that I ever returned), Notre-Dame of Paris was the school where I learned everything I know and became everything I am. I will not dwell on the great event of Christmas, 1886, with which you are already familiar. But the nearness of the cathedral (at that time, I lived on the ile Saint-Louis) allowed me daily to be its faithful visitor; and the Blessed Virgin, in order to force me, after a long struggle, to kiss the ground at her feet, wanted no other angels and no other ministers than her little white-robed servants. With what desperate nostalgia I watched them serving mass, and when one of them came to me asking whether I wished to receive "Holy Communion," how I longed to answer Yes! At least, every Lenten Friday I was able to tearfully kiss the relics of the Passion! These are powerful memories, and they make forever dear and sacred to me the dark and deep cavity where I found life! And I nearly forgot to tell you about that magnificent procession of the first days of Advent, which I so often followed with a taper in my hand!

One does not easily return from a path where skepticism and doubt, kept alive by Kant and Renan, have stifled the aspirations of the intellect, and paralyzed the impulses of the heart. Even while he listened to a pure voice deep within himself, the song of the eternal child, he could also hear, with a mesmerizing and depressing insistence, what he called "the most horrible blasphemy ever uttered by human lips," these words of Renan: "Perhaps the truth is sad." Neither could he entirely close his ears to the teachings of the university, on the strength of which he had believed in good faith "that there was no mystery in the world, that everything could be explained by 'the laws of science,' and that the mechanism of the universe could be disassembled like a weaving loom."[5] He loved this inner God, ever present within him, and yet at

[5] Letter to Gabriel Frizeau (Gallimard), p. 33.

the same time he considered absurd the "dogmas" and "legends" which "thrust themselves forcibly upon the wretched little fool—vain, pitiful and corrupt—that I was at that time."[6]

The setting of Notre-Dame meant a great deal to the convert. The Gothic place of worship built in the twelfth century under the initiative of Bishop Maurice de Sully; the metropolitan basilica to which Saint Louis had brought the Crown of Thorns; where the vow made by Louis XIII received its official consecration; where Turenne renounced Calvinism; where Bossuet pronounced the funeral eulogy of the Great Condé; where the Concordat first went into effect—nine years after the sacrilegious homage paid to the goddess Reason; where Lacordaire and his successors had given their famous Conferences. . . . But this distinct and tangible house of God conjured up for him the "celestial city," the "vision of peace," the "living stones," "the happy bride made beautiful by her husband."[7]

> The Great Book open to me and in which I studied [wrote Paul Claudel] was the Church! Praised be forever that great and noble Mother at whose knees I learned everything I know! I spent all my Sundays at Notre-Dame, and stopped there as often as possible during the week. I was then as ignorant of my religion as one can be of Buddhism, and here was the sacred drama unfolding before me with a magnificence surpassing all my imaginings.[8] It was no longer the poor language of devotional books, but the deepest and greatest poetry, the most august gestures ever entrusted to

[6] Ibid.

[7] Mentioned in an anonymous eighth century hymn: *Caelestis urbs Jerusalem*.

[8] Claudel does not mean that he knew nothing of Catholicism, since religion played an important part in his childhood, from the days when he celebrated mass in the garden of Villeneuve and when Sister Brigitte taught him Sacred History, until his first communion, for which he seems to have been adequately prepared. What he implies is that until 1886, his knowledge of religion was superficial, without any deep and intimate communication between man and his Creator.

human beings. The sight of the mass was an endless source
of inspiration to me, and each of the priest's movements
etched itself deeply into my mind and heart.

The reading of the Office for the Dead or of the Christmas
Service, the sight of the ceremonies during Holy Week, the
sublime hymn of the *Exultet*—next to which the most ec-
static lines of Sophocles and Pindar strike me as insipid—
all this overwhelmed me with respect, joy, gratitude, repent-
ance, and adoration. Little by little, slowly and laboriously,
there took shape in my heart the idea that art and poetry
were also divine, and that the pleasures of the flesh, far from
being necessary to these great pursuits, are actually detri-
mental to them. How I envied the fortunate Christians at the
communion table. . . .[9]

To the educative influence of the cathedral of Notre-Dame
must be added the part—although it is a secondary one—
played by all the books which young Paul Claudel undertook
to read in the course of these crucial years.

First and foremost he read the Bible. After returning home
on that momentous Christmas evening in 1886, (he had left
the cathedral in darkness and rain, "drunk, staggering and
dazed"[10]), he opened at random a Protestant Bible lent to his
sister Camille by one of her German friends. The account of
the evening at Emmaus fell before his eyes. And then the
eighth chapter of the Book of Proverbs, which revealed to
him the symbolism of Woman, a symbolism he would never
forget: she was the Virgin, the Church, the human soul. He
would always see Woman in this sacred light, even when he
went astray under the influence of a consuming passion.

Pascal was one of the authors whose works he medi-
tated over at great length, whose example was beneficent
to him, but against whom he always seems to have had
certain objections. In particular, he believed (and in this
Claudel was mistaken) that Pascal failed to give enough im-

[9] "Ma Conversion," *Contacts et circonstances* (Gallimard).
[10] *Paul Claudel interroge l'Apocalypse* (Gallimard), p. 232.

portance to the Blessed Virgin and to the Eucharist. He felt
a strong affinity for Dante, who was also an exile (although
for different reasons). Claudel was later to comment upon
Dante's works as though he were speaking of himself, and
placed him among the five poets who, in his opinion, "seem
to deserve the title of imperial or Catholic." Newman helped
him to strengthen the sense he had of the presence of the
personal or immanent God. Aristotle pruned and ordered
Claudel's philosophical knowledge. So did Bossuet, particularly through *Les traités,* and young Paul liked the round-
ness, the fullness and the simplicity characteristic of the
Eagle of Meaux's writings and orations; a style in keeping—
Claudel felt—with the accents of our old chanters intoning
the *Credo* of the mass written by the seventeenth century
composer, Henri du Mont. Through her visions, Catherine
Emmerich, who was dear to his entire generation—and
who was often quoted by Léon Daudet, Claudel's schoolmate
at Louis-le-Grand—increased his awareness of the unfolding
of the evangelical episodes, and especially of the Passion.
Among the other books which were also helpful to him he
mentions an "admirable work which can fill a whole library,
the great catechism by Father d'Hauterive." But he rates
above all else the *Parishioner,* "the best of all books."

4

FIRST DIPLOMATIC
AND POETIC VENTURES

DURING THOSE YEARS IN PARIS STEPHANE MALLARMÉ
reigned over a group of young writers. Here was a master
who had entered into poetry as one enters into religion, and
who attempted to subordinate his entire existence to the most
disinterested cult of art. He taught at the lycée Charlemagne,
and every Saturday, starting in 1875, there gathered around
him in the snug sanctuary of his fourth-floor apartment, at
89 rue de Rome, men such as Maeterlinck and Henri de
Régnier, Marcel Schwob and Oscar Wilde, Pierre Louÿs and
André Gide, Camille Mauclair and Téodor de Wyzewa and
a number of others.

The Grand Priest officiated and cast over his admirers, in
the words of one of them, Francis de Miomandre, "a luminous magnetism which left one in a trance." Mallarmé had
very fine eyes, and a voice worthy of his rank as master and
pontiff. He affected a dark-blue flannel jacket over which
he wore, like a stole, a plaid in a tartan pattern. His feet
were shod in Muscovite slippers. His utterances were received amid religious silence as though they carried divine
oracles. Even Lilith the cat, an animal with a flair for literature (according to an eyewitness), and who was descended
from a feline said to have inspired a poem by Baudelaire, respected the gravity of the place and circumstances. The

fervent participants hardly noticed Mlle. Geneviève Mallarmé occasionally fleeting by; golden-haired and ethereal, an evanescent vision who, we are told, resembled one of Edgar Allan Poe's heroines.

Claudel was introduced into Mallarmé's circle around the year 1887, but appeared at the rue de Rome three or four times only. Camille Mauclair, who saw him there, assures us that the young man looked like Bonaparte. Later, he was to cast off the Magician's influence, but on approaching Mallarmé for the first time he received a kind of psychological shock. By his own admission, Claudel continued to learn from Mallarmé, who taught him that Verse is "the best possible means of transferring reality from the field of the senses to that of the intellect; from the realm of fact to that of definition; from time to eternity; from chance to necessity, by capturing it in an unbreakable numerical combination."[1] He was to remember Mallarmé's teachings when much later, in Shanghai, he wrote *Connaissance de l'Est*. In the long run, however, the artificial and contrived quality which in Mallarmé's works was allied to an unquestionable power of dazzlement, could but disappoint Claudel, who was concerned first and foremost with more substantial realities; and who found Jules Laforgue more in harmony with his own deep feelings.

Mallarmé was fond of him, believed in his star, was thoughtful and attentive toward him. As for Claudel, he became fascinated with the explanation of the universe attempted by the would-be decipherer, an attempt which proved hardly more than an abortive venture. It is clear from *Connaissance de l'Est* that he profited from Mallarmé's admirable example of observation and attention. Claudel, too, dared to try explaining the world, but he did so in positive terms. . . . There is a story about a small gathering impro-

[1] Paul Claudel, "La catastrophe d'Igitur," *Positions et propositions*, p. 204.

vised in honor of the Master, during which an album of poems composed for the occasion by the members of his group was presented to him. He was saddened to note that Claudel's name did not appear and inquired about the reasons for this absence. In actual fact Claudel had been "neither forgotten nor forgetful," but was in China at the time. A few days later his poem arrived and was placed in the folder with the other expressions of homage.

Meanwhile, Paul Claudel had set his sights on a diplomatic career and had prepared for the competitive examination which leads to it. He had first thought of becoming a professional interpreter and had applied for admission to the School of Oriental Languages. But his age—he was barely twenty-one—would have meant a long wait. The council of state had also appealed to him, but he had finally decided, on closer consideration, that it was "a deadly bore." Throughout his life he never quite got over the surprise of coming out first in the foreign service examination.

His feet were already firmly planted on the ground, so that it did not bother him in the least to have the practice of a career as his foremost preoccupation. In this he stood apart from those romantics who feel they must sacrifice everything to fulfill what they consider their mission. Claudel was a born administrator and civil servant. He liked the smell of ink, and loved records, filing systems, archives, questionnaires and forms. "My life was divided among different interests," he told Jean Amrouche,[2] "but I have never had the feeling that I was unhappy or sacrificed, or that I was victimized because I could not busy myself from morning to night with literature."[3]

[2] *Mémoires improvisés.*
[3] He never served in the army. A faulty vision made him unfit for duty: he was far-sighted and also suffered from astigmatism in the right eye.

Another young man, two years Claudel's senior, entered on the same career at the same time he did. His name was Philippe Berthelot and they were later to become close friends. Son of the famous chemist, Marcelin Berthelot, he belonged to one of those great Parisian middle-class dynasties which, in the course of the ninteeth century, gradually took the place of the aristocracy and overcame social differences through a taste for the arts, for literature and for science. At the time, however, although the challenge of the examination might have been expected to bring them together, it seems that the acquaintance between the two young diplomats remained superficial. After serving as trainees at the Quai d'Orsay, they were both posted to the Far East. At first Claudel's attitude toward Berthelot was marked by a kind of deference, which went less to the senior than to an exceptionally gifted human being and to the representative of a family already visited by fame.[4] He wrote: "It would never have occurred to me to call him *tu*, or to overstep that secret limit which is the condition of any virile friendship." Many things might have kept them apart. Like his father, Philippe was a kind of mystical pagan, an austere secularist. All Marcelin Berthelot's faith had been channeled exclusively and forever into the prospects of science. Service to his country and devotion to all cultural solicitations were to occupy his son's faith entirely. Rationalism had dried up and destroyed their original family Protestantism. In their view everything in this world took place as though God were absent, and in their preoccupations there was absolutely no question of another world. Claudel, on the other hand, was to evolve toward a living religion; toward integral Catholicism.

[4] Claudel, however, had this to say: "A prevalent misconception is that, in diplomatic life, social contacts are of prime importance. This is not at all true. Really important people who know the ropes and lead the game are few and very busy. One seldom meets them in drawing rooms, where the atmosphere is not very favorable to useful meetings."

Young Claudel was starting to assert himself strongly as a writer. At the age of fifteen he had composed *L'Endormie*, the first rough draft of his future *Protée*, in which the comic element—highly valued by the budding author—reached the point of buffoonery. The manuscript shows that his handwriting was already fully formed and had acquired all the characteristics it was to keep throughout his adult life. *La messe des hommes* was a poem written during the year of his conversion, and foreshadowed *La messe là-bas*. Two years later he composed *Une mort prématurée*.[5] In August 1889, an article he wrote on the Isle of Wight, under the pseudonym of Paul Serveau, appeared in *La Revue Illustrée*. Among these early works there was also *Fragment d'un drame*, published in 1892 but written somewhat earlier.

This "Fragment" calls for several comments. It predates the "dreadful experiences" he went through, which have left their mark in *Le Partage de midi*, yet seems directly inspired by those very experiences. Which proves, according to Claudel, "the highly mysterious nature of poetic inspiration." In addition, one senses through this work the extreme despondency which at that time pervaded the young writer's life, as well as the struggle he was engaged in to adjust his decisions, his mental habits and his way of life to the demands which Catholic truth made on his whole being. The full weight of death is felt here. He wrote: "Why is this Life given to man . . . ? So that he may become a laughingstock and a token among all the others, more wretched than the half-exhumed skeleton whose powdery ribs are a playground for field mice, under the cold rays of the moon?" This fragment, which is only a few pages long, made Claudel aware of his power and ability and gave him the confidence he needed to go forward in his literary ventures. "It was," he declared, "the first awakening of what I call my intellectual puberty."

[5] The same year, 1888, when his sister Louise was married; and he seems to have destroyed the manuscript for family reasons.

To widen and strengthen his cultural foundation, he gave himself a second classical education. He had kept bitter memories of the lycée, and was determined to make a clean sweep of everything which reminded him of it. A strong will and a remarkable literary discrimination became his twin guides in this major undertaking. As far back as 1881 he had been reading Shakespeare—what is really called reading— pencil in hand, underscoring, annotating, closely studying methods, images and even mannerisms and idiosyncrasies. In writing *Tête d'Or* he remembered Shakespeare, and it was the Bard who led him toward the Greek tragic authors and particularly toward Aeschylus, to whom he turned for a proper training in prosody. Later he was to consult the works of Aristotle at the Bibliothèque Nationale.

His enthusiasm for Shakespeare gradually lost much of its intensity, however, whereas he returned to Racine, whom he had scorned for many years and of whom he was to write: "In none of the world's languages, not in Greek literature nor anywhere else, do I find anything to match Racine's three great dramas, *Britannicus, Phèdre,* and *Athalie."*

During this period of re-education, he also received the revelation of Dostoevski. He developed a deeper insight into Bossuet, "the only French author," he said, "who exerted an influence on me and whom I admire unreservedly." Some of Claudel's letters to Jacques Rivière, his speech on Dante and several other of his prose writings, show that there existed a kind of affinity between himself and Bossuet.

Tête d'Or,[6] his first really complete work, helps one to gauge, better than anything else could, the spiritual night in which young Claudel lived at that time. A darkness occasionally broken by rays and flashes of light amid which he advanced with the support of religious certainty, but where he compelled his turbulent and rebellious nature to bow before

[6] Written in 1889, published anonymously in 1890.

the injunctions of the living truth. He was twenty-one years of age when he wrote this play.

Tête d'Or is Simon Agnel, a man of Herculean strength, whose authority and prestige are felt by all those who approach him. The drama opens and ends under the sign of death. In the first act, Simon carries the body of his beloved wife, who has just died, to the grave. A passer-by named Cébès meets him unexpectedly and recognizes him. Cébès lives intensely with nature and the seasons, drinks in the wind (reminiscent of that of Villeneuve-sur-Fère, which Claudel often recalls), and admires *the temple of trees*—just as the author himself marveled at the forest of Compiègne and the woods of Fère-en-Tardenois, where he liked to wander as a child. Simon and Cébès conclude an alliance in order to lend support to an empire threatened by barbarians; Tête d'Or thus hopes to take his revenge on destiny for the death of his wife. But when victory is won, and when, thanks to him, civilization is preserved, he loses Cébès, his ally and friend. Fury breeds an inordinate ambition in him, and he decides to conquer the whole world. Carrying out his plan, he brings all Europe under his sway. He invades the Caucasus and, flying from victory to victory, challenges and threatens all Asia.

This might be contemporary history. In the recent past the world witnessed a comparable Odyssey. Claudel can rightly be listed among the writer-prophets, with Blanc-de-Saint-Bonnet, Hello, and—more recently—Louis Veuillot who, a century before Hitler, painted in ten lines an amazingly accurate portrait of the German dictator.

Just as victory seems within his grasp, Simon perishes. At the same time death claims the Emperor he has mortally wounded and the Princess he has abandoned, but whom he has just designated as Queen. On the battlefield an officer draws the conclusion of this tragedy of human ambition:

Three kings dead! Strange events!
The laws of custom broken, human weakness overcome, the
　　obstacle of things
Dissipated! And our endeavor, reaching a vain limit,
Falls apart of itself, like a fold of material.

True, the author of *Tête d'Or* did not in this play indis-
criminately condemn human will and its attempt to accomplish great feats, but he made it abundantly clear that man
cannot effectively usurp the place of God. Man can do nothing for man unless he clothes himself with the divine armor.
Simon's capital mistake was to have neglected the Princess,
who symbolizes his very soul. As a matter of fact, all Claudel's dramas hinge on this presence of woman to man. He
once declared: "To me, woman always represents four
things: either the human soul, or the Church, or the Blessed
Virgin, or sacred Wisdom. And it is in *Tête d'Or* that the
blind, untutored and instinctive force often found in the
young is defeated by the princess, and is obliged to submit
to her, not without a gnashing of teeth!"[7] As for Claudel's
prophetic quality, it should be pointed out that he also appears to have foreseen the advancement of woman—who is
only just beginning to make her influence felt—so as to re-
store to a sex-obsessed mankind its lost purity; not an insipid
and negative purity, but an energy like that of fire.

Until 1890, which ended one of the major phases of his
life, Claudel was in some ways one of the young barbarians
he describes. As we have seen, he had lived for several years
in skepticism, immorality and despair. He had escaped from
these shackles, and had received the sudden revelation of the
supernatural world to which he now had to adapt himself.

[7] See *Mémoires improvisés*. *Tête d'Or* has a political significance
far surpassing the Boulangist enthusiasm which young Paul shared with
his father. General Boulanger was Minister of War in 1886, attempted
a *coup d'état* in January 1889, failed and committed suicide.

In the meantime, however, although he had steadfastly pursued his studies and was to come out first in the foreign service examinations[8] he had not in the least neglected the obligations arising, he felt, from the miraculous event through which God had shown His interest in him. If anything, he took these obligations too seriously. He pondered over the end of his literary career, either feeling that he should sacrifice it to God or fearing that publishers would henceforth reject his manuscripts.[9] He continued reading most avidly, and had added to his classical list a number of spiritual works chosen among the most beneficial: *The Imitation of Christ*, Pascal's[10] *Thoughts, The Divine Comedy* and the writings of sister Anne-Catherine Emmerich. Peace returned to his soul in Saint-Médard, the old Parisian church of the Mouffetard district, which has other claims to distinction beside the questionable antics of François de Pâris, the miracle-working deacon and his convulsionaries. Claudel's own account is deeply moving:

> The years went by, and my position was becoming intolerable. I secretly and tearfully prayed to God, and yet dared not speak. Each day, however, my objections grew weaker and God's demands harsher! Ah, how well I knew Him during that time, and how strong were His strokes on my soul! How did I find the courage to resist them? The third year [1889], I read Baudelaire's *Ecrits posthumes*,

[8] Success in this had alleviated his feelings of inferiority. He now looked rather condescendingly upon his sisters, and had rented an apartment on the ile Saint-Louis, very near the cathedral of Notre-Dame.

[9] During this period he wrote a paper entitled "L'impôt sur le thé en Angleterre" which appeared in the *Annales des Sciences Politiques* Vol. IV, in 1889, pp. 640-653.

[10] His opinion of Pascal fluctuated widely throughout his life. At first he admired him and was grateful for his spiritual help. Later he deplored Pascal's Jansenism to the point that he reputedly thought of writing against him. According to Jacques Chevalier, Claudel finally reverted to his original views, believed that Pascal had never really been a Jansenist, was pleasantly surprised by his filial devotion to the Virgin Mary, and was ready to write in defense of the author of *Les Pensées*.

and saw that my favorite among all French poets had regained his faith during the last years of his life, and had
struggled amid the same feelings of anxiety and remorse as
myself. I gathered my courage and one afternoon entered a
confessional in Saint-Médard, my parish church.

The minutes I waited for the priest were the bitterest of
my life. I was faced with an old man who appeared unmoved
by a tale which seemed so interesting to me. He spoke of the
"memories of my first communion" (to my deep vexation)
and, before giving me absolution, ordered me to tell my
family of my conversion, for which today I cannot blame
him.[11] I left the box in a mood of humiliation and anger and
did not return until the following year, when I was positively
forced, reduced and driven to desperation. This time, in the
same church of Saint-Médard, I found a young, compassionate and brotherly priest, Father Ménard, who reconciled me;
and later the holy and venerable Father Villaume, who was
my director and beloved father, and whose protection from
Heaven where he now dwells I never cease to feel over me.
On that same day of Christmas, 1890, I received Holy Communion for the second time in my life, at Notre-Dame.

Regarding Father Villaume—"whose wise, salutary, strong
and cruel hand" he wrote about[12]—when this good priest
died on October 9, 1904, Claudel was to feel at last free from
the terrible hold exercised on him by the drama transposed
in *Le partage de midi*. The father had told Claudel that he
was going to die and would draw him closer to God. There
are signs which deceive and delude but this one flashed
through Claudel's life with all the evidence of a prodigious
reality.

The poet surrendered to his God. And at the same time
he truly found himself again. He would never forget

[11] This was Father Jouin, and this confession took place in Dec. 1889.
[12] *J'aime la Bible*, p. 111. The same priest "forced" Claudel, in spite
of his reluctance, to join the Society of Saint Vincent de Paul and to
attend the meetings of the rue Planchat Sodality, where he met Father
Anizan.

. . . those dark winter afternoons at Notre-Dame. I [was] alone. . . . lighting up the face of the great bronze Christ with a long candle.

All men, [continues Claudel, addressing God] were against us, science and reason too, and I did not answer. Faith alone was in me, and I gazed at You in silence, like a man who prefers his Friend.

In his renewed heart, which once again had become that of a child, gratitude broke forth in inexhaustible songs of praise which quite naturally borrowed Biblical images, powerful, bold and vivid.

Shortly before leaving France on his first foreign assignment, Claudel entrusted a few friends—among them Camille Mauclair—with the manuscript of *La Ville*, which he had just completed and which was accepted by the publisher Edmond Bailly, thanks to the efforts of these devoted agents.

Even more than *Tête d'Or*, this play expresses the state of soul the poet found himself in between his inner illumination and his final conversion. A whole social community breaks down, one in which men faced each other in fierce antagonism: lover and poet, magistrate and engineer, politician and scientist, bourgeois and artisan, man and woman. A "prison" collapses, the very prison in which the author was confined and from which he desperately longed to escape. The city, and particularly Paris—his long solitary walks covered all districts of the capital—was to him the enemy, the antagonist to be overthrown; the oppressive world which in turn had to be smothered.

Once again, one cannot help thinking of the old apple tree in the Villeneuve garden where Claudel faced the call of the four horizons. He anticipated and sensed the boundless universe which inspired in him a vehement passion. Disciplined in spite of his independent nature, he never thought of blindly escaping like Rimbaud who, during this period, passed furtively through Paris and whom he might have met. Instead, Claudel sought a profession, a career thanks to which a socially acceptable and honorable escape would become possible. He did not think of the Americas, but fancied himself living in China. The Director of the School of Oriental Languages advised him to prepare for the entrance examination to the diplomatic service, instead of persisting in his plan to take the examination for the council of state, which had at first appealed to him, but now struck him as being unbearably dull. With the guidance of a private tutor he came out first by a wide margin, as we have already seen.

In *La Ville*, Claudel can be recognized under the features of the poet Coeuvre who gives the play an optimistic conclusion. Coeuvre is the man of the future, the rebuilder, God's delegate for the rehabilitation of His creatures. At the poet's side a woman named Lala continues the role filled by the Princess in *Tête d'Or;* in the second version, written later, Claudel makes her speak these words, which admirably define woman's mission:

"I am the promise which cannot be held. . . ."

In 1893 starts for Claudel "the great official road which unrolls before me at full speed and without accident." He is first sent as deputy consul to New York, which he considers "a railway terminal":[13]

> Houses have been built between the tracks, a landing pier, a jetty flanked by wharves and warehouses; like the tongue which takes and divides food, like the uvula at the back of the mouth placed between the two lanes, New York between its two waterways—North River and East River—has on one side, on Long Island, placed its docks and bunkers; on the other side, through Jersey City and the twelve railway lines which marshal their depots along the embankment of the Hudson, it receives and ships the wares of the whole

[13] "La Maison fermée," *Cinq grandes Odes,* p. 165.

continent and of the West; the active tip of the city, entirely composed of banks, exchanges and offices, is like the extremity of that tongue which—to follow the figure of speech—endlessly moves from one point to another.[14]

He must have reached the United States in the early months of the year, since on April 23, 1893, he wrote to Marcel Schwob—the friend he often met in Paris at the Café d'Harcourt with Léon Daudet, Jules Renard, Maurice Pottecher and others—and told him of a "voluminous report" he was bringing forth on the New England fisheries. This kind of work delighted him. He identified himself with his activity as a civil servant, trying to be objective and accurate. One may assume, however, that the poet in him was not entirely forgotten, and that a discreetly whimsical note occasionally crept in to enliven the purely technical aspects of this assignment. "This kind of work," he wrote to a friend, "is like macaroni, which begins everywhere but has no ending." In his spare time he translated the Greek tragedies, and particularly Aeschylus. He had been interested in them ever since his first steps in the humanities. He had also always been fascinated by the Greek Fathers of the Church, whose rather simple style had reintroduced him to the Hellenic language, and who had played a definite part in his return to God, for he was impressed by the doctrinal coherence and soundness of their arguments.

From New York he was transferred to Boston as acting consul, at such a low salary—seven or eight thousand francs a year—that he sometimes had to do without lunch. Seventy years ago Boston was not, as one can well imagine, that great capital city of Massachusetts which today has a population of over 800,000 inhabitants, and has added to its memories of Franklin and Poe the more prosaic presence of tentacular industries. This is how the young consul saw it:

[14] *Connaissance de l'Est*, p. 43.

Boston is composed of two parts: the new city, pedantic, miserly—like a man who displays his riches and virtue, but keeps them for himself—as though the streets, in the bitter cold, became quieter and longer so as to listen with more hatred to the footsteps of the pedestrian. . . . opening avenues on every side, gnashing its teeth in the icy wind; the hill of the old town, like a snail, contains all the secret recesses of commerce, debauchery and hypocrisy . . .[15]

The consul who was to have been Claudel's chief died on his way to occupy his new functions. Through an extraordinary attention of providence, Claudel—as pointed out in a lecture which his son Pierre devoted to the poet's diplomatic career—never had a superior to report to in any of the posts he occupied.

In Boston Claudel saw quite a bit of a most unusual person, Christian de Larapidie. It is not clear whether the consul had known him before going to America. Larapidie, who for a time lived at 21 St. Germans Street, was a music teacher, violinist and maker of violins. He would spend entire days in forests looking for extremely rare woods. He was the son of an actor—who it seems enjoyed a brief spell of notoriety—and dressed most unconventionally. This was a source of considerable amusement to Claudel, who at one time gave much attention to sartorial elegance until one day he saw, in a tailor's shop, an absurd dandy more elegant than he could ever hope to be. Larapidie later left Boston, and taught in the Junior Lycée of Ben Aknoun el Biar, in Algeria. Claudel, who by then had received a new assignment, wrote to him, taking him to task over religious faith and practice. His friend the violinist answered:

Why should I be offended by what you say to me about religion? You do not appear to remember clearly who I am, and even less what is expressed in my music, which you had seemed to understand, however. . . .

[15] Ibid., p. 45.

Rejoice when you learn of my death: it can never come too
soon. . . . Allow me to repeat some of your own words: "Let
us hope that God, Who has His eye on you, will lead you
back to Himself," and to let you know that I have in fact
been led back to Him quite some time ago . . ."

Although Claudel had no immediate superior to report to,
his life in Boston was not an easy one. It has already been
mentioned that he sometimes went hungry and had to be content with one meal out of two. Moreover, he was faced with
an alien culture and unfamiliar customs. To be sure, he met
some families who were of the European pattern, having
maintained a sense of tradition. But his duties brought him
into contact with businessmen who of course have their coun-
terparts in France, but with whom he had not until then had
much opportunity to associate. For these people the important values are not those of the families which have kept a
link with the past. Money and trade on the one hand; love
and loyalty on the other. From this duality Claudel drew
L'Echange, which was written in Boston, and in which—by
his own admission—something of himself animates each
character. Through the voice of Marthe Laine, the faithful
wife with a passion for duty and service, the poet translates
the nostalgia of exile into these bitter and solemn lines:

I salute you, O distance!
I stand on this land of the West, O land which was found
beyond the rain.
O land of exile, your countryside is dreary to me, and your
rivers seem insipid!
I will remember you, country which I mourn! O land of
wheat and of the mystic grape! And the lark rises from
your fields, glorifying God.

L'Echange portrays several main protagonists: Louis
Laine, an American who represents pre-Columbian America;
his wife Marthe, a Frenchwoman who has been taken out of
her peasant environment by him; Thomas Pollock Nageoire,

an American tradesman descended from European pioneers; and the latter's wife, Léchy Elbernon, an actress of the "vamp" type, who has a grasshopper mind. For a large sum of dollars, Louis Laine is willing to sell his wife to the tradesman, who until then has known love only through the emotions inspired in him by a person as unstable and peculiar as Léchy. Before Marthe, an admirable woman who embodies the wife in her sacramental reality, he is disconcerted and dumbfounded; but seems to believe that his gold can abolish a marriage which, according to the Church, is indissoluble. As far as he is concerned everything can be bought and sold. Trade is almighty. Through Marthe, however, he appears to receive the revelation of an unfamiliar value, of a modest and tender beauty, of an unknown and fresh attraction:

> What is this elusive charm in you? Unlike other women, you
>   do not make one want to talk and boast,
> But to remain silent and ponder past events,
> And to reveal things of old, left unsaid but kept in the heart,
> And to hide nothing.

Like Violaine and Sygne de Coûfontaine, Marthe is "visited" by the cross of her God. For this reason she does not throw herself into distress and despair, nor resort to the illusive liberation of suicide which Léchy suggests to her. Neither can one say that she is resigned. She trusts in the justice of the Father. She consents to the burden of the present. In darkness, but also in the reality of faith, she accepts the bitter hour inserted in the heart of eternity.

To gain a fuller understanding of *L'Echange,* it may be useful to quote Claudel's own explanation:

> The slavery which was mine in America was most distressing to me, and I pictured myself under the features of a young man who sells his wife to recover his freedom. Out of the perfidious and multifold desire for freedom I fashioned

an American actress, contrasting her with the legitimate wife in whom I sought to embody the *passion for service*. All these roles issue full-grown from the theme, just as in a symphony one part is entrusted to the violins, and another to the woodwinds. In short, I myself am all the characters: actress, forsaken wife, young rebel and scheming tradesman.

In the same way, he would later be the mystical architect Pierre de Craon and the practical-minded peasant Jacques Hury, the idealistic nobleman Louis de Coûfontaine and the vulgar upstart Turelure, whose sudden rise on the social ladder was brought about by the revolution.

Beyond the realm of signs, symbols and parables, however, one may recognize in *L'Echange* a tragedy illustrating the roles of Europe and America. In spite of certain reprehensible attitudes, Claudel makes it clear that there are valuable qualities in Thomas Pollock, who embodies pioneering America. And Marthe, the French peasant woman, shows a generous and peaceable understanding of that which is best in this man. Jacques Madaule expressed this most strikingly in his remarkable study entitled *Le Drame de Paul Claudel:* "The hand she holds out to Thomas Pollock Nageoire is a hand which will not be withdrawn, and whose grip cannot be loosened. Over the unfathomable oceans and the awesome solitude of mountains, mankind, through this gesture, proclaims its authentic unity."

5

FROM CHINA TO THE
PROMISED LAND

AFTER HIS AMERICAN EXPERIENCE, THE YOUNG DIPLOMAT
dreamed of an assignment which, for a time, would take him
to Japan. His sister Camille, no doubt inspired by some imperious artistic predilection, held that empire in boundless
admiration. Her opinions carried great, even excessive,
weight with her brother, and convinced him that no other
post was more desirable. He requested an appointment to
the land of the chrysanthemums and the samurai. But there
was no vacancy for him in Japan, and he had to be satisfied
with a consulate in China. Early in the winter of 1894, after
three months of leave in France, he sailed for the Far East.

In Shanghai, his destination, he had to take up quarters
in a hotel room with the bitter sadness of feeling isolated,
separated, cut off from all things and all people.

The young vice-consul had left France determined to carry
out his task with that painstaking, professional conscientious-
ness, that invincible sense of duty to his estate, from which
he would never deviate and which must have been largely
inherited, for it appears not to have cost him too much of an
effort. But his true path was elsewhere. For him the call received in the cathedral of Notre-Dame went far beyond the
limited prospect of a mere conversion. Perhaps he was destined for a full commitment, transcending the world and all
its concerns, to the uninterrupted praise of the Only One.

He tried to see clearly within himself with the help of the good curate of Saint-Médard, Father Villaume, who had been instrumental in his return to God. On the priest's advice Claudel had taken with him to Shanghai the two *Summae* of St. Thomas Aquinas.

> At the height of my strength and youth I went to China and lived in a fullness of body, soul and senses, a voluptuous delight difficult to explain or describe today. Everything there pleased me, even—or indeed mostly—the confusion, negligence, filth, anarchy and idiotic wisdom; this good-natured civilization resting entirely on tradition and established practice; this artistic sense everywhere as natural and spontaneous as an animal industry; the revolting, sophisticated and delicious food; the religion, for which I continually felt a reprehensibly sympathetic tolerance; the magical and magnificent script; and above all that intensity of the intrinsic human quality, of what I would call the *humanita*.[1]

Claudel thus makes one understand his peculiar partiality toward Southern China; his curiosity stimulated by a poet's love for everything colorful or picturesque. And he continues with these descriptions rich in vivid imagery:

> This was the time of the Taotais, of mandarins wearing peacock feathers and buttons of many colors, the time of sable coats and of examinations, which every year during the cholera season set into motion a multitude of writing brushes. I refer to civil tests, for the army ones took stone-throwing into consideration for promotions—as in the days of the *Iliad*—and also archery. The uniform of their troops included a red blouse emblazoned with a huge velvet symbol, bold and black; and their armament was composed of a trident and a cage in which a small bird chirped (this reminded me of a line by Alfred Jarry which I had read that very morning in *La Revue Blanche: Le gazouillis de l'oisillon, le gazillon de l'oisouillis* . . .).
>
> A few of these rascals (the *Satellites,* to use missionary

[1] *Sous le signe du dragon,* pp. 235-236.

language), preceded by a brass thunder, formed my escort when I went to pay a call on the viceroy or the Tartar marshal. I remember being put down in my green sedan chair —after an hour's ride through the fantastic city—in the shade of the great litchi trees laden with their red blossoms. How often I exchanged ideas with the giants painted on the gates of the *yamen* who vainly tried to frighten me with their horrible grimaces![2]

As soon as he was able to get more or less settled his life was not without a certain comfort or a certain delightful freedom. It was so hard for him to accept any restraint, obligation or discipline not self-imposed! After a year he was sent to Foochow and moved into a house with a veranda, where the shrill chorus of the cicadas and the croaking of the frogs drowned out all other sounds. He had a number of servants who lived in a basement: "a small village emitting a faint odor of opium." A cemetery was near by. Claudel's duties consisted in preparing reports on products such as tea, or on the state of the currency, keeping up the accounts of the consulate, and answering the mail. There was no typewriter, but he was assisted in the latter task by the marvelous penmanship of Mr. Chao, a Chinese scholar and miniaturist. The Catholic mission, led by a Catalan bishop, Monsignor Masot, experienced endless difficulties. The diplomat related how, in an unbearable heat, he wrote to this prelate in Latin, "stripped to the waist, a towel wrapped around my brow, armored with blotting paper to avoid perspiration stains":

Venum datus est ager Tien-cho-Tang pretii quinque millia patacarum—Lis composita est—Irruperunt satellites in Petrum catechistam cum fustibus et sclopetis—Comperi cito advenire quamdam navem vapoream Gallicam munitam viginti quatuor tormentis bellicis—Et coetera.

He returned to Shanghai, then had to spend some time in Hankow, which left him with the worst kind of memories: it

[2] Ibid., pp. 236-237.

was an "infernal place," with a small group of dissipated cosmopolites; he may have suffered also from a certain spiritual aridity, a heightened self-loathing. Finally, after a visit to Japan (which is reflected in his *Art poétique*), and another stay in Foochow, he sailed back to France for a much-needed leave.

Jules Renard's *Journal* draws a picture of Claudel as he was in that year, 1895. At times he appears to seek forgetfulness, or simply amusement, by revealing to those around him only what he is willing to disclose of his inner self. In Renard's works the prevalent naturalism had become mocking and caustic. His *Ecornifleur* is an unsuccessful man of letters, an unreliable friend, a questionable lover. His *Poil de Carotte* is the child-victim surrounded by beings who would all be despicable but for the saving grace of caricature which arouses merciful compassion. If Claudel associated with this writer it is presumably because he found in him a man capable, in his acute and terrible lucidity, of being moved to pity. These are excerpts from Renard's *Journal*:

> March 7, 1895
> At Pottecher's, in Bellevue, Claudel reads us his literary translation of Aeschylus' *Agamemnon*. At first he modestly required pressing, then he started in the voice of a talking machine, and his lips open like heat lightning. His head is ash colored. One would think that he has been singed. He admires or hates like a child. He says: "There is nothing more beautiful in the world than the Chinese theater. Everything else fades in comparison."
>
> Then he reads us a revised version of *Tête d'Or,* on which he will work throughout his life.
>
> He finds Boileau a great poet of the picturesque, the only one who really knew how to write poetry.
>
> March 13, 1895
> Jules Renard: "I love solitude."
> Claudel: "You do not know the meaning of solitude. But

I have experienced it in an American desert, eighty kilometers away from Boston, where my friend the violinist wrote a tune expressing the very essence of that desert."

Claudel reads La Bruyère aloud. Impression of utter novelty. Claudel wants to crush all inspiration within himself. . . . He speaks of the Indians who with their mouths imitate the sound of an insect eating into wood, and who believe that the rabbit is a great magician. He stays at his office through duty, writes reports which have not been requested.

March 19, 1895

Weird dinner and evening in Claudel's apartment. Mlle. Claudel.[3] She hates music.

Studio with crossbeams and lanterns hanging by strings. We light them. Wardrobe doors set against the wall by Mlle. Claudel. Candlesticks in which the candle is placed on an iron spike—these could serve as daggers—and sketches lying on piles of laundry.

The musician who has shared Claudel's apartment for two years has just learned that Claudel is a man of letters.

Jules Renard's prestige was such in Claudel's eyes that the diplomat did not hesitate to recognize in him one of the greatest writers of his time. He was to say as much to André Gide, with whom he struck up a friendship in 1899.

Among the passengers on the steamer there was a Carmelite nun, bound from Marseilles to Saigon. Claudel held memorable conversations with her on spirituality and the conventual life. The Saigon Carmel, first of all the Carmels in missionary lands, had been founded in 1861. In 1896 there was to be talk of sending to that Indo-Chinese convent two of the sisters of the future Ste. Thérèse of Lisieux, Mother Agnes and Sister Geneviève.

The summer was to see Claudel back at his post in China. The ocean voyage "was pleasant and dull." His ship, the

[3] This is obviously Camille. Louise was a dedicated musician.

Jarra, touched at several "magnificent" ports of call, "under
the glorious sun of the Orient: Alexandria, Aden, and finally
Colombo," whence the steamer, detained by a fouled anchor
chain, seemed reluctant to depart:

> We stayed there nine days in spite of St. Expedit, patron
> of urgent causes, whose medal the good sisters . . . had tied
> to the helm. What a country! I can still see the flamboyants,
> the byssus waving crimson lilies among its leaves (lilies
> with a corolla like the male and female organs), the
> jack-trees with their fruit as large as a pumpkin hanging
> tied to the trunk, and finally the banyan and the coconut
> palm, sublime trees which would deserve an entire study by
> themselves. (I sent Léon Daudet a few lines on the coconut
> tree.) Saigon, completely flat in its abundant vegetation,
> beneath an enormous sky full of mountains and monsters,
> with the burning blackness of those nights, has also left in
> me a lasting memory.[4]

In Shanghai his consul general was a certain Mr. Dubail,
"a large and kindly man," with whom he hoped to get along.
This hope must have been fulfilled, in fact, for Claudel was
able to say much later that, thanks to circumstances, he had
never had any difficulties with any of his superiors. He wrote
this short but pithy answer to his friend Maurice Pottecher,
who had asked him for his impressions of China:

> These are the two deepest. The first is the elusively fresh
> and milky quality of the deep and radiant atmosphere whose
> first caress I felt in Singapore. The second is that of a nation
> doing everything by its own devices and with its own hands.
> I find this very striking. It gives me many new ideas and
> changes many others which I had allowed to take shape in
> me. This sight alone, of a nation which has eliminated all
> animal and mechanical aids, has struck me since my ar-
> rival. . . .[5]

---

[4] Letter to Maurice Pottecher, August 1, 1895.
[5] Ibid.

The poems of *Vers d'exil* attempt to express this unutterable sadness:

Paul, we must leave on a more beautiful journey!
For the last time, accepting their embrace,
I have of the weeping parents kissed the holy face.
Now I am alone under a new sun.

So much waiting and tedium, so many tiresome hours,
The morning entrance into a golden harbor, the naked men,
The smell of flowers, the taste of unknown fruit,
So many stars and lands left far behind. . . .

Day and night, the golden lamp astonishes me.
If I eat, the bread remains between my teeth.
I speak and am silent; I am deaf and I hear.
And last of all, pride itself forsakes me.

I have lived. The noise of men is foreign to me.
All is finished; I am alone; I wait and stay awake.
Lamp, all I have left is your bright red glow.
I sit like a man who has been judged.[6]

On March 23 of the following year—a year marked by the death of Verlaine, one of the writers for whom Claudel felt an abiding admiration—the diplomat was temporarily placed in charge of the vice-consulate in Foochow. This assignment carried very extensive duties and responsibilities. As French representative he had to negotiate and sign the contract for the Pagoda-Anchorage arsenal, where he had succeeded in bringing back a French mission. The war was to force three great powers—Russia, Germany and France—to intervene in the complexities of Chinese affairs. In Foochow events brought together Philippe Berthelot and Claudel, and established bonds of friendship between them. For the young vice-consul, this relieved the sadness of exile. In his loneliness it was a providential development. Later, *La messe*

[6] *Vers d'exil* "Théâtre IV" (Mercure de France).

là-bas was to recall those China masses, "for which the priest wears on his head a kind of cylinder devised by the last of the Mings." In these lines the new convert presses his former celestial opponent, through ardent soliloquies:

> You have defeated me, my beloved! My enemy,
> You have taken in your hands my weapons one by one,
> And now I have no defense at all,
> And here I am naked before you, my Friend.

During the same period he wrote *Le repos du septième jour,* his most typically Oriental work, with *Connaissance de l'Est,* which he started at about the same time. Ever since his grandfather's frightful end he had been obsessed by the idea of death. The Chinese, who delight in imagining the terrifying presence and the persecutions of the "cold ones," suggested to him the atmosphere most fitting to his meditations and investigations. The words of an Emperor—who found in the underworld, together with the precept of Sunday rest, the very secret of resurrection—are a comforting answer given by Claudel the adult and the believer, to Claudel the adolescent locked in the "materialistic prison."

But if we seek to surprise him in his innermost self, to penetrate his secret being, we must study Claudel, not only in his philosophizing moods, but also as he was every day, at his desk or during the long walks he enjoyed so much. This is how he experienced his own being, how he described and painted himself, how he told his own story:

> My living quarters are on the top floor, in the corner of the spacious and square dwelling. I have fitted my bed against the window recess. When evening comes, like the bride of a god who silently climbs onto the couch, I lie down, stretched out and naked, my face against the night. At some moment, lifting an eyelid heavy with the semblance of death, my gaze mingles with a rose-colored light. . . .
>
> It is midday, and everything which occupies a dimension

in space is sheathed in the soul of fire, whiter than lightning. The world is obliterated. . . . Prisoner of light, I keep
the diary of my captivity. Now I write, with hand on paper,
an activity in no way different from that of the silkworm
producing its thread from the leaf it consumes; now I wander inside the dark house, from the dining room, through
the parlor where for a moment I rest my hand on the cover
of the organ, to that bare study in the middle of which, formidable and alone, stands the work table.[7]

In June, my hand armed with a crooked stick like the god
Bishamon, I am the enigmatic wanderer met by the naive
group of red-faced peasant women. And at six in the evening, as the storm cloud in the sky endlessly continues the
monstrous ascent of the mountain, I am that man alone on
the rutty road. . . . I am the Inspector of Creation, the
Verifier of the present thing; the solidity of this world is the
substance of my beatitude . . . ! I walk on and on . . . !
For me, the even movement of my legs serves to measure the
power of more subtle calls. I experience the attraction of all
things in the silence of my soul.

I understand the harmony of the world; when will I grasp
its melody?[8]

He was to retain a sovereign dislike for Hankow, that "infernal place" where he was sent in 1897 to negotiate the plans
for the Hankow-Peking railway. There was nothing in this
inland city to comfort him from the worst days spent in
Shanghai, where he felt—once again, how well we recognize
him in this—that he had to attend too many dinner parties.
Hankow, reputed to be the city of tea, had nothing much
else to commend it at that time.

Last December I left that pleasant town of Foochow and,
after two months in Shanghai, was sent to Hankow, an important city on a dreary river bank, where I am kept busy
organizing a muddy little concession under the protection of

[7] *Connaissance de l'Est*, pp. 179-181.
[8] Ibid., pp. 162-164.

our flag. I find diversion from my duties conversing with a few cowhide and pigskin merchants, whose crude and scanty company I do not yet enjoy as much as I should.[9]

Hankow offered him a compensation. It was there that he met Emile Francqui, the Belgian consul, who was to become his friend. In his *Mémoires,* Jammes painted a curious portrait of Francqui, but it is one which may not be entirely faithful or accurate. Be that as it may, this Belgian made a deep impression on Claudel, a great admirer of all business-men and executives who knew how to face and solve difficult problems and situations. "What I admired in him," wrote Claudel, "was the mass and unity which produced this power-ful organizing ability, whose dominant features were an in-spired common sense and an almost diabolical imagination, an impact or power of penetration which was practically invincible."

In the first rank of the great missionary figures Claudel met in China stood Father Robert, of the Paris Foreign Mis-sions. He was born in the Jura district, and his wisdom and activity were always available to worthy causes. He won Claudel through his wonderful spirit of sacrifice, which would not have hesitated if faced with martydrom (a prospect the good Father had accepted in advance); this spirit also suf-fused the accomplishment of his humble duties and simple tasks. He worked in detail just as willingly as in great under-takings. In 1888, as a young priest of twenty-two, he had been sent almost immediately after his ordination to Hong Kong, where he served as Assistant Procurator for Missions. In 1891 his superiors sent him to Shanghai, where in 1903 he became Procurator General, replacing Father Martinet whose militant apostolate would long be remembered. Claudel was appointed consul in Shanghai in 1894 and this is presumably where they met. Between the diplomat and the missionary there grew a close friendship, marked on both sides by strong

[9] Letter to Stéphane Mallarmé, July 9, 1897.

feelings of trust and affection. Once he became Procurator General, however, Father Robert was again required to reside in Hong Kong, and when he returned to Shanghai in 1910 Claudel had already left China.

They were to meet again, nevertheless. The missionary continued his career, and in 1920 became first assistant to Monsignor de Guébriant, the Superior General, at the mission's Paris headquarters. I remember being received by him, around 1925, in the famous Missionary House on the rue du Bac. I have forgotten his features, his voice and his eyes, but I recall his kind courtesy and an impressive quality compounded of intellectual power, spiritual greatness and marvelous simplicity. The Chinese and French governments recognized his exceptional services by decorating him with the Golden Spike and the Cross of the Legion of Honor. I will not go into the vicissitudes of his many campaigns, travels, missions and conferences, for they could easily fill a whole book. After Monsignor de Guébriant's death in 1935, all of Father Robert's qualifications marked him as best suited to take over as superior of foreign missions, a position he held until 1945. He died in 1956 in his nineties, leaving behind him a luminous trail of good works, enduring achievements and trials endured with rare equanimity.

Father Robert shared in the main events of the Claudel family life. He had been godfather to the eldest of the children, a daughter born in Tientsin in 1907. He was to celebrate the nuptial mass of the poet's youngest daughter Renée, whose marriage to Jacques Nantet was blessed by Cardinal Verdier on February 16, 1940, in the chapel of the Archbishop's residence. In the letter by which Claudel asked Father Robert to officiate (a letter dated February 8 and written from 4 avenue Hoche), these significant words stand out:

> I have spent the better part of my life protecting the missions. It would mean a great deal to me if their most

qualified representative could be once more associated with
this family event. If by some unfortunate chance you were
unable to attend, would you ask one of your priests to officiate in your place? [And in another letter, written on the day
after the ceremony:] It is a new bond which you have thus
created between my family and yours, that great family of
the foreign missions, whose life I have shared on the highways and byways of Asia.

Even after they were separated by events, Claudel and
Father Robert remembered the problems which they had so
often discussed during the time when they were both far from
their common homeland. They were especially absorbed in all
questions concerning China. The diplomat kept them in mind;
the missionary experienced them as part of his life, even
from afar. Claudel wrote Father Robert from Brangues on
August 18, 1928:

> Circumstances have kept us apart for a long time, dear
> Father. They have led me westward and kept you in Paris
> far from the field of action where you spent all your life
> and where you could, at the present time, do so much good!
> Through a kind of fascination, everyone is deluded about
> China. . . . I am returning to Washington at the beginning
> of October. I would be very happy if before leaving I could
> see you for a few moments, and even happier if you could
> pay us a short visit in America, where you would see so many
> interesting things.

On the world scene these were eventful years. Felix Faure,
the French President, was invited to Russia on a state visit,
and the Franco-Russian alliance was proclaimed at Cronstadt
amid a general feeling of confident optimism. China was in a
complete state of anarchy; following an intervention by several European powers it became possible for foreigners to
travel through parts of the country with some degree of

safety. A massacre of missionaries had brought about the occupation of Kiaochow by a German naval detachment, and Germany was to obtain a ninety-nine-year lease on this port. Russia took over Port Arthur under a similar arrangement. France was granted the right to extend the Langchow railroad, and received Kwangchow bay under an identical long-term lease. Japan was to sign an agreement with Russia recognizing the independence of Korea. Another important event took place on June 27, 1898, and was of particular significance to the young consul. Théophile Delcassé, who was to play such a dominant role in French diplomacy, entered the Brisson cabinet as Minister of Foreign Affairs.

A short time earlier, Francis Jammes and Claudel had started corresponding, and this exchange of letters was to lead to a deep understanding and enduring friendship. Jammes lived in Orthez, in the Basses-Pyrénées, which his poetic imagination adorned with melancholy autumnal gardens and naive but tender maidens. He wore a pince-nez and an imposing beard. His handwriting was curiously shaped and very large, so that ten lines covered a full page of commercial size paper. Musicians and painters gathered around him. Later, young poets were to kiss the threshold of his house. Although a pagan, he already loved leaf-clad churches. Although impure, he longed for purity. He would not find it easy to part from Theocritus, but St. Francis of Assisi had already claimed him for all eternity. *Tête d'Or* had made no sense to Jammes. Then, ambling among the street of Bordeaux one day, he found a periodical in which he read a page of prose by Claudel, entitled *Le cocotier*.

> In reading it, I was illuminated with a light so clear, so green and so pink, that I fancied myself carried onto Robinson Crusoe's island, or into a garden at the dawn of the world. I remain forever dazzled by that tropical page, and

immediately hurried to tell my faithful friend Charles Lacoste about it. He admired it as much as I do.[10]

Two days later, returning to Orthez, he received a card from Hankow bearing congratulations from Paul Claudel, who had read and admired a page by Jammes. The diplomat borrowed a few lines from Theocritus to express the feelings which this page had inspired in him: "How sweet, goatherd, the murmur of yonder pine tree, singing by those springs, and no less sweet is the melody of your flute."

Such correspondence occasionally enlivened the dreary days in Hankow and allowed the Consul to escape in spirit from the dismal city "where an international group of good-natured men, rather like the California forty-niners, bivouacked among playing cards and bottles of gin."

His stint of duty in Southern China was drawing to a close. In 1898, he visited Japan for the first time. And the following year, on his way back to Europe, he made a pilgrimage to the Holy Land. In this he was no doubt prompted by that otherworldliness which little by little turned his attention exclusively to the truly important realities, and directed his wishes toward the order of St. Benedict. In the Church of the Holy Sepulchre, he served mass for the bishop of Philadelphia. More often than not, and particularly from Nazareth to Jerusalem, he traveled on horseback. At every turn he was assailed by literary memories, by the shades of Chateaubriand, Lamartine, Michaud and Loti (who, three years earlier, had written *Jérusalem, la Galilée,* the testimony of a desperate soul deprived of faith). But he was attentive mostly to the presence of Christ, Whose voice still echoes along the shores of the lakes, in the heart of the mountains and on the desert paths. He remained in the Holy Land for one month:

[10] Francis Jammes, *Les caprices du poète,* p. 87.

Of my stay . . . the strongest impression I have brought
back is that of the Dead Sea and the high rectilinear wall
of the Moab, "*murus cocti lactis*." The Holy Places now give
the impression of a bazaar and this was, I must admit, most
distasteful to me. Obviously, a religious benefit must accrue
from a visit to the Holy Land. But what kind of benefit? I
do not quite know. It is striking, however, to realize that
there is one place on earth where those three great religions,
Judaism, Christianity and Islam—which all stem, in the
final analysis, from the same revelation—continue to inter-
cross. . . .[11]

In other letters and writings, Claudel emphasized how
moved and proud he felt, as a Frenchman, to see so many
signs and relics of the great contribution made by Medieval
France in a land where, it is true, some excesses were committed when the Crusades—although pure in their original
intent—degenerated into a self-seeking venture:

One fact stood out for me, a fact which has struck all
travelers: it is the abundance of masonry, of religious and
military remains which one century of occupation by the
Crusaders left on the land they clung to with such a powerful embrace. Even today these remains form the land's most
characteristic feature. . . . For a son of the Ile-de-France, it
is deeply moving to find again, in the heart of the Promised
Land, those great solid walls best compared to large pure
pages; this innate taste for stone, akin to our peasants'
predilection for wheat; this bold and generous use of the
vertical; all of which are the glory of Laon and Beauvais. It
can be said of any sincere Catholic that he is at heart a
builder, or more accurately a maker, a poet.[12]

But where would it lead him, this road on which Paul
Claudel silently wandered, thoughtful and troubled? To what
heights would his temporal career ascend, a career so bril-
liantly inaugurated? What literary destiny stood before this

[11] Letter to Father Brunot, of the Sacred Heart of Betharam, s.d.
[12] *Les aventures de Sophie*, pp. 198-199.

poet and playwright, whose past achievements would have been ample enough for the glory of another writer? It is doubtful, however, that fame, recognition and a "successful" future in the conventional sense formed the subject of the whispered conversation between himself and the Voyager he met on the road to Emmaus. A Voyager resembling the mysterious Friend Who, in the cathedral of Notre-Dame, had one day revealed Himself to Claudel's heart.

At the very time when China stood battered and ripe for the revolution, Claudel's years in that country left him with an entirely favorable balance. Much later, examining some photographs taken by Madame Hélène Henri-Hoppenot of "imperial China—the China of the yellow wind, the yellow air, the yellow water and the yellow earth," he commented without regret on these days of disintegration which he had witnessed:

> I knew China at its supreme moment when Peking, emptied of its ancient authority, was to join its cemetery to those of Singan-fu and Laon-yang in historical nullity. I attended the simultaneous funeral rites of the last Manchu, of the poor little emperor and his horrible stepmother; which were to be followed by so many other collapses—so many other funerals of Emperors and Empires—Japan, Russia, Austria, Germany, Spain, Italy. From one end to the other of the Old World, the wind of catastrophe blew. Dynasties collapsed one after the other, all those weakened trees uselessly occupying the earth.[13]

The book from which this quotation has been drawn is made up of a lengthy report prepared for the French Foreign Office by Claudel, when his stay in China drew to an end. At a turning point in Chinese history this document sums up the situation from the viewpoints of civilization, religious life, European interests in the country, commerce and industry,

[13] *Sous le signe du dragon*, p. 239.

finance and currency. By reason of the circumstances, this report constituted a milestone. When he wrote it Claudel could see in his mind's eye the forests like that of the Fokien, where he took pleasure in studying and classifying the countless varieties of woods; the ports like the one where seventy-two middlemen took part in one single lumber transaction; the mines such as that of the Shan-si, through the narrow tunnels of which he is said to have crawled; the "great achievement" of the Peking-Hankow railroad, which was to contribute to the spreading of the French language . . . . It becomes clear that he could have been *the right man* at each place and under any situation; one understands the words of his friend Francqui, who was one day to say of him that, "if he were not an ambassador, I would make him the manager of a railroad."

6

THE MERIDIAN YEARS

THE YEAR 1900, WHICH USHERED IN A NEW CENTURY, witnessed events as varied as the Paris World Exposition, the assassination of King Umberto I of Italy, the re-election of President McKinley in the United States, President Kruger's trip to Europe and the wedding of the Belgian crown prince.

After completing his pilgrimage to the Holy Land, Claudel spent the year in France. He had turned his back on the world, and had made up his mind to enter into religion. On April 17, he lunched with Jammes and Schwob at the Lapérouse restaurant, on the quai des Grands Augustins, in Paris. Neither of them suspected that, although physically with them, he no longer lived among men. His diplomatic leave, however, was far from providing him with the serenity he required. His inner mood—that of a believer yearning for perfection—was disturbed by the fear that he might be called back to his post. The Boxer Rebellion had broken out in China, and it had become necessary to organize an international expeditionary force. In April, the Boxers were thrown back from the Chi-li by the international army under the command of the German Field Marshal Waldersee. Clearly, Claudel's final choice could not be delayed much longer.

After a stay in the country he returned during the early part of August to Paris where *L'Echange* had just been published in the literary review *L'Ermitage*. He then went on to Solesmes for a retreat, and in the time left over from the spiritual exercises started to write *Les muses*—the first of his

Cinq grandes Odes—in which he sets forth a prosody illuminated by the longing to reach the eternal Being. These lines describe the thirst and eagerness of Terpsichore, muse of the dance and the song, but they betray Claudel's own feelings:

> "It has lasted too long! Take me, for I cannot endure!
> It is too much, too long have I waited!"
> I looked around me, and saw myself suddenly alone,
> Unattached, refused, forsaken,
> Without task or duty, outside amid the world,
> Without right or cause, strength or admission.
> "Do you not feel my hand on your hand?"
> And in truth, I felt her hand on my hand.

This is probably the time when he put down his pen or broke it in two, determined never to write again.

During this cruel inner struggle he exchanged a few words with his neighbor at the guest table, Algar Labouchère Thorold, a young Englishman of thirty, the son of an Anglican bishop, a former Etonian and Oxonian who later was to join the foreign office, and who in 1920 served on the staff of the press attaché to the British Embassy in Paris. Thorold was converted to the Catholic faith and became deeply interested in Ste. Catherine of Sienna. He served as editor-in-chief of the *Dublin Review,* and died on May 30, 1936.

It is not known why Claudel left the Benedictine abbey of Solesmes, near Le Mans, for Ligugé, the other monastery which the spiritual sons of St. Benedict maintained in the immediate vicinity of Poitiers. Whatever the reason for this move may have been, he spent eight days in Ligugé for a retreat during September. This abbey had been placed in a somewhat anomalous situation, for a secular pastor had just been appointed in the locality. But it attracted many writers and artists who seemed to be drawn there as though by the inspiration of the Holy Ghost. Huysmans stayed in the Notre-Dame guest house, right by the cloister. Louis Le Cardonnel also came to Ligugé, and contemplated entering the Benedictine order. Claudel met several of the Fathers, whom he would never forget—Dom Moreau and Dom Pottevin, and particularly Dom Besse, his spiritual adviser, who was instructing the novices at the time.

Dom Besse, an unusual and curiously arresting figure, was to die in 1920. At the age of forty, at the height of his vigor, he was engaged in numerous activities. He founded several papers and periodicals such as *La Revue Mabillon, L'Univers, La Vie et les Arts liturgiques*. As an historian interested in both temporal questions and spiritual manifestations, he studied the Salic Law, Marxism, the Revolutionary Decalogue; and also the status of Catholic schools in France, Catholic support for the Republican regime, the abbeys and priories of old France, the life of Cardinal Pie and many other subjects. He wrote treatises on the Mass and on the Benedictines. Before all else he was a monk, and worked tirelessly for a Counter-Encyclopedia, a Counter-Reformation and a Counter-Revolution.

Dom Besse was described by Antoine Lestra,[1] who had known him well:

> He had strong features stamped like a Gallo-Roman medal. During the hours of silent study his face was severe, but it would quickly light up in the presence of others and especially at the arrival of a friend. A wide smile, mischievous and gentle, subtle, open and vivacious, played on his lips, which immediately expressed kindness, even before he spoke. The same smile seemed to shine forth from his deep-set and piercing eyes. In a flash his entire face was illuminated by this gaze and all his features sparkled with intelligence in the golden light which sprang from his pupils. Those eyes penetrated history, scrutinized the foundations of society and illuminated souls.

The good father took charge of young Paul Claudel, and no doubt studied his case with that feeling for vocations for

[1] "La vie et l'oeuvre du R.P. Dom Besse," *Revue des Jeunes,* Aug. 25, 1920.

which he was known and because of which he had been
chosen as novice master. I remember hearing Louise Claudel
tell me, some thirty years ago, that when Paul told their
mother of his wish to leave diplomacy and embrace the religious life, she strongly advised her son against giving up his
career and urged him to return to China for a year, during
which he could think the matter over at leisure .... Although
their viewpoint was probably somewhat different, the Benedictines also dissuaded their guest from his design, and made
him realize that he would serve the Church better by remaining in the world. Actually it seems that Paul Claudel felt too
great a love for life to renounce it, yet was too strongly attracted by the cloister to give himself fully to the world. He
was never to feel completely at home anywhere. Much later
one of his friends, who had gone with him to Solesmes, told
me that Claudel, a few days after the beginning of the retreat,
longed for a breath of fresh air and wanted to stretch his legs
on a highway, and to leave the atmosphere of the abbey,
which was rather confining for a man such as he, who needed
space and freedom.

The most enlightening documents on this spiritual crisis
—which was to be heightened and brought to its peak by the
Ligugé retreat—seem to be these excerpts from various letters he later wrote to his friend Louis Massignon:

> There is no convert who has not wondered with deep anxi-
> ety whether God, who ordered him to take a first step, will
> not demand a second. This anguish was so great in me that
> at one time I had asked to enter Ligugé as a novice, *after
> having made the complete sacrifice* of a poetry which I
> deemed useless to God's service. This was in 1900 and my
> Superiors ordered me, in view of events, to wait and return
> to China. I was then thirty-two, the really critical age, and
> the two first acts of *Le Partage de midi* are nothing but an
> accurate account of the horrible adventure in which I very
> nearly lost my soul and my life, after ten years of Christian

living and of absolute chastity. It is likely that if I had been really firm in my request to stay at Ligugé, I would have been allowed to remain. But I lacked determination, and this sacrifice of the main gift, which was probably my personal vocation, proved to be beyond my strength.

November 19, 1908

After a retreat at Ligugé, I understood that God did not want me as His priest and rejected me from His altars. It was a very bitter moment in my life.

October 12, 1909

And yet Ligugé alway remained in his memory. Nearly fifty years later he wrote to Dom Basset, one of the fathers:

I was deeply moved by your letter from Ligugé, a name linked in my mind with pathetic memories. Like you, I believe that God did not intend me for the monastic life. He clearly told me so on the last day of my stay at the monastery, in that little chapel of the novices placed under the invocation of the Child Jesus of Prague. This gave rise in my soul to a deep and possibly beneficial turmoil which for many years left a mark within me.

Brangues, April 12, 1946[2]

Claudel was profoundly vexed and disillusioned by the decision of his spiritual advisers. He felt that God considered him a useless servant, as it were, and that to a certain extent he was cast aside and rejected. He had led a life of self-denial and sacrifice, and had even steeled himself to give up his art on which he set such high value. Had all this counted for nothing? And yet deep within himself, he knew that he was and would always remain a man of God. Nothing else interested him. Any other ambition seemed pointless. Nothing mattered to this man of strong will and faith except his longing to partake in the power of eternal love.

[2] *Lettre de Ligugé*, No. 51, 1955.

Such was the frame of mind in which Claudel returned to his post in China early in 1901, on the S.S. *Ernest Simon*. On board he remained aloof and silent, probably even more than usual. He did, however, enter into conversation with a certain Mr. Castagné, who was on his way to Indo-China, where he had been appointed governor.

Another meeting which took place during this trip has been transposed in *Le Partage de midi,* and its known circumstances deserve to be related in some detail. This meeting forms the preamble to what Claudel called "the frightful humiliation of his life."

On deck he stood apart, unhappy, indifferent and silent. Other passengers were boisterously enjoying themselves. Amid gales of laughter, they played the English game of *Hunt-the-Slipper,* and the woman's shoe fell to the stern-faced diplomat, much against his will. The episode, although in doubtful taste, may have inspired the basic idea of *Le Soulier de satin*. On board Claudel also met a young man of excellent family background, whom he knew slightly. This young man who had squandered a great deal of money in the island of Réunion, was on his way to China where he planned to leave his wife (who was also a cousin) and four young sons. At their first meeting, the young woman—a dazzling beauty—surprised the reserved traveler, who was torn between physical desire and a wish to avoid any possibility of an involvement. He conversed with her about the Bible and *The Imitation of Christ,* with which she seemed to be very familiar. Her deeper interests and tastes were in sharp contrast to her gay and somewhat frivolous appearance.

The crisis brought about by this chance encounter was to last more than twenty years. It was unbelievably violent, until the day in 1905 when, conscious of being the obstacle between God and this man, she decided to leave him and never to see him again. In this she held to her promise. If Claudel suffered a punishment, he and God kept the secret of its nature and intensity. But evil can lead to a providential outcome, and the following lines written by the poet-diplomat show that this was the case: "To tear man away from himself down to the roots, to give him a taste for the Other—who is grasping, hard and selfish—to make him monstrously prefer that Other to himself, to the extent of forsaking body and soul, Woman is the only appropriate instrument. She is the lever."[3]

During these tragic years the young diplomat was sustained by the vigilant, fraternal and active friendship of Philippe Berthelot and the woman who had become his wife.

Philippe and Hélène Berthelot came to visit their friend in Foochow during the summer of 1903, as Claudel's translation of Aeschylus' *Agamemnon* was being published by the widow Rosario, a Portuguese woman suffering from leprosy, who operated a small printing establishment. The solicitude and devotion of the Berthelots was unfailing. They did everything in their power to save the distraught poet from himself. (Philippe Berthelot was then thirty-seven years old, and had been sent by the foreign office on a special mission to investigate conditions in Indo-China. He started his tour of that French dependency in February of 1904, going from Ching-foo to Signanfoo, and venturing as far as the borders of Tibet. As for Claudel, he undertook several trips to Indo-China and Japan while stationed at Foochow: in his *Art poétique, Connaissance du temps* describes the long climb from Nikko to Sezenji, and mentions the sacred huts of Nikko.)

Even more important was the support he received from afar from Father Villaume who—as we have already mentioned—was to be called back to God just as the crisis was about to be resolved; that is to say, in October of the year 1904. It was then that Claudel understood the value of an

[3] "You have not accepted me," he was to say to God, "and it is the Other who has taken us." *Partage de midi*, Act 3.

authority, a discipline and a rule. He even wrote to Elémir
Bourges (on June 23, 1905): "I am for the legitimate authority, with Jupiter, against Prometheus."

One should read *Le Partage de midi* in the light of these
events, bearing in mind the esthetic requirements of the
factual transposition. Mesa, the main character, a customs
superintendent, is a smug and self-centered member of the
middle class, utterly impervious to the wishes, the needs and
the solicitations of others. He is interested only in himself.
Only his little personal affairs preoccupy him. It seems that
the Grace of God, suddenly received, is given to him in vain,
and that it remains, in the words of St. Paul, fruitless within
him; so great are his pride and complacency. The talent entrusted to him is unproductive. He had wanted to give himself
more completely to God, but God has scorned and rejected
him, as it were. Mesa has understood nothing. He will finally
see the light when, on the ship carrying him back to the Far
East, he meets a woman, a beautiful stranger, Ysé de Ciz.
She is not free, and her husband is a second-rate man. She
remains deeply attached to her children, but they do not
absorb her entirely.

This woman will draw Mesa out of his indifference to
others; through sin she will break down within him all obstacles to his concern for his fellow men; she will bring about
in him a major spiritual crisis comparable to the one which
shook Claudel's own life during the year 1886. With all his
energies Mesa will strive toward this communion with another
being, an adulterous and sacrilegious communion. Like King
David, he does not shrink from a criminal decision: against
Ysé's wishes he sends her husband away on an assignment
to a distant land where the climate is unhealthy, even dangerous, and from which the poor man will surely not return. But
the happiness of the lovers does not last. Ysé falls into a
panic, no longer knowing what to do, blinded by too much
light. She flees in terror, bearing Mesa's child, and meets a

former friend, Amalric. Although a rake and a kind of free-thinker, he represents a new security. Ysé unburdens herself to him. She hears that her husband has died; and Mesa returns to the scene. Ysé is now free to marry again, but Mesa's thoughts are only of peace, forgiveness and reconciliation on a high plane. In the beleaguered city where the three of them are thrown together, there is an opportunity for only one person to escape. Amalric takes this only chance. All that is left for Mesa and Ysé is to die. It is no longer the separation at high noon, the sharing of love, but the parting at midnight. Two separate prides have clashed and pride dominates this terrible drama. It is the passage of death, which represents another form of love. For love and death are closely connected. Ysé cries out:

> Oh, Mesa, here is the parting at midnight, and here I
>   am, ready to be set free,
> The sign, for the last time, of my long hair
>   whipping in the wind of death.

And Mesa answers:

> Farewell! For the last time have I seen you!
> By what long and arduous paths,
> Separated but weighing still on one another,
> Shall we lead our souls in travail?
> Remember, remember the sign!
> Mine is not a vain lock of hair in the tempest,
> Nor a small kerchief fluttering for a moment,
> But myself, all sails dissipated, the strong
>   bright flame, the great male in the glory of God,
> Man in the splendor of August, the victorious Spirit
>   in the Noonday transfiguration!

It is understandable that Claudel once said of *Le Partage de midi*: "This is not a play like any other. I have written it in my blood."[4]

[4] *Cahiers Barrault*, 1955, p. 81.

7

PURIFICATION

In 1905 PAUL CLAUDEL ENTERED ONE OF THE CRUCIAL YEARS of his life: the long nightmare through which he had lived was to be left behind him, at least to a certain extent, as he progressed toward spiritual peace and purification. Literature afforded him some measure of escape, and he found the process valuable although not entirely adequate. He gathered inspiration from Pindarus, whose triumphant *Odes* exerted a marked influence on his own *Cinq grandes Odes,* a task which he took up again after the interruption of Solesmes, through the evocation of his "shipboard love" and of the days when, "separated from the earth, they were alone with one another."

After Delcassé's resignation, Rouvier the opportunist had replaced him at the Quai d'Orsay. The new foreign affairs minister valued the young consul's numerous and abundantly documented reports, which until then had been judged so detailed and copious that only a poet could have written them. On one occasion, a foreign office member even penciled in the margin the single word *Insane,* which might have broken Claudel's career if other more open-minded readers had not recognized the true worth of the report.

Springtime brought him back to Paris. He still experienced difficult and discouraging moments. In a letter to his friend André Suarès, he spoke of a certain night of the Sexagesima when he felt "most keenly . . . the ineffable kindness of the Saviour, His sufferings, His simplicity," and against all this,

his (Claudel's) own "weakness, vanity, frivolity, shameful sins." Perhaps France would draw him out of these bitter feelings welling up from the past. He saw his mother and his sister Louise at the 37 quai d'Anjou apartment. On April 17 he returned to Ligugé where he had been received as oblate. He also revisited Villeneuve-sur-Ferè, the scene of his early childhood, and planned other trips during the summer without, however, neglecting his literary activities.[1]

Francis Jammes had been his friend for eight years when Claudel, in June 1905, journeyed to Orthez to meet him. Jammes lived with his mother in a large old house surrounded by a garden, and commanded a limited but fervent public through his moving elegies, written in prose or verse, which pictured young girls reminiscent of the illustrations in the *Magasin des Demoiselles*.[2] It is said that a certain youthful poet once stopped in front of the Orthez house at nightfall, and kissed its threshold. Jammes wore a drooping mustache and a beard which had not yet turned to snow; a pince-nez softened the ardent gaze of his tender eyes. His face shaded by a wide-brimmed hat, he was often seen walking along the banks of the Gave, carrying a fishing pole or a gun. He was gradually becoming a legendary figure. Claudel was a Christian who had just spent a season in hell, and who was resuming the path of faithfulness with considerable difficulty. Jammes, who had been christened and was a believer of sorts, actually lived like a pagan and rated nothing above the love of creatures. But his soul was filled with disappointment, torment and even anguish, and he longed to enter the leaf-clad church. On September 1, 1904, he had sent his friend this call, this cry which arose from deep within his heart, "Claudel, I need God."

[1] His friend Marcel Schwob died during that year. "[He] drank in Claudel's words like a water of Grace which offered him the certainty of an eternal and blissful life." (Jammes, *Les caprices du poète*, p. 45.)
[2] An illustrated periodical, much in favor with the French middle classes and aristocracy during the last century. It was known for its romantic color plates, which are now greatly in demand.

"We are both emerging from great sorrows," wrote the young consul. He always remembered that he was the "delegate for light," the "missionary of truth" barred from the priesthood, although he had renounced much to give himself entirely to God. In person, he brought an ardent answer to his desperate friend. At the same time he rejoiced in the return to God of another dear friend, Gabriel Frizeau, a Bordeaux art lover who sent him long letters showing 'a remarkable grasp of Claudel's thought and works, and who shared all his hopes and ambitions from afar. Claudel saw them both in Orthez during the last week of June 1905. Then he went on to Eaux-Chaudes, a spa in the Pyrenees where delightful public walks correct an initial impression of severity. Jammes joined him there, then brought him back again to Orthez. In the silence of a modest drawing room looking out onto the garden and a country road, the elegist, delighted to have his friend all to himself, read his latest poems to Claudel.

They did more than read and listen to poems. They confided in each other and, although the secret of these talks has been preserved, their friendship was raised to the highest point of mutual trust and affection. A private chapel belonging to Madame Lafourcade, at La Bastide-Clairence, near Hasparren where he later settled, witnessed the essential act of Jammes' conversion. Mass was celebrated by Dom Michel Caillava,[3] of the Benedictine Abbey of Belloc, and was served by Claudel. The two friends received Holy Communion side by side, with a deep feeling of regained peace. Jammes relates that later that day Claudel, so justly proud of his faith, said to him, "If there are only two left, then let us be those two."

At the end of July, after a stay in Paris, Claudel returned to Eaux-Chaudes, where he was distressed not to meet

[3] Dom Caillava had founded the Abbey of Belloc-sur-Joyeuse. Claudel was to consult him on the advisability of writing Le Partage de midi. Later, Msgr. Baudrillart, to whom he related the whole tragic episode, dissuaded him from having this play staged.

Jammes, who had promised to join him there. He did not mince his words in expressing his displeasure and disappointment. "This month," he wrote, " is probably the only part of our lives we were meant to share, and you are going to spend it almost entirely with some family in the Gers."

Lourdes brought them together again, however. For two days they both took part in the national pilgrimage, and were fortunate enough to see a miraculous cure. During a procession an old man who had been confined to a wheelchair suddenly stood up before them, and a little girl started following the Holy Sacrament, "triumphantly holding aloft a pair of boots whose use she had regained." Eaux-Chaudes was to offer them more pleasant hours, in the company of Philippe Berthelot and of Claudel's friend Francqui, the Belgian financier, a giant of a man known for his superhuman exploits.

This season, following the season in hell, was extraordinarily beneficial to Claudel and truly brought him a new life. He found that he had become a new man, made wondrously whole and younger. "I feel overflowing with vigor and ideas," he noted, "after this long, four-year crisis; it seems to me that I am eighteen and that my life has just begun." Using all his faculties of mind and heart, he wrote about his talented sister Camille, who was dangerously ill: "Her life has been so full of disappointments and humiliation that its continuation is not to be desired." In a later chapter we will relate the heartbreaking story of this inspired woman, who was an accomplished artist and lost her reason through a tragic love affair. Claudel generously shared in her ordeal and suffered from his inability to break the chains of this love.

In Paris the center of his existence was his beloved Notre-Dame. He wrote that the great cathedral was to him "haven, teacher, home, doctor and nurse." But other holy places also played an important part in his spiritual development and stood as milestones along his path. In particular, Notre-Dame-des-Victoires seems to have been instrumental in one of the leading events of Claudel's life. It was there that he confided his personal preoccupations and anxieties, and called down heavenly assistance for the Church and his country (like Péguy, he felt a physical and almost carnal love for France). A relentless religious persecution was in full swing all around him, and some of the men who conducted it were his superiors in the foreign office. He sensed an increasingly dangerous trend, a definite threat which might even lead to physical violence and loss of life. On December 25, 1905, at midnight, he attended Christmas Mass in that church—which is possibly the most intimate in Paris—built by King Louis XIII to commemorate the capture of La Rochelle, under the name of Notre-Dame-des-Victoires. Three days later, he was engaged to be married.

Almost twenty years earlier, in Notre-Dame cathedral, the Blessed Virgin had smiled upon him, and it was to her that he turned for the choice of a bride, a choice of which he felt incapable. She "brought [to him] by the hand"—in his own words—Reine Sainte-Marie-Perrin, one of the daughters of her Fourvière architect. Claudel's future father-in-law, who was to die in 1917, was a real patriarch surrounded by his fifty children and grandchildren. An elder daughter had married Doctor M. Gaillard, a physician who practiced in Annecy. The eldest of his sons, an officer in a Dragoons regiment, had graduated from the Saumur Cavalry School and was to die for his country in 1914. A second son, Antoine, an architect like his father, had married Elisabeth Bazin (one of the daughters of René Bazin), who would one day write *Introduction à l'oeuvre de Paul Claudel*. A second daughter was to become the wife of Doctor Millon, and would later own an estate[4] at Hostel-en-Virieu in the Bugey, which played an important part in Claudel's life. Reine was the fifth and last of the family, whose mother was to die prematurely.

[4] This remained joint property for many years, but now belongs to Pierre Desjardins.

The Sainte-Marie-Perrins were strictly practicing Catholics, and the atmosphere in their home was intensely religious. Claudel felt perfectly in his element with them, although he came from a family where God's presence was barely perceptible, where observance was intermittent and purely formal, and where an ill wind had swept away all deeper faith. One day, during one of his conversations with me, Claudel praised those "right-thinking" *bourgeois* of Lyons, who may have been cut off from the main stream of life, but who at least generously provided God with priests and nuns; while their detractors are often notable, in their pretentious intellectualism, for a deplorable sterility. In a poem entitled *L'Architecte,* he was to draw a portrait of his father-in-law: "powerful and straight," with his "white beard" and "big bushy eyebrows," whom "the children, at the golden hour of the morning all came to salute, standing in a line before his drawing board."

Paul and Reine had known each other before, but they met again in Paris and received Communion during the mass we have already mentioned at Notre-Dame-des-Victoires. In the glow of his engagement, Paul translated the poems of Coventry Patmore, an Englishman who was married three times and who extolled in lyrical terms the sacrament of matrimony. In his neighborhood, on the quai des Célestins, Reine's fiancé found a priest after his own heart, an Oratorian named Father Baudrillart, who was to become Cardinal. Claudel found in him a confessor who may have been gruff—like himself—but who was straightforward in his ideas and advice, aware of life's problems and familiar with the difficulties of young intellectuals, since he had studied at *Normale* and been a fellow-student of Bergson and Jaurès. In addition, he was truly kind, faithful and even tender in his affections.

Several setbacks and complications occurred between the engagement and the wedding. After having undergone major abdominal surgery, one of Reine's uncles hovered between

life and death. Paul, who had gone to Lyons and was staying
at the hôtel de l'Europe, on the rue Bellecour, came down
with influenza and was confined to his bed for several days.
All arrangements had been made for the ceremony to take
place on March 19, the feast day of St. Joseph—which meant
a great deal to Claudel—in the church of Saint-Martin
d'Ainay, in the parish of the Sainte-Marie-Perrin family. The
date was advanced, since it was feared that the uncle would
die. The wedding[5] was celebrated on March 15 at eleven in
the morning, in the chapel of a hospital for young incurables,
at 6 rue Jarente, founded by one of Reine's great-aunts.

Three days later, on March 18, the newlyweds sailed for
China. The young bride uncomplainingly accepted the fate
which separated her so soon from her family. She did not
claim to be an intellectual, but was well educated, highly in-
tuitive and proud of her husband. She was to help him im-
measurably in his career through her tact in handling people,
a quality as essential to a diplomat's wife as it is to her husband. In this particular instance, since tact was not one of
Claudel's outstanding attributes, although he had many
others, she had to show enough for two. She created a gracious
setting for him, knew how to entertain, how to organize and
maintain social relationships, how to extend and continue his
personality through a home where, during his absence, she
took care of everything just as though he were still present.

The atmosphere in France during this second half of March
was anything but idyllic. A parliamentary interpellation on
the church inventories had just brought about the fall of the
Rouvier government. Sarrien was to become premier, with
Clémenceau as minister of the interior, and Léon Bourgeois
as minister of foreign affairs. The Conference of Algeciras,
on the straits of Gibraltar, was in session, trying to settle the
Moroccan question. At the end of the month the horrible

[5] An article on the wedding appeared in *Le Tout-Lyon*, No. 541,
March 25, 1906.

catastrophe of Courrières, in the Artois district, was to cause the death of twelve hundred miners. Intellectual life was enlivened by a few new names and titles. Paul Claudel would probably have looked vainly in book shops for the first volumes of his theatrical works. But he would have found, among the recent best-sellers, *Le voyage de Sparte,* by Maurice Barrès, *Les Roquevillard,* by Henri Bordeaux, and *La fille de Jorio,* by Gabriele d'Annunzio.

The young couple traveled with Monsieur Bapst, the new French minister to China. Claudel was to be his first secretary, but remained at the legation in Peking for only a few weeks. He was then sent to Tientsin where he became, as it were, administrator, mayor and even a kind of viceroy, with the title of consul, first class. It was then a city of forty-thousand inhabitants. In July 1906, he wrote to Jammes: "The consulate is rather pleasant and comfortably appointed. The countryside is horribly poor and ugly. It is really an *edging* of a country, as one would speak of the edging of some material, all eaten away by sand and salt water." In this environment he applied himself assiduously to his consular duties, to the organization of his home—a haven in his busy and eventful life—and to the daily accomplishment of his mission as a poet and a man of God. He forgot neither the souls left behind in France nor those which, in this foreign country, could not be a matter of indifference to him. During this period his major poetic work was the ode he entitled *L'Esprit et l'Eau.* Written beneath the walls of Peking, "near a marigold-colored palace," it describes the sea and the enchantment of water, a symbol of "infinity and liberation," and even more of the spirit's higher aspiration which leads to God. Although invisible, He is not absent, and "we are connected to Him through that fluid element, spirit or water, which pervades all things." In a merciless self-examination, Claudel rued his past transgressions and errors. But he had turned a new page, and a fault can be redeemed by tears. In

silence, he was now attentive only to the uninterrupted voice
of Wisdom:

It is the soul receiving the soul, and all things in you
                                have become clear.
Here is the Word, like an eternal virgin, on the threshold
                                of my house!
Throw the door open! God's wisdom stands before you like a
                    tower of glory and a crowned queen!
O my friend, I am neither man nor woman, but love, which
                    is greater than any word![6]

On January 20, 1907, Paul and Reine Claudel's first child
was born. They had hoped and wished for a boy, who would
have been named Joseph. But it was a daughter, Marie, "our
Chouchette." The father had insisted on being present during
the delivery, and wrote to Gide: "[It is] a very beautiful and
moving thing, and not the horror and the filth depicted by that
disgusting Zola." In a third ode he let his heart sing a *Magnificat*. He thanked God, who had saved him from death, a
spiritual death toward which he was hurtling, the outcome of
the philosophies of nothingness, of homicidal theories. Obe-
dient to the divine will and ordination, he exulted before the
new-born infant:

Be blessed, for You have given me this child, and with me
    have provided the means of returning to You this life
    You have given me,
And now I am her father with You.

His fatherhood reached beyond flesh and blood, beyond
the concrete realities of his family, soil and race. In this man
of forty, who through trials and struggles had found invincible
and radiant certainties, distant souls—anxious ·about their
eternal destiny—quite naturally recognized a father capable
of bringing them an answer, The Answer. So it was that in
March he received an anguished letter, the heartbreaking ap-

[6] *Cinq grandes Odes*, p. 74.

peal of Jacques Rivière, a young intellectual smothered and all but destroyed by the pernicious philosophies of the day. Rivière, the son of a professor at the medical school of the Bordeaux University, had been a brilliant student at the lycée Lakanal, and was a friend of Alain-Fournier (whose sister he later married). This young man in his early twenties was strongly influenced by Gide. And like Gide, he had until then refused to *choose* between a boundless freedom and the acceptance of the disciplines inherent in the Catholic faith, a faith after which he aspired with all his energies. He was already planning a treatise on apologetics, which was taking shape in his mind; but the keystone was missing. He wrote of God: "I need Him, for everything to fall into place." Humiliating refusals followed his fervent impulses. With one hand he took back what the other had given. He needed a steadiness of purpose, of which he seemed wellnigh incapable. Who could give him this perseverance if not Claudel, that tower of strength, that Christian of singularly powerful genius, who appeared to have solved for himself the problems tormenting the younger man?

The consul's reply was strikingly firm and even demanding. But it was also marked with true fatherly affection and contained sudden references to himself and to his particular struggles. Claudel wrote this answer in the light of the birth with which his home had just been blessed, and of a faith which found a source and a support in the fathomless depths of prayer.

Meanwhile, Claudel was bored by this severe and mediocre Chinese city and by his distressingly monotonous administrative duties. His most rewarding hours were in the morning. After taking a look at his child, "a very pretty little girl— in my opinion, at least— . . . a new exeperience . . . ; very new and very strong emotions," he would take his place in church in his consular armchair, within the chancel, to the right of the Gospel, "facing a horrible painting of a deathly

pale St. Louis burying corpses which look like children's
'gollywogs,' in view of a castle resembling a gasoline storage
tank."[7] In this church what favors did he ask of God? To take
him away from this place where he could not lead his spiritual
life or conduct his literary activities as he wished, and where
he was beset by too many obligations. He broached the subject to Philippe Berthelot, then assistant head of the personal
staff of the foreign affairs minister, and soon to be appointed
assistant director for Asian affairs at the Quai d'Orsay. Berthelot felt that it might be possible to arrange his friend's
transfer to Calcutta, a prospect which delighted Claudel.

The summer brought back solitude. He sent his wife and
daughter to Shan Hai Kwan on the seashore, at the end of
the Great Wall. He resumed his bachelor habits, rediscovered
his monastic tastes and propensity for meditation in a cell,
and even wrote to his friend Suarès, "Absurd as this may
seem, I have a kind of idea that I will end my days as a
priest."[8]

News from France reached him in surprising and contrasting variety. He had already heard of Husymans' death, on
May 12, which had affected him deeply, for he saw in it the
passing of one of Christ's few witnesses in contemporary literature. A witness who gave a heroic denial to those who had
doubted the sincerity of his conversion. Claudel considered as
a miracle comparable to those of Lourdes this acceptance of
a horrible death (eyelids sewn together, tongue eaten away
by cancer) by a man who previously had been oversensitive
to a multitude of minor physical ailments and discomforts.
Shortly after this sad event Francis Jammes imposed on his
life the discipline of matrimony. In Bucy-le-Long, not far
from Villeneuve-sur-Fère, he married Geneviève Goedorp,
an admirer of his works. Having read some of his books, she
had written to him, on her own initiative. "Tired of Art and

[7] Correspondence with André Gide, p. 91.
[8] Correspondence with André Suarès, p. 109.

artists," (as he wrote to Suarès on August 5) Claudel remained faithful to those fraternal hearts who did not hesitate to acknowledge values transcending literature, and to subordinate everything else to those values, as he himself had done once and for all.

During that period Bergson's works were the rage. In Tientsin, Claudel followed *L'Évolution créatrice*, which probably interested him even more than he ever admitted. Perhaps he saw in it the characteristic expression of the new philosophy. The consul, who in the Chinese mountains had studied and pondered the *Summae* of St. Thomas, detected in Bergson's book various sophisms, oversimplifications and weaknesses; but he also found in it, and did not hesitate to say so, some "profound and fruitful" views, such as the theory of space and life. He even saw in *L'Évolution créatrice* a certain similarity to his own conception of time, but nevertheless felt and emphasized important differences between Bergson's ideas and his own.

Claudel was to remain in China several years more. An important national event there was the death of the Empress Tzu Hsi in 1908. She had stubbornly and fiercely opposed the modernization of her country. Pu-Yi, a child of two, succeeded her and was the last emperor of the Manchu dynasty. His reign ended three years later through revolution, but he was to reappear from 1934 to 1945 on the throne of Manchukuo, as a puppet of the Japanese. Claudel lived these historic days intensely, when a great nation was in travail on the eve of Sun Yat-Sen's rebellion, which was to bring in a republican form of government. Indeed, although a man of the past, a traditionalist, Claudel was also and quite obviously a man of the future to an equal degree. In September 1907, when he was able to join his family at the seaside resort of Shan Hai Kwan, it was with a joyous optimism that he wrote his *Processional pour saluer le siècle nouveau* in the form "of those sequences of the early Church"

which he so admired. The future is temporal destiny, with its
heavy weight and the difficult commerce of men. But it is
also the second coming of the Redeemer, the Judgment of
the world, the entrance into Peace.

> Be therefore neither tormented nor jubilant within yourself,
> but seek first the Kingdom of God and its justice.
> The rest is unimportant. Sufficient unto the day is the
> malice thereof.
>
> And life is more than bread, and the body more than
> clothing.
> I am at peace with all beings under the vault of heaven.
> Half of my life is already done, and I am released from it
> forever.
> It will not start again. I see before me the end of the road
> and of the day. . . .
> I see my wife next to me, and my child clear and triumphant,
> who vigorously kicks her cradle, and laughs in the rising
> sun.
> My child babbles in the rising sun, little heart filled to
> the brim with innocent joy,
> Because God has not created it for death, but for the life
> of the living vision!

And in his *Cinquième Ode*, Claudel shows himself imbued
with the idea of a "world finite and closed, an earth alone
inhabited by living and intelligent beings." In the past he
had been disturbed by the problem of the plurality of inhabited worlds. He now seemed free of this concern. The
eternal silence of infinite space no longer alarmed him. He
contemplated the universe "with a familiar confidence, realizing that God, Who has made only perfect things, has no
use for what is finite, and that, knowing the number of His
sparrows, He is also aware of the number of His stars."[9]
Claudel had hardly completed his odes before he started work
on a kind of lyrical breviary, the "songs arising as the sacred
hours unfold."

[9] Correspondence with André Gide, pp. 91-92.

On February 4, 1909, writing to Jacques Rivière, Claudel said among other things, and without further details: "I have met a most beautiful soul, a certain L.M., a convert and a student at the Cairo School [of archeology]. . . . I receive from him letters worthy of a saint." This was Louis Massignon, then twenty-five years old, who was to devote his entire life to the study of Islamic religion and civilization. In recognition of his competence and authority he was to receive a professorship at the Collège de France. Massignon was tall, had solemn and unforgettable eyes, and was a born mystic. During those years as a student he had faced problems and trials in which Claudel recognized something of his own spiritual crisis. With his flair for vocations, the poet-diplomat soon realized that this dedicated Orientalist belonged to the race of those men chosen by God for heroic conquests and inner sacrifices. Perhaps Massignon would be the Columbus of a secret Asia and Africa which would bear witness in God's own time. Around 1908, he was to write: "The traveler who sees those great inert Oriental civilizations understands what an invaluable ferment Christianity has been, precisely because there is no part of human nature which it has left untouched."

They met during the year 1908, marked for the young consul by several memorable events. His friend Rivière was engaged to be married, which made even more pressing the obligations he had assumed toward that serious and sensitive young man who was so unstable spiritually! In May, Claudel read the life of the Curé d'Ars by Vianney (a pseudonym of the Saint). This book led him deeper into the mystery of priesthood, over which he had already pondered so much, with such agonizing introspection. On July 23, he experienced an ineffable joy: the birth of his first son, Pierre. In the fall an extensive tour allowed him to see the entire district placed under his consular jurisdiction. He visited the area as no one else could have done, with a deep attention to all questions and all details, and gathered valuable information; a summary of which, on the religious plane, is contained in a letter he wrote to Massignon (October 12, 1908):

> You know what an admirable movement of conversion is taking place at the present time in Northern China. In the Peking vicariate alone—one of the four vicariates of Chu-Li —there were nearly fifteen thousand adult christenings last year, and it is necessary to slow down the rate of conversions on account of the limited number of missionaries. Who knows whether the light is not now returning toward the Orient, and whether the West is not going to enter one of those periods of sabbatical fallowness mentioned in Leviticus? We see that Persia, Russia and hither Asia, which seemed buried forever under the sands of Islam, are once again receiving the winds from Europe; those winds dissolving to everything but truth. Who knows whether you yourself are not one of the laborers . . . chosen for the great task which seems to be starting?

Every conversion manifests the divine intention of creating new instruments for designs which go far beyond the immediate beneficiary. There have been cases of small towns where a complete change of spiritual atmosphere was brought about simply through the apparent agency of an antireligious schoolteacher struck by Grace, as though by lightning. All that was still needed was this surrender, for the last obstacles to give way and crumble. On a much larger scale, the future St. Paul had to fall from his horse on the road to Damascus for the Gentiles to embrace Christianity; and St. Augustine had to be mysteriously prompted to open and read the Book of Truth so that Africa might start on the way to the discovery of Christ. After the skepticism of the years during which Renan dominated the French intellectual scene, Claudel had to experience that sudden inflow of the supernatural, in Notre-Dame Cathedral during Christmas vespers, so that new generations of French youth might confess the faith. Louis Massignon had become a convert while studying the martyrdom of a Moslem won over to Christianity. His Tientsin correspondent felt that this was the indication and the omen of an important providential design:

> A conversion is always an astonishing miracle, a direct call through which God addresses us personally. And He is an artist too sparing of His means for any of those rare and dramatic developments to be useless to his great plans. When the ashes of this martyr bring forth new flowers in your heart, it is God Himself Who speaks to you and tells you to resume His work. I know full well that God is served through holiness, rather than through any special talent or human science. But each one [of us] does what he can and uses what he has.

Such prospects helped Claudel not to lose heart in this diplomatic post where he remained much against his wish. The same letter to Massignon describes "this rather austere place, which has the nakedness of the desert without its grandeur, and the barrenness without the solitude. No intellectual company, no stimulation for the mind; as occupation, the miserable quarrels of my nationals to be settled; to write poetry [here] one must really draw everything from oneself. Only the sky is beautiful, always offered to the eyes, always admirably pure . . ."

But a kind of peace had come to his soul. The echoes of the storm had gradually died down. He sometimes suffered—and complained about it—from a spiritual aridity which left him helpless before the new problems facing him. He had become capable of directing his attention elsewhere than into his soul, however; of taking interest in history, in the past, in other human beings.

His theatrical works were to benefit from this newly acquired serenity, and objective, nonpersonal elements would henceforth occupy a larger place in them, while his torn and suffering ego would play less and less of a part. His curiosity became universal. English literature always fascinated him and he read it avidly. After Robert Browning, who was— Claudel felt—wonderfully imaginative, it introduced him to Robert Hugh Benson, admittedly not a writer of the first rank, but one whose *Master of the Earth* interested the young diplomat greatly, for he recognized in it certain viewpoints resembling those which had occupied his own mind when he wrote *Tête d'Or*. At that earlier time in his life he was anxious above all to project his ego into his dramatic works, a heavy and cumbersome ego of which he needed to unburden himself. Probably because the storms in his soul had gradually subsided, the dramatic author now gave a dominant role to more objective themes. He occasionally utilized personal memories and experiences, but only for the purpose of adding color, of introducing a shade of meaning, of connecting the products of his inventive genius to realities drawn from actual life. In this spirit he undertook to write *L'Annonce faite à Marie*, the purest and highest among all his dramatic works and certainly the most beautiful steeple of his lyrical edifice. As in *La Jeune fille Violaine*, a rivalry between two sisters forms the basis of the plot. One can recognize in it something of the atmosphere of his own family, of his village swept by furious winds, of the folklore of Champagne, his native province. Everything in this drama leads toward a miracle. The play is like a stained-glass window representing the coronation of the King of France in Rheims, in which Claudel took great liberties with historical truth. In the filigree of the plot one can perceive a chronicle of the author's own life, marked by the miraculous event of a Christmas night. These are not the essential aspects of the play, however. *L'Annonce faite à Marie* is the tidings brought to Violaine, as it was the tidings brought to Joan of Arc, who in 1908 had just been beatified and whom one cannot help thinking of throughout the four acts. Violaine is the exceptional creature, the chosen woman, designated from all eternity to co-operate in the redemption of men. Her sublime *fiat* echoes throughout the play, with the mystery of love which stamps its terrible consequences. Mara, who deserves pity rather than contempt, stands in contrast to Violaine. In her way she is a believer; she has no doubt of her sister's holiness, nor of the possibility of miracles.

While Claudel was composing this drama, a campaign was carried out against him, and all Philippe Berthelot's authority was required to save his friend. The consul had been obliged to dismiss a dishonest employee, who took his revenge by denouncing his superior for alleged clericalist plots. During that period, clericalism was, to use the word of Gambetta, "the enemy." The various government offices in Paris, where Freemasonry was all-powerful, took a decidedly dim view of any civil servant suspected of religious zeal. The matter reached the point where Berthelot had to threaten to hand in his own resignation to avoid any sanction against Claudel. It seemed doubtful that the poet-diplomat could remain in China, although without these unfortunate developments he probably would have received a new assignment in any case. There was talk of appointing him to Damascus. He had to be extremely careful, and the fragments which he sent to *La Nouvelle Revue Française* were even published under his initials, instead of his full name.

Amid these contradictions and vicissitudes, how could Claudel help feeling more exiled than ever? He experienced the need to forge a spiritual link between himself and so many friends who shared his present or past difficulties, who sought God with the same ardor which had been and remained the motive force of his own life. In increasing numbers, young people and priests wrote to him, and this correspondence no doubt formed an infinitely precious bond with the vast world of living souls. Obsessed with the certainty of the Communion of Saints, which was precisely the theme of

L'Annonce, he wished for something more. For many years I
believed that this interest on his part was only intermittent
and secondary. After reading many letters dealing with this
plan I came to understand that, on the contrary, Claudel
attached the greatest importance to the project and that it
played a major role in his life as a man and a believer. He
spoke of it for the first time in a letter to Louis Massignon,
on February 4, 1909: "Many young people write to me, and
some have become converted. I would like us all to be among
ourselves like a *Co-operative of Prayer,* in all the parts of
the world where we live, asking God that we may always
do for His service what is most immediate, what is closest
with regard to those who are closest to us: *'Proximum erga
proximum.'* "

At about the same time, Claudel told another friend of
his plans. This friend was Charles Henrion, an extremely
gifted student at the University of Nancy. One day the desert
was to call him and to keep him forever, in a destiny comparable to that of Father Charles de Foucauld. A study on
Claudel by Jacques Rivière had filled him with enthusiasm,
and he had wanted to know the poet. Massis and Maritain
greeted him, and he was to participate in the famous investi-
gation of Agathon. Henrion later guided Cocteau toward a
conversion which unfortunately proved short-lived, and
acted as spiritual adviser to Eve Lavallière, that entertainer
of the boulevards who also became a target for the Holy
Spirit. Subsequently Francis Jammes, and then Gabriel Frizeau, were informed of Claudel's plan and were asked for
their suggestions and advice. In the consul's mind it was not
a question "of a confraternity or of a special devotion, but
simply of people scattered to the four corners of the earth,
and linked through bonds of affection and mutual esteem,
who agree on a way of thinking of each other every day, of
benefiting each other if possible, and of offering to God in
collective homage one single flower, composed of them all."

A little later (October 4, 1909), he added in a letter to Louis Massignon: "Let us draw together by the thread of prayer, like rosary beads, or like mountaineers who are in danger of falling."

The idea gradually took shape. Claudel was not the kind of man to abandon easily a plan he was really attached to. It took three years to reach fruition. We will follow its slow evolution in another chapter. Meanwhile, his long stint of duty in China was about to end. In May, in the magnificent city of Peking, he attended the pitiful and carnival-like (these are approximately the adjectives he used) funeral of the Emperor Kwang-Su. At the beginning of the summer he received news of a new assignment. Although worried about his wife, who was expecting another child, and about his very young children, he left joyfully for Paris. On August 16 he boarded the Trans-Siberian railway.

8

"BOHEMIA, SEATED BETWEEN ITS FOUR FORESTS"[1]

WHAT A JOY TO SEE FRANCE AGAIN, TO FEAST HIS EYES ON the familiar countryside! After a thirteen-day journey, Claudel arrived in Paris, stayed briefly at the hôtel de la Trémoille, and soon left for Champagne. He was eager to return to his roots, and to absorb the atmosphere he required in order to undertake the writing of *L'Otage*, a major work to which he devoted much thought during those inspired months. He stopped at Rheims, which represented for him the crown, the scepter, the Holy Ampulla, the lilies of France, the royal standard; all witnessed by the double flame of the noble cathedral of the coronation. Laon showed him another great medieval church, rising on the top of a hill from the depths of a land which fed the rustic imagination of the Le Nain brothers. At Goudelancourt, near Liesse, he discovered one of the cradles of his family. Liesse itself is the site of a centuries-old pilgrimage to the Virgin of Champagne. He decided to stay there a while and to fulfill a wish dear to his heart: the preparation of what was to be the charter of his *Co-operative of Prayer*. He wanted the association to be rooted in this land of faith. He submitted the charter to Father Baudrillart, his confessor, and on October 4 wrote to his friend Louis Massignon: "I hope that you sometimes think of that little Co-operative of Prayer which I spoke about in one of my letters

[1] *St. Wenceslas, roi et martyr*, poem dedicated to Zdenka Braunerova.

to you. I had mentioned it in rather general terms to another friend, and the idea has developed on its own, as it were. This small sodality now includes Jammes, Frizeau, a converted student from Nancy named Henrion, Th. de la Rive [a convert from Protestantism], a Benedictine monk, a Carmelite nun and a few others."

At the beginning of October, after a short stay in Villeneuve-sur-Fère—which had hardly changed at all and where so many memories came to life under his fervent contemplation—Claudel was off again to Hostel, in the Bugey, the family estate of the Sainte-Marie-Perrins. It is not too much to say that a kind of mysterious rapport would henceforth link him with that district. Although he belonged to the province of Champagne through all his ancestral ties, through all the fibers of his being, through his physical and spiritual make-up, his language and his accent—and although he enjoyed returning frequently to Villeneuve—there was in him a kind of implicit rejection of those elements in his memories of the past which were alien, and somehow inimical to his personality. He had suffered too deeply through his family and early environment—even though he still felt toward them a filial, fraternal and Christian attachment—not to turn toward a new land better attuned to the new human being he had become. He belonged both to Bugey and to Champagne, as Barrès belonged to Auvergne and Lorraine.

Hostel lies near Artemare, between Nantua and Belley. It is a happy place amid happy landscapes, which is exactly what Claudel needed. He spoke to his friend Gabriel Frizeau "of the face of this country of joy, next to which all others are but darkness" [June 14], and "of the most admirable landscape one can see anywhere" [October 14]. On October 12 he wrote to Louis Massignon: "I also live amid the most beautiful countryside one can imagine, in the threefold glory of autumn, mountains and glaciers. God has made my life very sweet, and treats me like a spoilt child, it seems." A local historian describes the locality in the following terms:

> Rising on a wooded peak, the château of Hostel, situated northwest of Artemare, forms one of the most magnificent vantage points of this region which is studded with many country houses as picturesque as they are livable. Facing away from the western slopes of the Val Romey [these heights are called the Hauteville plateau] and from the pine forests framing the Col de la Lube, one beholds from the terraces of Hostel the imposing mass of the Colombier [last foothill of the Jura] which, starting at Hotonnes, borders the Val Romey to the east. To the southeast, beyond Béon and Culoz, one catches a glimpse of the Alps of Savoy enclosing the Lac du Bourget, so dear to Lamartine. To the south, Belley is hidden from view by the Bugey hills, the castle of Grammont and Ceyzérieu. Paul Claudel compared the valleys converging toward Artemare to the spokes of a wheel meeting at the hub." (*Cantate*, p. 27)[2]

Claudel's father-in-law, Sainte-Marie-Perrin (he was the architect of Fourvière), had bought the estate from Count de Lauzière. As an artist, he had been captivated by the magnificent view which it afforded. And as a Christian he delighted in a spectacle which quite naturally directed his thoughts toward the God of beauty. As I write these lines, I have before my eyes a sketch of the castle and of its immediate surroundings, drawn in the romantic manner by the architect's son Antoine. Paul Claudel endlessly explored the neighboring countryside, always on foot, with his usual patience, attentiveness and acuity of observation. He drew parallels and comparisons with what he had seen elsewhere, and these almost invariably turned to the advantage of Hostel and Bugey. He grew to know all the country roads, footpaths and passes. Fascinated with plant life almost as much as his friend

[2] *Yggdrasill Review*, November 25, 1936, article signed A XXX.

Jammes, he would question the local people about new flowers he noticed. A connoisseur of wine to the extent that he later challenged the vinegrower Ramuz, he marveled at the grapevine, "daughter of the Flood and mysterious sign of our salvation." Tasting the wine of Ceyzérieu, he exclaimed: "A god, I tell you, and not a man . . . invented how to gather in a glass the heat of the sun, the color of the rose, the taste of blood and the temptation of cool, clear water; and gave us in one and the same drinking cup, in order to unburden our souls, both the water which dissolves and the fire which consumes."[3]

Returning to Paris he first lived with his mother at 37 Quai d'Anjou, then in a furnished apartment which he rented at 7 rue La Trémoille. He was happy to see his literary friends again: André Gide, Gide's brother-in-law Drouin, Jacques Copeau, Jacques Rivière and Charles-Louis Philippe. Gabriel Frizeau joined him in Paris. Claudel sensed the workings of Grace in many of these souls. At that time Gide was not without a certain religious fervor. Philippe, more secretive, was torn between two opposite tendencies, the son of the Cérilly sabot maker, the friend of Jacques Chevalier, preferred the voices of peasant loyalty to those of Parisian nihilism. Rivière hesitated between the author of *La Porte étroite* and that of *La Jeune fille Violaine*. Claudel noticed also that "this period seems to be [religiously speaking] that of the laity." On December 4, 1909, he wrote to Louis Massignon: "See what a [large] role it has played for the past hundred years, which has no counterpart in any other era: Chateaubriand, de Maistre, Veuillot, Ozanam and many others." During these years Claudel's mission as a Christian, rather than his literary activity, was the most important element in his life.

Instead of returning to China, Claudel was appointed French Consul in Prague. Czechoslovakia did not yet exist

[3] "Cantate," *L'oeuvre poétique* (Gallimard, La Pléiade), p. 338.

and the capital of Bohemia was then under Austrian domina-
tion. It owed its name *(Praha)* to the war cry of John of
Luxembourg, King of Bohemia, who died like a hero on the
French battlefield of Crécy-en-Ponthieu (August 25, 1346).
This was a sacred link between Bohemia and France, one
that the new consul liked to recall. Nor was it the only historical bond between the two countries. During the same
fourteenth century, French cultural influence in this Central
European kingdom had been strong, and the Cathedral of
St. Velt, which overlooks Prague, was designed by the French
architect Mathias d'Arras. In the more recent past, in 1871,
when Germany annexed Alsace-Lorraine, the protest raised
by the Czech deputies was a comforting gesture of solidarity
with the French people. The famous *Sokols* (falcons)—members of the patriotic societies originally founded in Prague,
which later spread to so many other countries, and whose
purpose it was to foster the practice of athletics by the young
—were actively supported in France. The Sokols performed
at the Universal Exposition of 1889, in particular, and
during the following years in various French provincial
cities.

But it was only around 1895 that the French government
decided to open a consulate in Prague. At first its existence
seemed precarious, for commercial relations between France
and the kingdom of Bohemia were very limited, in both ton-
nage and value. In 1906 a certain French senator—concerned
exclusively with trade interests, it would appear, and insensi-
tive to both moral influences and historical memories—suggested that this consular office be closed. This brought an
almost immediate answer. A detailed pamphlet by Louis
Léger on *French Interests in Bohemia* was distributed to
the members of parliament, and the inopportune suggestion
was fortunately rejected. When Paul Claudel reached Prague
he was welcomed most cordially by Mr. Srb and Dr. Gros,
two old and faithful friends of France. And he was delighted
with the opportunity to sit at that "table d'hôte" of Europe

represented, in his view, by the declining Austrian empire.

Goethe called Prague "a magnificent precious stone set in the crown of the earth," and Chateaubriand saw in it "a cheerful city where twenty-five to thirty graceful towers and steeples pyramid skyward." Claudel made a preliminary trip to his new post around December 4, and from the first admired the sumptuous baroque architecture of the city where he was at once surrounded with warm sympathy and friendship. The first few weeks were far from pleasant, however. He was officially installed on the feast day of the Immaculate Conception, was unable to occupy immediately the apartment set aside for him, and had to be content with temporary quarters which were cramped and mediocre, at 8 *Riegrovo nabrezi*. In addition, the winter was gloomy and bitterly cold. He wrote Louis Massignon on December 13, 1909:

> I live under a horrible snow and in continuous darkness. This is certainly a change from Tientsin, where the sky is always clear as the purest crystal. Add to this all the difficulties of a temporary encampment in a small apartment—the one we were to occupy will only be available in February— my wife who is pregnant and tired, and finally a sick child whose continuous cries break my heart. I commend my family and myself to your fraternal prayers.
>
> The people of Prague are very friendly, and their city itself is most pleasing. The Jesuits have strongly left their mark on it. On every side are statues in the manner of Bernini, making nobly pathetic gestures in a great flourish of billowing cloaks. The small and devout churches are dark and warm as nests, filled with little cherubs and great rays of gilt wood. Above all this, a long palace crowned with a pointed spire: the *Hradschin*.

Central Europe proved to be a highly enriching experience for Claudel. This cannot be overemphasized. He learned to know and understand baroque art, a style admirably suited to his temperament. He witnessed at closer range the sufferings of the Jews, and became the friend of authors such as Milos Marten, an admirer and propagandist of French literature. The Roman Catholic discovered the realities of the Counter Reformation.

To his family worries and household troubles was added a new grief. On Christmas day, as he returned from Mass, a letter brought him the news of Charles-Louis Philippe's death.[4] The suddenness of the event, and his own uncertainty concerning the ultimate frame of mind of that young novelist of goodwill and considerable talent (who might well have succumbed to the prevailing Parisian mood of skepticism) were a great personal blow to Claudel. The poet had very much hoped to lead back to God the younger man, for whom he had deep affection. This was his answer to the friend who had sent him the sad news:

> I had left him in Paris, a few weeks ago, full of life and gaiety, and now, of all the small group of my friends, he is the first who silently leaves me. God have mercy on this good heart, on this noble soul full of simplicity and of tenderness for the poor! After the inequities of life, death now leads him to his proper place. But what bitter desolation for all of us! Our friend has not been harvested, but brutally uprooted in full fruit, just as *Croquignole* heralded the great works of maturity.
>
> Five years ago I had a long and earnest conversation with Philippe. May he on his deathbed have remembered those words, admittedly so inadequate, but which at least were most sincere and came from the heart of his Christian friend. I felt that this soul, so noble and religious, was made for total enlightenment. I firmly hope that this great light was not denied him at the final moment, *in ictu oculi, in sono tubae.*
>
> I thank you most sincerely for having immediately thought of me when you heard the horrible news; I am deeply touched

[4] This letter was published in the periodical *Les Davidées*, June, 1934.

by your kind thoughtfulness. I would be even more indebted
to you if you could tell me everything you may learn on the
last moments of our poor friend.[5]

The plot of *L'Otage*, the drama written largely in Prague,
is so closely related to Claudel's personal life that it deserves
to be outlined.

As we have already explained, one of his ancestors, at the
peril of her life, had hidden a priest in her house during the
revolutionary terror, and had made a vow to offer her son to
God if the priest escaped his persecutors. Moreover, as soon
as he reached manhood, Claudel had felt deeply the conflict
created in him by his partly aristocratic and partly plebeian
ancestry. Through his Cerveaux grandmother he was descended, as we have previously pointed out, from the de
Vertus family, which traced its lineage directly back to Louis
d'Orléans, brother of King Charles VI. But he also counted
among his forebears vulgarians like the Chamborands; one of
these, an hussar, had been known for his "extremely brutal
and adventurous temperament," and had "left a memory of
terror in the district" where Claudel spent part of his childhood.[6]

Besides, a book written by Count d'Haussonville on the
Pope had made a profound impression on him. Once again
he had found in it "this conflict between two races, a conflict
which had more or less as arbiter and battlefield the religious
question, in the person of the Supreme Pontiff, namely of
the Pope, who at that time was truly tossed between various
[opposite] influences."[7]

It appeared to Claudel that a situation like that in which
Sygne, his heroine, was to find herself toward Turelure still
held "present significance." This was confirmed to him in
Prague, when he came into contact with members of the

[5] Letter to M.E., Christmas 1909.
[6] *Mémoires imaginaires.*
[7] *Ibid.*

declining Austrian aristocracy. A *grande dame* to whom he had described the theme of *L'Otage* said to him quite frankly, "You do not know to what a degree the tragedy of Sygne has been that of a large section of the Austrian aristocracy."

In childhood, Claudel had been deeply and durably impressed by the figure of Pope Pius IX, who was deprived of his Roman states and confined to the Vatican. Paul was only two at the time, and ten when the Pope died, but the subject was often brought up in Bar-le-Duc by the nuns whose pupil he was. Since then he always recognized in the person of the Vicar of Christ "something permanent, and a kind of arbitration in those periods of mankind when precisely there is a complete change in currents and attitudes."

In 1908, while he was still in Tientsin, he drew up a general plan for his future literary efforts, in which *L'Otage* played a major part. This outline satisfied his need for order and clarity. In it he wrote:

> I am now tired of fragmentary works, and would like to limit myself for many years to one large undertaking. Being unable to write an epic poem, I would like to compose a cycle of dramas bringing forth not only characters, but all the strange, multiple and converging means by which these very characters are brought forth for the purposes arranged by God. I may quite possibly take as setting a freely treated episode of nineteenth century history, in which I distinguish three interesting phenomena: (1) The French Revolution, which I will call the revolution against chance; (2) Knowledge of the world; (3) The separation between the world and the man who has no more ties in it . . . One would have to express all this deeply and vividly, avoiding above all else a horrible doctrinal approach through the interplay of three or four series of parallel ideas resolving into increasingly wide agreements.

L'Otage is the first part of a trilogy. It shows what can be called the condition of the Christian, who is outside the world through his belonging to the kingdom of God, and yet of the world by the fact that he lives in it as a social being, faced with temporal problems. In this play we are introduced into an atmosphere of revolution. The revolution as such has already taken place and a new world has begun, in which Georges de Coûfontaine still represents tradition, faithfulness and a certain temporal order founded on the Monarchy; and Turelure embodies the rise of democracy, the ascent of yesterday's have-nots demanding their place in the sun. Georges' sister Sygne considers the grievances of these malcontents, weighing what is fair and legitimate or unjustified and outrageous in their demands. She realizes that the essence of her tradition resides in Christ and in His representative among men, Pope Pius, who under her roof becomes precisely the Hostage. To pour new wine into old bottles, is this not the purest form of Christianity? Through self-sacrifice Sygne allows the ancient race to gain new blood, without losing anything of its original worth. From apparent betrayal she rises to true loyalty. She cannot carry this out without mental reservations and loathing, however. To marry Turelure is more than she is capable of. She reluctantly consents, but does not give herself freely. *Le Pain dur*, the second part of the trilogy, seems to indicate the futility of this heroic sacrifice: it marks a kind of night of waiting in a tomb. In a third panel of the triptych, entitled *Le Père humilié*, Easter morning illumines all prospects: mankind returns to the path of Rome where tradition regains significance, and where at the same time human progress becomes possible because on this path God is revealed each morning, ever more resplendent and ever younger.

In spite of everything which separates and even opposes them, Turelure and Sygne clearly share certain traits. Turelure, the man of the soil who for a time entered a monastery, appears to sense something of the mystical and aristocratic superiority of Sygne de Coûfontaine. He is moved by a nostalgia for what she has and what he lacks. Sygne, daughter of a long line of landowners, cannot fail to understand, in some ways and to some extent, this coarse but authentic product of the soil of Champagne. If one really wishes to fathom and explain Claudel's own personality, I would say that he synthesizes within himself Sygne, Georges, Turelure, Father Badilon, the king and even The Hostage, without however embodying all the elements they represent. Claudel was a mystic and a realist, both feudal and plebeian. He was ecclesiastical, royal and papal. Let us not forget his persistent longing for the priesthood, nor the bitter disappointment he felt throughout his life because this ardent wish of his remained unfulfilled.

While day after day he continued working on *L'Otage*, Paul Claudel sought to make himself at home in the capital city of Bohemia where he still occupied temporary quarters. He occasionally left Prague for short trips to the neighboring countries or provinces. He surrendered to the lure of Vienna where he met Dumaine, the French Ambassador, and saw a performance of *Tannhäuser*. The Austrians he was introduced to interested him at least as much as the art treasures of that city and the memories of a great historical past, perpetuated through so many impressive monuments. He was to remember the sight of Count Walstein descending the grand staircase of his mansion of Mala Strana to meet the future Emperor Charles I. This was a vision of an empire already doomed to collapse.

On February 9, 1910, his third child was born: Reine-Amélie-Zdenka, later known as Gigette to her family. The name of Zdenka was included as a token of gratitude to Zdenka Braunerova, sister-in-law of Elémir Bourges. A distinguished artist, she was to draw the frontispiece for *L'Otage*, and had on several occasions been particularly kind and thoughtful toward the Claudel family. Gigette "made her

appearance in this world one month earlier than we expected
her. A true child of travelers, she arrived in the middle of a
move, and we made her bed in a trunk." This is how the
consul described the happy event to his friend Jammes, who
had just sent him a copy of the tender and touching *Ma fille
Bernadette*. The feelings of a father before a newborn
daughter, before her first looks of recognition, first smiles,
first signs of intelligence and first sorrows, are depicted with
poetic exuberance in this enchanting book. And Claudel himself, a little later, expressed the essence of his paternal joy
in that short but intense masterpiece, *L'Enfant-Jesus de
Prague:*

> December snow is falling. The wide world seems dead.
> But how cosy, O God, is the little room!
> The fireplace filled with glowing embers
> Colors the ceiling with a sleepy reflection.
> Water sings in the kettle.
> Up there, on the shelf above the two beds,
> Under a glass bell, a crown on His head,
> One hand holding the world, and the other ready
> To protect those little ones who trust in Him,
> So lovable in His wide solemn gown
> And magnificent under that huge yellow headdress,
> The Child Jesus of Prague reigns as though enthroned. . . .[8]

Although favored in his family life, and although his old
and new friends were dear to him, he always felt the weight
of a double exile: exiled from France by his diplomatic missions, he was also exiled from the only kingdom where his
soul breathed freely; and it was not without sadness and
regret that one day, in the Benedictine abbey of Emmaus,
he witnessed the ceremonies of a religious profession. "My
solitude weighs heavily on me," he wrote on July 27 to Louis
Massignon, who himself was led by God toward great de-

[8] *Corona benignitatis anni Dei.*

signs but through perilous paths. As Claudel explains in the
same letter, even his art could not provide him with a sub-
stitute for the contemplative life:

> If we have written a few articles, or composed—as I have
> —a few dramas replete with artificial sentiments, *quid hoc
> ad aeternitatum?* What are these accomplishments, even in
> comparison to the temporal glory of the sun rising each morn-
> ing? What does not die is the love of God, the deep joy of
> thinking that for another soul—and, who knows? for a multi-
> tude of poor heads leaning against your heart—you have
> been, you, perishable and mortal, a source of joy and eternal
> life. What a gift God allows us to make if we want to, if we
> only consent to give ourselves, and to let Him take our own
> place in our hearts, a place we surrender to Him.

A convinced Roman, constantly turned toward the light
held and offered to the universe by the successor of Peter,
Claudel saluted in Pius X "a great Pope," and was grateful
to him for his decisions that year concerning the first communion of children. He gave them even more thought than
the papal decisions concerning *Le Sillon*, a movement of
which he did not approve. He wrote Louis Massignon, on
September 1, 1910:

> I share your opinion completely on the new pontifical de-
> cree relating to first communion: it is quite true that these
> ceremonies, in spite of their deeply moving quality, were more
> often than not the concluding act of Christian religious prac-
> tice. Who is more worthy than little children to receive the
> bread of angels? And who can doubt the value in the eyes of
> God of these millions of pure communions which the new
> decree will bring about? The Master Himself finds it is time
> for Him to take the place of His priests and teach these pure
> souls from Heart to heart. Moreover, the decree once again
> asserts a doctrine most comforting to us, that *the Eucharist
> is not a reward, but a help against human frailty.* This re-
> lieves many scruples and anxieties of the heart.

There is something distressing about conversations between believers consisting largely of derogatory comments on the shortcomings of the Church and the unworthiness or mediocrity of the clergy. Claudel, during the same year 1910, protested against this kind of attitude, and took pleasure in gratefully acknowledging the blessings of the divine institution and the services rendered by the men of God he had known:

November 30, 1910

It is certain that all is not perfect in our poor Catholic city. We suffer all the ills which afflict a harshly oppressed minority. But what virtues also! The souls I have met in sodalities and at the lectures of the St. Vincent de Paul Society when I attended them, truly refreshed me every time I think of them. As for priests, it is true that I have endured many dull sermons, but how much good I have received from them! Just recently in Paris, deeply unhappy and worried, I went to the Church of Saint-Sulpice to confess my sins to an unknown priest who spoke to me so kindly, in such a comforting and fatherly manner, placing his hand with such compassion and perspicacity on the sore spots (of my soul)! I had the feeling that God Himself was talking through the priest's mouth, and I left the confessional deeply grateful. I will never see the failings of those who have done me so much good.

But if anyone went too far in belittling the officially atheistic France, Claudel—who suffered as much as any other Catholic from the anticlerical policy of the government—never failed to point out that, under the superficial hostility to the Church, a true Christian revival had come about among the intelligentsia and was gaining momentum on every side. He was soon to learn of the conversion of Charles Péguy, who almost regularly sent him copies of his books. From Coutances, Joseph Lotte, one of Péguy's friends, mailed Claudel the *Bulletin des professeurs catholiques de l'université*. It was a revelation to him, for he did not suspect the existence of these professors, nor their influence. Still few in numbers, they were among the most important and influential: Pierre de la Gorce in Lille, Jean Guiraud in Besançon, Maurice Blondel in Aix, Pierre Duhem in Bordeaux, Pierre Grasset in Montpellier, Georges Dumesnil in Grenoble, Jacques Chevalier, Philippe Gonnard and Pierre Heinrich in Lyons, Victor Giraud in Fribourg, Emile Baumann in Sens, Léonard Constant in Pau and Théodore Quoniam in Coutances. Whole groups of students from the *Grandes Ecoles* received Easter Communion together. With Maurice Denis, George Desvallières and their disciples, art placed itself at the service of religious faith. Persecution was bearing abundant fruit, but did not cease, as Claudel could testify. He wrote to André Gide that he was afraid to see his "personal enemy," the cabinet minister Maurice Berteaux, accede to power.

Also in 1910, his friends in the Académie Goncourt (Elémir Bourges, Léon Daudet—with his usual vehemence— and Octave Mirbeau) voted for him, but the famous annual prize was awarded to Judith Gautier.

This setback did not leave Claudel indifferent, but he knew how to turn the page, forget and set off once again toward work, struggle and possibilities of success and victory.

9

LUMINOUS SUMMERS
AND BITTER STRUGGLES

At this time something like a breath of abnegation, heroism and holiness swept through the thickets of mediocrity which had sprung up on every side and obstructed the French scene. Deeply conscious of his own unworthiness and shortcomings, Claudel urged youth away from the dilettantism which for too long had been the delight of his own generation. And although he was aware of his personal limitations, he nevertheless felt entitled to proclaim a message consonant with what he knew to be the truth, this truth born in him through tears and inner agony. Writing on February 6, 1911, to Louis Massignon, whose difficult path he was attempting to illuminate, Claudel did not hesitate to make these comments, which are closely matched by some of the advice he gave Jacques Rivière:

> It is said that youth is the age of passions. This is not true, for youth is the age of heroism. And if you want to love and be loved, what could you ever hold in your arms to compare with the weakness, with that sweet oath which your God Himself makes to you for all eternity, at the instant of Holy Communion! It is not only His heart which is joined with ours, it is His precious flesh, His very blood which mingles with our blood like the sun through a sparkling cup of wine! How weak in comparison is the love of any human creature;

what regrets, what suffocation, when we leave this source of gushing life, *aquae scaturientis,* for horrible stagnant ponds.

The year 1911 which, until the autumn Claudel spent partly in Prague and partly in France, was essentially the year of *L'Annonce faite à Marie* and of *Poèmes d'été.* He completed *L'Annonce*—a luminous transmutation of *La Jeune fille Violaine,* an earlier drama—in the Villeneuve barn, mistakenly referred to as the barn of Combernon, which later became the billiard room of the family house. "Every morning," wrote Claudel to Jacques Rivière, "on the straw the hens would lay their eggs, and I would produce a few pages." He used a carpenter's bench as a desk and labored methodically, facing the beloved horizon of Champagne, which had been that of his childhood. Jammes relates that, "shortly before his departure, as he was working in this manner, a huge farm horse tethered there, probably his Pegasus, broke away and, with a thrust of its powerful breast, sent drama, author, chair, inkstand and table rolling four paces away."[1]

It was in Tientsin that he had first contemplated this adaptation of one of his first tragedies. He brought the idea to maturity in Prague, while remembering a German mystic of the Middle Ages, Mechtilde of Magdeburg, who had been granted the miraculous privilege of nursing the Child Jesus; and also St. Bernard, who had been nursed by the Blessed Virgin. Mara, filled with bitterness, is jealous of her sister Violaine, whose name, "compounded of Yolande and Ghislaine, suggests the viola and the violet, music and flowers."[*] Mara wants to steal the other young woman's fiancé, the kind, loyal and simple ploughman Jacques Hury. She sees Violaine kissing the brow of the architect Pierre de Craon, builder of churches, in a movement of pity, because she knows he is

[1] *Le Patriarche et son troupeau,* p. 54.
[*] Pierre Mazars, *Le Figaro littéraire,* March 6, 1948.

a leper, and of kindness, because she senses his hopeless love for her. Violaine in turn contracts leprosy, and loses her sight. She gives up Jacques, and withdraws into the solitude of a forest. Much later, Mara seeks her out: she has married the ploughman, and their child has just died. The grieving mother asks Violaine to bring the child back to life, for she knows the power of holiness. The miracle takes place, but the child's eyes have become blue, like those of Violaine. This infuriates Mara, and she murders her blind sister.

L'Annonce is an attestation of faith. Man nearly always neglects the prodigious resources at his disposal: prayer, which brings God's command into play; charity, through which *everything* becomes possible, and whose inexhaustible source is in Christ; and miracles, which can still occur, when violently solicited, and supersede the laws of nature. Sustained by a strange, primitive and violent faith, this woman, whose heart is full of hatred, believes in her sister's sublime superiority and in miracles worked by holiness. The miracle occurs on Christmas night, as it did for Claudel when he was eighteen. And the author, disregarding historical chronology, depicts yet another Christmas miracle in the liturgical and medieval fresco of *L'Annonce,* when he shows King Charles of France, until then the pathetic King of Bourges, off to Rheims to receive the crown.

In this play Anne Vercors, the father of Mara and Violaine, and Pierre de Craon the architect, each represent contrasting facets of Claudel's personality: Anne embodies the peasant tradition with the monolithic faith which inspires the great pilgrimages of Christendom; Pierre is the new man facing the future, whose exalted religious ideal yearns to find expression in original concepts and undertakings.

On June 8, at the beginning of a summer which he described as *wonderful,* Claudel started his vacation leave. He wished to remain at Hostel for a full uninterrupted month. But he had to leave for Villeneuve shortly after his arrival to help his parents in the sale of a farm, and for a short stay in Paris.

During this period, dazzled by the beloved landscape and by a wealth of returning memories, he composed, in the form of a dialogue, the Songs of the Rhône, of the Inner Chamber, and of Shadow. They are even dearer to me than Claudel's other poems, perhaps because they introduced me to his art and thought. He himself indicated their meaning in the course of a lecture given a few years later at the *Université des Annales:*[2]

> During the night of June 21 [1911], at that moment poised between spring and summer, at that mysterious moment when the sun stops in its course before retracing its steps, three young women are seated on the terrace of a castle in the Alps surrounded by sweeping glaciers, vineyards and fields: they are Lacta, Fausta and Beata. The first is engaged to be married, the second is an exile and the third a widow. All three are separated from those they love. They talk to each other in the night and from time to time each one of them, in a long *Cantique,* gives vent to the thoughts and emotions filling her heart.

It is there and in *Les Cinq grandes Odes,* rather than in certain liturgical hymns, that Claudelian lyricism reaches its peak. These songs of praise conjure up the golden-white expanse of high glaciers visited by the sun. Bold metaphors, new and glorious images, glowing and concise evocations capture and hold the attention. Just as Lamartine's *Le Vallon* will always remain linked with the landscape it describes, these *Cantiques* will forever leave their stamp on Hostel and the Bugey.

At the end of this exceptional summer of the year 1911, Claudel made an extensive trip throughout Germany. He was no doubt already aware of the foreign office's intention to give

[2] On March 27, 1915. This lecture was published in the *Journal de l'Université des Annales,* No. 13, Vol. II (1914-1915 Academic Year).

him an assignment in that country. On September 22 he was officially appointed to the French Consulate in Frankfurt.

That Rhineland city built on the Main, which now numbers nearly six hundred thousand inhabitants, was already important as a commercial, industrial and banking center. The new consul's first impression was excellent: he admired that "very pleasing city, full of flowers and foliage,"[3] and declared that he was not sorry "to have left Prague, that beetroot silo."[4] He had previously acquired rather an unfavorable opinion of the Frankfurt bankers, those holders of the "anonymous and vagabond" gold, in the words of Philippe, Duke of Orleans. Yet a visit to Baroness de Rothschild proved of great interest to him, and he was surprised to meet among those magnates one of the men who best understood his works. And this man was Jewish!

Once again, the move was slow and difficult. His wife and children joined him on October 22. He gradually came to appreciate the German people, whom he had hardly known until that time. He noted, and this was unexpected, that the prestige of France—defeated forty years earlier—remained high, and the Germans he approached seemed to him full of kindness, joviality and understanding. "Do you know," he pointed out to Suarès, "that since 1870 more Germans died in the service of France, in the foreign legion or elsewhere, than [as enemies of France] during the *Année Terrible?*"[5]

His relations with French intellectuals and French Catholics were not always as smooth as he might have wished. He had hoped for a more sympathetic and intelligent attitude and for a moral support which was often denied him. Hostile campaigns were launched against him, and some of these scored heavily. Pierre Lasserre, who was to deal with Claudel

---

[3] Correspondence with Jacques Rivière, p. 241.
[4] Correspondence with André Suarès, p. 171.
[5] Ibid., p. 173.

quite bluntly in *Les Chapelles littéraires,* had already written
an antagonistic article about him. It is true that he spoke as
a positivist and an unbeliever. But some believers allowed
themselves to be influenced. . . . *L'Annonce* was to be coolly
received by many Catholics, and at one time the very orthodoxy of Claudel's religious ideas was questioned. Fortunately
he had a distinguished defender in the person of Monsignor
Baudrillart, Rector of the Catholic Institute. In an entrance
talk to his students delivered on November 3 and entitled
Piété agissante, piété éclairante, piété animante, the prelate
did not hesitate to comment warmly on Claudel's *Magnificat.*
And in literary circles Péguy, who had recently returned to
God, proclaimed in ringing tones his friendship and admiration for Claudel, "poet of the Hymns and of *Les Cinq grandes
Odes.*"[6]

Undiscouraged and comforted, true to his work and inspiration, the author-diplomat pursued the completion of his
Cantate the following year (1912), singing the intense happiness which a Christian poet can savor and express.

He also wrote *Physique de l'Eucharistie* and a study devoted to his sister Camille, and reworked the comical, grossly
humorous and satirical play which he called *Protée,* after the
name inscribed by Aeschylus as an unfilled promise.

When the good weather returned, Claudel decided to undertake alone a pilgrimage which he had set his heart on
many years earlier. It has already been pointed out that
Arthur Rimbaud played an important role in his life and was
a determining factor in his conversion. Around the middle
of July the consul took his hiking stick and left for the
Ardennes, intent on finding and following the earthly traces
of that prodigious initiator. He stopped at the farm of Roche,

----

[6] The following spring, when he sent Claudel a copy of *Le Mystère
des Saints Innocents,* Péguy wrote in it this dedication: "For this great
quinquecentennial year, and as we enter this doubly great week of May.
Non solum poetae sed quod solum interest christianus christiano."
April 25, 1912.

"near Attigny, where the poet's mother was born, then at Charleville occupied the room of the author of *Les Illuminations*, replete with so many visions and struggles." He delved into photographs and drawings, became saturated with the Rimbaudian atmosphere, as much as the locale, his imagination and his almost filial disposition allowed him to. Few things moved him more than the sight of a "radiating cross carved with the point of a knife" into the wood of the table where *Une Saison en Enfer* had been written.[7] And soon he felt "adopted."

On August 24 his home was brightened by a new birth, that of a second son, Henri, the only one who was to follow in his footsteps and become a diplomat. Claudel would have wished to return to his beloved Hostel with his family. But the weather was unfavorable, and besides, he had to make definite arrangements for the opening of *L'Annonce faite à Marie*, which was scheduled for the late fall.

These arrangements brought the author much worry and perplexity, and required all his care. He was deeply conscious of the play's merit, and knew that it was the favorite child of his mind, soul and genius. He had no doubts on the validity of the innovations it brought to the stage. But he was concerned about the acting. Who would impersonate Anne Vercors? Lugné-Poë had taken charge of the casting, and deserved the author's confidence. The cast included several actors who could be counted on, like Madame Frappe and Marie Kalff. But there were others Claudel was less sure of. Above all, how would the public receive this large-scale tragedy in which miraculous events run directly counter to contemporary skepticism and might be interpreted as a defiant challenge? Besides, Claudel was retiring, misanthropic and unsociable, and he dreaded the theatrical world, which was largely unfamiliar to him. "In what a sea of vanity and

---

[7] Commentary by Robert Mallet on the *Correspondence of Paul Claudel and André Gide* (Gallimard), p. 349.

chatter I will be thrown!" he exclaimed in a letter written to Louis Massignon on December 2, 1912.

His fears regarding the public's response proved justified, much to his chagrin. The opening performance of *L'Annonce*[8] took place on Christmas Eve, in the Malakoff hall which at the time had been rented by the Théâtre de l'Oeuvre. It is true that the spectators were deeply impressed, and Paul Souday, a witness who as a rule was not kindly disposed toward Claudel, did not hesitate to recognize that "this performance was to most of them, and perhaps even to a few critics, a true revelation." But the Catholics, already bewildered by the novelty and daring of Claudel's works and prejudiced against him, again raised the issue of orthodoxy. This was far from being the explosion of enthusiasm and fervor which a play of such mystical significance should have evoked, and which years later actually did occur. It was not until 1914, when *L'Otage* was staged, that Claudel finally received overwhelming public and critical acclaim, and that the unfortunate bias against his plays died down.

For several months past, a new and beneficial influence had entered his life. It was that of Father Daniel Fontaine, pastor of the parish of Notre-Dame Auxiliatrice, in Clichy, who was to become his spiritual director. Claudel once spoke to me of the difficulties he had experienced throughout his eventful career in finding priests to whom he could freely confide the cares of his soul. Trust, sympathy, friendship and affection are not enough in this field. A very special rapport or affinity is needed, an element which escapes both analysis and definition. Among the many priests and religious he met,

[8] Lugné-Poë, who had originally been approached on Claudel's behalf by the great actress Marie Kalff, deserves the credit for staging *L'Annonce*. Jean Variot contributed a plain and stark scenic system (utterly devoid of settings) which he had thoroughly studied in Germany. To put his actors in the proper mood, Claudel took them on a tour of the Tardenois district.

Father Fontaine was one of the very few who represented that advice of God which facilitates something Pascal summed up in these words: "Full and docile submission to Jesus Christ and to my director."

When Claudel met him, Father Daniel-Marie Fontaine[9] was about fifty. He had been the last confessor of Huysmans, who had met him through their mutual friend Louis Massignon. As pastor of the Clichy church, this "simple, intelligent and kindly man" (in the words of Claudel) lived "among railway workers, ragpickers and prostitutes."

After the death of this spiritual father, Claudel composed, while in Copenhagen during February 1921, a memento in which he describes the true role played in his life by this evangelizer of ragpickers, whom he had known in the "red belt" of Paris industrial and proletarian suburbs:

> Happy who, behind the altar, has found a healer, and not a judge but a father.
> The priest in deep humility, without surprise ever, and without anger,
> Patient, and his purse once more open for this prodigal son to draw upon,
> Knowing that Grace is always more plentiful than sin. . . .
> . . . And here again is the unrelenting Sunday, and how bitter it can be
> To brood over this sin, with its taste of ashes, this sin we had promised not to commit!
> May God then give us a father, and not this master staring at us in open-mouthed dismay.
> It is his business to delve into all this, and it would take more than me to frighten the apostle of the ragpickers.
> Here I am again kneeling before you. Look at me, O priest!

[9] Father Fontaine, who had previously been director of the charitable society of the Auteuil Orphans, was to die as pastor of Saint-Antoine des Quinze-Vingt on November 10, 1920. Two years before his death he had revived the Society of the Heart of Jesus, founded in 1791 by a Jesuit, Father de Clorivière, with the purpose of sanctifying the clergy through the practice of the evangelical precepts.

Look at my soul, father of the poor and consoler of literary
  men.

(Feuilles de Saints, p. 25)

Once more Claudel reveals himself in this memento as he
really is: a Christian of good will, but a sinner. Not a
Pharisee, certainly. Some are scandalized that this devout
believer—and he was one—occasionally showed shockingly
un-Christian attitudes. But we know (or rather, we should
all know) that intention and actual practice are two entirely
different things. Let us rather imagine what Claudel might
have been without the Christian discipline which he did his
utmost to follow.

Father Fontaine found in Claudel a spirit of never-failing
docility, and enlisted his help for various parish activities in
spite of the difficulties entailed by the diplomat's habitual
absence from Paris. In particular, Claudel was asked to contribute to the editorial work of a local newspaper whose articles, although generally unsigned, were of a quality which
many larger papers might well have envied.

Le Réveil municipal de Clichy, founded in 1907 to serve
local interests, conducted the anticlerical battle in the name
of the radical, radical-socialist and independent-socialist political groupings, under the editorship of a certain Georges
Moitet. A rival newspaper, founded one year earlier under
the label of "independent republican," once a week gave *Le
Réveil* the answer. But its staff was inadequate and it was
necessary to fight with the most effective weapons possible.
Claudel had the temperament of a polemicist and would have
made a singularly pugnacious and pertinent journalist; he
contributed articles and even took part in the activities of
the editorial team with Louis Massignon, François Mauriac
and several others. This was obviously not his vocation and
he preferred other tasks, although he sometimes envied someone like Louis Veuillot. Let us say that he accepted this involvement as a kind of penance, and because he felt that

providential signs should be obediently followed. He was of course forced to be very discreet by his official position, and it seems that his actions were kept under close and constant scrutiny by suspicious and small-minded government officials.

In this new role he found many opportunities to avenge the persecution which reached all Catholic circles and activities in France. During Poincaré's tenure as foreign minister, the government ordered the closing of all Catholic orphanages. They had offered charity under the sign of the Cross. *L'Echo de Paris,* a daily by no means associated with the anticlericals, published under the name of Count d'Haussonville, a member of the Académie française, an article bowing down to the politicians responsible for this order. Claudel's blood boiled. He took up his pen to unburden his conscience. On the twentieth anniversary of Renan's death he once again gave free rein to his indignation: would this commemoration not be taken as a pretext for renewed harassment of Catholicism? He was ready to follow Father Fontaine's wish and launch a counter-attack on the ideas of the skeptical thinker who long ago, at the lycée Louis-le-Grand, had crowned him with a wreath. But as a member of the Church, accepting all its laws, he inquired about the formalities necessary to be dispensed from the interdiction of the Index, which prevented him from personally consulting the condemned works. On another occasion he denounced what he called the bankruptcy of the lay schooling system, as it showed itself during those years when young teachers admitted individually to the absence of any moral doctrine in their thinking. Concluding five articles devoted to this failure, Claudel ended with these generous and enlightened lines:

> We do not blame the members of the public teaching profession, but only the pedantic and evil theorists who try to make them into their tools. The teachers should realize that in the final analysis their real enemies are not so much the

Catholics, with whom they could always reach an understanding on the level of practical reality, as the political mountebanks whose dupes they have been for so long. All we ask of the teachers is that they remain truly neutral and refrain from dispensing a moral teaching for which they themselves admit their incompetence.

One cannot, however, recognize the stamp of Claudel's genius in those articles which he signed with the initial M. He depersonalized them to such an extent that they resemble anything else one might have read at the time under the pen of a small-town lawyer. Claudel the polemicist emerges much more clearly in his usual prose which he dates, signs and authenticates.

Another member of his journalistic team—Louis Massignon—urged him to write an article on Jean-Jacques Rousseau, the bicentennial of whose birth was being celebrated in 1912. Claudel gave his colleague this lively and amusing answer, which has the merit of showing that, when all was said and done he was not sorry to have been persuaded into this avocation of journalism:

> Don't you think that the good people of Clichy have had more than enough of Jean-Jacques, whose works they have probably never read? (Just between us, I am somewhat in the same position, for I am familiar with only the *Confessions* and *La nouvelle Héloïse,* which I read during that "larval" stage of ravenous literary hunger when one would devour even wooden building beams!) This is to say that I really cannot give you the information you wish. But you will find an entire issue of *La Revue critique d'Art et de Littérature* (July 15, I believe) completely devoted to the philosopher. I will gladly let you take the pen for any additional blows which remain to be struck. But do not think that I lack the time [for such an article]. I have only too much of it on my hands, and am happy to do a little "soldiering" for the Church.

Let me know when I am needed to speak of Renan! I would
dearly love to settle his account.

Meantime, "the presumptuous Moitet," editor of the adverse newspaper, "beat a rather humiliating retreat." Claudel
felt that he could henceforth be left alone. Did Moitet suspect the identity of his contradictor? A sentence of his on
the anonymous journalist "most skilled in the art of writing"
leads one to assume that this was the case. Far from giving
up the fight, the French consul in Frankfurt and Darmstadt
continued it until the outbreak of the First World War.

In August 1913, Claudel, anxious for spiritual guidance,
was received for three days as a guest in the Clichy rectory,
delighted to spend this time with Father Fontaine and only
wishing that he had met him years earlier. Of this short stay
the good priest was to write: "Our true friend Claudel gave
me half a week. We were able to talk things over thoroughly.
I fathomed better that noble soul, which knows how to go
so uprightly to God." When much later he lived in Paris, the
ambassador-poet liked to spend a few hours in Clichy on
Sundays. And when he presented the father with his poem
entitled *Notre-Dame Auxiliatrice,* which his confessor had
urged him to write, he said to him, "It is you who are its
author; I have only arranged your ideas one after the other."
He attributed these two lines in particular to the priest:
"There is no true friend for a pauper, unless he finds another
poorer than himself. So come, my heavy-hearted sister,
and gaze upon Mary."

Claudel did not want to be the only one to benefit from the
help of his spiritual adviser, whom he consulted just as
naturally as he would visit his doctor. He gave the priest's
address to Jacques Rivière, who went most fervently to kneel
at the feet of the saintly pastor of Clichy. He also urged
Gide to seek out the good priest, and gave him this assurance,
"You will not surprise him." Gide promised to listen "with

respect, with piety even," but never took this step. As for Massignon, he sent to Clichy Father de Foucauld, who had no difficulty enlisting the pastor's interest in his apostolate of prayer for the infidels of the French colonies. And Johannes Joergensen, the Danish writer converted to Catholicism, also found his way to Father Fontaine's door.

In a closely related field, Claudel sought to carry out his plan for a Co-operative of Prayer. He devoted to this project the same methodical and meticulous care, the same common sense which marked all his activities, and in which the civil servant and the man of the soil in him pooled their resources. Jammes, Frizeau, Henrion and Massignon were the first friends he consulted, and from them he received suggestions and constructive criticism. Massignon was opposed to any printed publicity given to a strictly spiritual association with a specific and limited purpose. Claudel answered that this printed material was not public and that, "since the actual person and his face are unknown, the name and place are important." And he added, "We cannot pray effectively for a man who has no shape or substance in our thoughts." Moreover, the printed list of names and addresses made it easier for each member to consult a specialist on some particular point of theology, history or literature of interest to him.

This answer to Louis Massignon rightly emphasizes the isolation of the convert, which the association would attempt to overcome, at least in part. This isolation was and remained Claudel's lot, and in his case was compounded by an almost continuous absence from his homeland. He wrote Massignon on May 5, 1912:

> Personally, before making up my mind to become a convert, I spent four years of particularly distressing solitude and anguish. No one offered me a helping hand. In the fundamentally pagan frame of mind I was in, priests and religious literature could do me no good, and even after many years of

Christian profession I had great difficulty getting accustomed to the tone of the house. A conversion—this is my personal feeling, at least—is a kind of catastrophe. It is a little as though one were to change one's sex. The new convert is bewildered in a new world and goes through extremely trying moments. It is true that God's Grace is sufficient, but fraternal assistance is precisely one of the manifestations of this Grace. In this instance it is not a question of dogma, but of affection, of understanding of the sinful and pagan soul; and this is something a priest or an ever faithful soul, in the usual order of things, does not always possess.

In April, shortly before these lines were written, the first bulletin of the association had appeared. The five founding members listed were Claudel, Georges Dumesnil, who was editor of *L'Amitié de France,* Gabriel Frizeau, Charles Henrion and Francis Jammes. In August 1913, accompanied by Father Fontaine, Claudel asked to be received by Cardinal Amette, Archbishop of Paris, and requested his endorsement and blessings, which were granted. A new edition was then prepared. Georges Dumesnil, having been called back to God in August 1916, was replaced by his friend Emile Baumann. Among the priests and religious who became members were Father Barge (editor of *La Revue des Jeunes*), Louis Le Cardonnel, Monseigneur Deploige, Father Garrigou-Lagrange, Brother Gemelli, Father Plazenet, Father Ubald d'Alençon and Father (later Monsignor) Francis Vincent. Among the lay members were Thomas Braun, Eusèbe de Brémond d'Ars, Léonard Constant, Fagus, Henri Ghéon, Prince Ghika, Robert Valléry-Radot (later Father Irénée), Maurice Vaussard and Captain (later Admiral) Yamamoto.[10]

[10] In the rules of this Co-operative, it may be of interest to quote the articles which best define the nature and purpose of the Association (Bulletin No. 10, September 1923): I. This is neither a confraternity nor a special devotion: simply a group of people linked by bonds of mutual sympathy, and who agree to pray for each other, to benefit each other in this way and to offer themselves to God in collective homage. II. No obligation whatsoever. All depends on good will alone. But the

The great project which sprang from Claudel's heart was fulfilled.

Among the members of the Co-operative still living today are Father Garrigou-Lagrange, Father Lacaze, Monsignor Francis Vincent, Thomas Braun, Louis Chaigne, Albert Cherel, Albert Flory, Charles Henrion, Louis Massignon, Henri Massis, François Mauriac, Robert Vallery-Radot (Reverend Father Irénée) and Maurice Vaussard.

May these "survivors" revive, around the memory of Paul Claudel, a link which today would be more valuable than ever.

---

best will be for us to try and make this commendation to God daily, in the form each of us will have chosen (rosary, meditation, attendance at Holy Mass, etc.).

It will be a comfort to some members to think that if their prayers are imperfect there may be, in another part of the world, a friend who compensates for their inattention or negligence. III. It will be well if the Grace to be requested for each of us is not the highest, but the closest, the most immediate, the most practical. *Pietas erga proximum.* There is a *daily* bread which we are urged to request for the present day. IV. We will gladly welcome young Catholics who, undergoing an intellectual and moral crisis too painful to bear in solitude, believe they can find help and comfort in our association. V. Priests and religious will always be welcome among us. For the benedictions which they add to our prayers, may they receive hereby the assurance of our deep gratitude.

10

UNDER THE SIGN OF MARS

FATE HELD IN RESERVE FOR THIS MILITANT CHRISTIAN A
series of family trials, which affected him to the very deepest
of his being. Although he "supernaturalized" everything, he
nevertheless remained intensely human and was more sensitive and vulnerable than he cared to admit. During the night
of Sunday March 2 to Monday March 3, 1913, at three in
the morning he lost his father, who was carried off in a
matter of hours without realizing that it was the end. As soon
as the critical nature of his condition became apparent Claudel was warned, and hurried back from Frankfurt. It was
too late. Louis-Prosper Claudel had left this world without
the assistance of the sacraments—which he had wished for,
however—and had remained, in the words of his son, *distant*
from religion.[1]

Paul blamed himself for not having urged his father to
take the last step toward the Church, to cross a threshold
where no serious difficulties held him any longer, to obey an
inner wish which was sensed, so it seems, by this son attentive to the smallest spiritual manifestations in the one whose
salvation was so dear to him. Forty years later he wrote to
a nun who had just gone through a similar experience: "But
I did not lose confidence in *the Father*. After all, he is a much
tenderer Father than the best of our good priests whom we
know. And His son died for us . . ."[2]

[1] Letter to A. du Sarment, Jan. 22, 1954 (Gabalda).
[2] Ibid.

Besides, one must bear in mind the mood of this family where each member lived for himself alone, settled his problems without consulting anyone, concealed his worries and difficulties. Louis-Prosper was the archetype of the unsociable and fiercely secretive peasant.

A few days later, on March 10, Claudel suffered another tragedy and was again called back to France. This time the crisis concerned his sister Camille. She lived in an old building on the quai de Bourbon, in Paris. The shutters of her ground-floor apartment always remained closed. She had been a radiant young girl, bursting with talent and beauty, proud and self-confident, and showing a certain arrogance born of her feeling for greatness, her daring inventiveness and her overflowing joy of life. Now she was but a pathetic middle-aged woman, stealing down her street in the early morning in search of a few scraps of food. She had been Rodin's pupil and assistant, and he had made her his mistress, but had preferred to marry a woman less beloved but more willing to accept a subordinate position in his life. Actually he would have been ready to share his attentions but Camille Claudel had no taste for this kind of compromise and would not hear of the arrangement. Neither would her rival for the affections of the famous sculptor. After spending fifteen years by his side, this rival left him, and he remained cruelly distressed. As for Claudel's sister, the great love of her life was broken, the fire of her genius had been smothered, and her very reason gave way, so that her existence became a living death. "One day," her brother relates, "the hospital attendants entered through the back of the room [where she lived] and laid hands on the terrified occupant, who had been awaiting them for a long time amid dried-up plaster casts and clay figures. The confusion and filth were, as the phrase goes, beyond description. On the walls the fourteen Stations of the Cross, cut out from the front page of the rue Bayard newspaper and held up by pins. Outside, the ambulance was waiting . . ."[3] So it was that, on a horrible day of March 1913, Paul Claudel took his sister to a special nursing home near Avignon where she was to stay for thirty years until her death.

Paul was four years her junior. His grief was overwhelming. It is true that in the past he had suffered from the tyrannical will of this sister who would brook no contradiction. As we have already pointed out, however, his own genius owed much to that of this exceptionally gifted woman. She taught him always to believe in himself implicitly, and preceded him on the ascending path which leads to self-expression. He was proud of Camille, who used to call him "Mon petit Paul," and who uttered these words once again during the last moments of her life. He spoke of the *frequently cruel ascendency which she exercised over his early years*. After her death he wrote Louis Massignon this vivid description of her: "A noble brow over magnificent eyes of that dark blue shade so rarely found outside novels; a nose in which later she liked to recognize the inheritance of the de Vertus; a large mouth showing even more pride than sensuality; a powerful shock of brown hair of the real brown which the English call *auburn,* falling to her waist."

His own soul henceforth often turned toward "those imprisoned souls"[4]—his father carried off into the mystery of the beyond, and his sister locked in the night of an incurable insanity—Paul Claudel returned to his duties, his heart filled with bitter sorrow. During this critical time it seems that he received spiritual help from Dom Besse, whom he may have seen in Paris where the good father was living (at 20 rue Monsieur, a Benedictine convent), before leaving for his monastery of Chevetogne, in Belgium. With his friend Massignon, Claudel thought of approaching Father de Foucauld,

[3] Cf. Musée Rodin: Paul Claudel, *Camille Claudel, décembre 1864—octobre 1943,* introduction by Marcel Aubert (Paris, Nov.-Dec. 1951).
[4] Ibid.

whose humble and radiant holiness he knew of through the eminent Orientalist. But the diplomat was not at the end of his trials. The health of one of his sons gave cause for worry; the boy was thin and delicate, and a deviation of the nasal septum prevented him from breathing properly. An operation was necessary but the family was apprehensive of surgery. It took place early in May, nevertheless, and was completed during the summer. The child gradually recovered his strength and was to enjoy a normal life.

To a certain extent, Claudel's literary activities suffered from these family events. He continued writing, however, and maintained, whenever possible, the self-imposed discipline of his established pattern of work. At the request of Father Barge (editor of *La Revue de la Jeunesse,* which later became *La Revue des Jeunes*), and not without a certain reluctance, he wrote the account of his conversion in simple accents which sometimes reach the sublime. This account seems to have received from God an instrumental value, as it were, to touch the souls of countless other men. He continued his hymnal, which was to be published under the title of *Corona benignitatis anni Dei.* In addition, he completed the first version of *Protée.*

When summer came, deeply distressed by what he considered the poverty and mediocrity of his behavior as a Christian, he was eager to throw himself into the arms of Father Fontaine. Claudel's friend Berthelot introduced him to Maurice Barrès, then at the peak of his literary career and fame. It seems that Barrès was struck mainly by the "civil servant" quality of the diplomat, who rated more highly the brilliant journalist of *Leurs figures* than the unorthodox (in Claudel's opinion) author of *La Colline inspirée,* which had just been published. The consul esteemed Barrès neither as a thinker, nor as a poet, nor as a novelist. He tempered this extreme and rather unfair judgment, this uncompromising position, by admiring Barrès for having succeeded, obstinately and courageously, in drawing so much from a soil "which was not among the richest."

Claudel later elaborated on this point: "He was a man of great determination. . . . This is the mountaineer spirit. He was from both Auvergne and the Vosges: both are mountain lands, and there is always that fighting instinct. He had settled into an attitude which seemed to him likely to compel recognition." Claudel also had this to say: "He was turned toward the past. I am attracted by the future. 'The earth and the dead,' said Barrès. I would readily answer him: 'The sea and the living.'" Actually, the two formulations are not mutually exclusive, and Barrès would perhaps not have accepted being narrowly restricted to his.

Be that as it may, Barrès, who was well aware of Claudel's talent and who read much more than his secretaries (the Tharaud brothers) intimated, had shown himself most generous toward the friend of his friend Berthelot. He intended to write in *L'Echo de Paris* one of those articles whose secret he possessed, and which had launched Péguy, Mauriac and several others. He asked Claudel for some information on himself and his work. Alas, the answer contained an admiring reference to Rimbaud and this caused Barrès to drop the whole plan.

A mitigated success in Paris, *L'Annonce faite à Marie* was to be very well received in Germany. In September 1913 it was produced by two friends, Wolf Dohrn and Alexander Salzmann at Hellerau, near Dresden, the capital of Saxony. The warm and active support of these producers moved the author deeply, all the more so since he knew that one of them at least was an agnostic.[5] Claudel was present and experi-

[5] This refers to Dohrn, who was to die in 1914, and about whom Claudel wrote: "And God, Wolf, what do you say of Him now, this God you did not believe in as others do, naively and simply? And yet, you were so sincere, so naturally Christian from head to foot, that the absence of faith in you seemed only an enormous oversight, the result of an inconceivable carelessness; like a schoolboy who has forgotten the most important item of his equipment. Will God be without pity for

enced the satisfaction of witnessing the success of his play. In the first row of the audience sat Jules Cambon, French Ambassador to Germany, and Prince John-George of Saxony. This was the beginning of Claudel's fame in a country which was to remain always, or nearly always, most favorably inclined toward his works. Even today they are appreciated there more than anywhere else. And he found in Germany a keen and penetrating commentator in the person of Monseigneur Grosche.

In October of the same year Claudel was transferred from Frankfurt to Hamburg, a Hanseatic town and one of the oldest ports in all Europe, the free city which—with its extensions of Altona and Cuxhaven—forms the great nerve center of German sea trade. He was pleased with this promotion, which would not, it is true, greatly change his usual occupations: entertaining his compatriots and being entertained by them, carrying out the duties of mayor, notary and magistrate. From this incomparable observation point his professional responsibilities allowed him to conduct his personal studies and investigations in the economic field. In Hamburg he behaved as a realist, not as a dreamer. Every phase of this intense and enormous activity fascinated him; to enter more closely into contact with it he brought into play all the resources of his senses and intelligence. This is how he was seen by Alexis Léger (the poet Saint-John Perse) who accompanied him.[6]

Portents of the impending world-wide tragedy were already visible in the Hamburg sky. The French elections held in May showed a weakening of the national spirit and fiber, a new erosion of the political system, which inevitably would be taken advantage of by those who had secret reasons to

you? Will He be the only one not to love you? Ah, there would be no point to His being the Father, if He did not open His arms to this chubby boy." *Nouvelle Revue Française*, May 1, 1914.

[6] Cf. Paul Morand: "Un grand serviteur de l'Etat," *Le Figaro*, March 30, 1935.

redraw the map of Europe. Claudel was alarmed by this development, and at the same time, as a Catholic, he feared the consequences of this more active surge of sectarian irreligion. He was called to Paris, where the Théatre de l'Oeuvre was to give *L'Otage* at the beginning of June.

The performance was an apotheosis. It brought Claudel recognition and success, and made up for the lack of understanding which had greeted his earlier plays; for the setbacks, the disheartening failures and the faint praise. On the stage Lugné-Poë, with good-natured authority, embodied the role of Father Badilon, the village priest. And Sygne de Coûfontaine was played by the young Belgian actress Eve Francis, a dazzling beauty with a charming trace of an accent, a slight drawl. The *Tout-Paris* was there. The press, hitherto rather unfavorable to the author, was represented by some of its greatest names. Péguy and Gide were among the audience and so were a number of younger writers such as Mauriac, Robert Vallery-Radot and Henri Massis.

Much more than a simple victory, the evening was a triumph. Anticlericalism itself, although not actually shaken, sat up and took notice. In Senator Bérenger's newspaper *L'Action,* Joachim Gasquet did not hide his admiration, but expressed the fear that "Claudel's mysticism, advocating scorn for life and a return to the Middle Ages, might bar the way to the revival of pagan naturalism." Péguy, utterly loyal and incapable of pettiness or envy, was filled with enthusiasm, and dwelt on a character who could not fail to be his favorite. "No denying it," he exclaimed before some of his friends, "among all those fellows it is still that Turelure who has the most red blood in him." Gide was as though carried into seventh heaven and, in his lyrical fervor, uttered this prayer, "We will not leave You, O Lord, until You have blessed us."

Claudel did not expect this triumph, or in any case he never thought it would be as free and spontaneous. This is

how he accounted for it in a letter requested by the newspaper *Le Temps* and published in the theater section of
that great daily, whose editors were well-known Protestants:

> If my play was so favorably received it is because the
> spectators, most of whom probably did not share my religious
> convictions, nevertheless felt the tragic power arising from
> the intervention in our individual and daily lives of a call
> exterior and superior to us. The more or less miserable cir-
> cumstances under which we all live nevertheless leave the
> feeling that there is in us something unused, something which
> did not come out, and which is perhaps precisely the best
> and deepest in us. It is this need, this great latent yearning,
> which today's ordinary art cannot satisfy any more than
> ordinary morality. . . .

Not without reason, Claudel deemed that this art, "far
from utilizing all of man, discards the best in him and leads
only to the pessimism and dejection of helplessness." Naturalism, from which he had suffered so during the "sad
eighties," lingered on without producing any work of real
merit and led to a dismal and depressing dead end.

This sorry state of affairs had come about because men
had "forgotten the glorious faith, the great doctrine, the great
school of energy which made Europe what it is . . . the great
rule of conduct expressed in this verse of the Hymn to the
Blessed Sacrament: *Quantum potes, tantun aude* [make
yourself heard as much as you can], because, in a word, they
had ceased to be Christians."

Catholic daring, the orchestration of all the physical and
spiritual resources of Christian man: this is what Claudel
offered his contemporaries. Having at last found in the public
such a resonance, such a deep rapport, it was only natural
for him to be intensely moved and gratified after suffering so
much from the theatergoers' and critics' scorn, disdainful indifference and malevolent irony.

This is not to say that there were no adverse comments,

but these generally dealt with points of detail: some claimed that the sacrifice demanded of Sygne was insufficiently motivated, or that her attitude during the last moments of her life was more feudal than Christian. . . . But the Catholic press, led by *La Croix,* clearly showed that it had been won over and recognized in *L'Otage* "one of the most powerful masterpieces of the contemporary theater."[7]

After the opening performances of *L'Otage,* the playwright repaired to the Dominican monastery of Le Saulchoir, at Kain, in Belgium, for a few days of retreat. Did the intoxication of success generate scruples of conscience? Did Claudel suffer a recurrence of spiritual torment, a sickness of the soul stemming from his habitual sense of unworthiness as a Christian? Or was it, more simply, the need to seek advice for his exegetical work on the Bible? We are inclined to favor the latter explanation, for this reason: if he had merely sought religious help and solace he probably would have chosen the Benedictines of Chevetogne, with whom, as an oblate, he naturally felt a close bond.

Claudel stayed at Le Saulchoir at the same time as Henri Massis, then a very young writer who had published two well-received studies: one on the problems and attitudes of youth during that period (written with Alfred de Tarde, under the shared and single pen-name of Agathon), and the other entitled *L'esprit de la nouvelle Sorbonne.* Drawn to everything noble and generous, Massis, with his thin and rather solemn features, his restless eyes burning with a deep fire, his emphatic and ardent voice and his quick and nervous walk, had instinctively sought out masters or elders who could help him to find himself: Barrès and Péguy, Claudel and Maurras. He struck up a friendship with Ernest Psichari, who was to become his model: "We asked this solitary being for the secret of our destinies." He worked as part of a

[7] Julien Laurec, *La Semaine littéraire,* June 28, 1914.

team with Jacques Maritain, carrying out in the realm of literary criticism the same re-examination of values which the latter conducted in the field of philosophical criticism.

Claudel exerted a considerable influence on Massis, who turned proudly toward "the gruff man, thickset, rich-blooded and muscular . . . the massive creature of vehement passions, the sensuous and primitive artist . . . bowed down before his God, and who probably had not surrendered without a struggle." And Massis added, "His face and body bore the signs of this struggle," and his eyes were "direct and clear, brimming with a love so filial and tender."[8] Later, Massis was to describe their prayers side by side in a high gallery, their walks together along the paths and avenues of a large park, their conversations on poetry and art, "which are also divine."

In the course of these conversations a name was to arise at the mere sound of which Claudel bristled: that of Gide, an old friend to whom he had grown deeply attached, whom he had hoped to convert, but who had almost constantly resisted Grace. Gide was now spiritually frozen in an attitude of blind narcissism. He had just published a new book, *Les Caves du Vatican*, in a special edition limited to five hundred copies, which was a kind of answer to *L'Otage*. Learning that the Pope is held prisoner in the cellars of the Vatican, a Catholic family sends to Italy a certain Fleurissoire, who is to investigate the facts. On the way he meets in the train an unknown relative, Lafcadio, illegitimate son of the head of this family. A perverse and diabolical creature, Lafcadio throws his traveling companion out of the speeding train without reason, just for the thrill of committing a senseless crime. This attitude, which Gide seemed to approve of, naturally horrified Claudel. Moreover, Gide had the audacity of placing at the head of his book a quotation borrowed from

[8] *Revue des Jeunes*, Jan. 10, 1924. See also *De l'homme à Dieu* (Les Nouvelles Editions Latines, 1959.)

the author of *L'Otage:* "But of what king are you speaking, and of what Pope? For there are two, and it is not known which of them is the right one."

> Claudel [relates Massis] suffered from this [incident] as from an unspeakable injury [for he was] wounded in his overly tender heart; and thinking of his friend's book, he gruffly uttered these words, pregnant with meaning, which express the deep unity of art and truth: "There can be no compromise with evil."

After the evening service Claudel and his young friend would meet two scholarly monks—Father (later Monsignor) Gillet and Father Barge—in their cell. The poet had thought of someday writing a kind of *Paradise,* and questioned these theologians on the symbolism of water. It seemed to him that water could be considered the celestial element, just as fire is the infernal element. It was the idea of a lyricist and had to be harmonized with St. Thomas.

Meanwhile, war was drawing near. Premonitory signs followed one another. On June 28 Archduke Franz-Ferdinand, heir to the Austro-Hungarian throne, and his morganatic wife Sophia von Hohenberg were assassinated in Sarajevo, the capital of Bosnia. This was a major portent which did not deceive clear-sighted observers. At his post in Hamburg, Claudel remained vigilant. To his anguish as a Frenchman were added family worries: his elder daughter Marie fell seriously ill, and he was deeply concerned about her. On July 22, Serbia received an Austrian ultimatum which alarmed all Europe. The Austrian mobilization was answered by that of Russia, protector of the Slavs. Kaiser Wilhelm II was asked to use his influence in Vienna to bring about a compromise, but refused to act. On July 28 Austria declared war on Serbia. On July 30 President Poincaré returned hastily to Paris, cutting short a state visit to the Scandinavian countries. On the 31st, Germany proclaimed the *Kriegsgefahrzustand,* or state of readiness for war. Russia continued to mobilize. Anxious for her neutrality, Belgium assembled her forces. On August 1 Berlin issued a general mobilization order, and Paris followed suit the same evening. The next day Imperial Germany officially declared war on Russia and entered the Grand-Duchy of Luxembourg. . . . The inevitable had occurred.

The French consul general in Hamburg lived through days of anguish and felt definite threats hanging over himself and his family. While he was getting ready to leave the city a "howling mob" was out to get him. The crowd was "driven to a frenzy by the sight of a certain tricolor outfit [worn by his son Henri, who was one year old] and especially by a confounded bowler hat, the color of a pink pearl, insolently flaunted by one of the attachés."[9]

In his poem devoted to St. Martin, *Feuilles de saints,* Claudel lyrically related his last days in Hamburg, "when the trains loaded with soldiers started, and the sun was that red ember in the sky. . . . And that wordless crowd, all those people in straw hats on the *Jungfernstiege* waiting for news . . . ! And as the wind by sudden gusts ripples the entire surface of the Alster. . . . So these heads suddenly undulate, and the white sheets of the *Extras* spread from one end to the other of the crowd, waving in the breeze. . . . The monstrous torso of War appears at the end of the street, and with a toss of its powerful shoulders uproots the gates of the city. . . . The ships' sirens are silent, and already all exit from Germany has been stopped."

His superior, Jules Cambon, French Ambassador in Berlin, who had himself been roughly treated by the Imperial Police, awaited him in Copenhagen. The return to France was to take place through Sweden, Norway and England. Claudel

[9] Cf.: *Souvenirs de la carrière,* VI. "L'absent professionnel," *Le Figaro littéraire,* Feb. 12, 1938.

was sent ahead to carry out a reconnaissance, shepherding the personnel of the embassy.

Soon he saw Villeneuve again while waiting for a new assignment. His faith in France stood firm during the tragic days when the French front gave way, and Paris itself, threatened by the enemy, was in the grip of terror. He made it a point to dissociate himself from certain Catholic writers filled with resentment and imprecations, who seemed to feel a vicious and almost sadistic joy at the sight of their "guilty" country punished by God. Claudel was aware of the French failings and was not reconciled to the official atheism; but he saw, under the surface, under dismaying appearances, the active faith of countless families, the devotion of so many officers and men who were to shed their blood for the coming of a better world and thousands of whom, as a matter of fact, had already laid down their lives.

On August 8 the newspapers announced the capture of Mulhouse, and on the 10th the French lines extended from Maubeuge to Belfort. By the 15th public opinion was alarmed and disappointed, for it had expected a quick advance through Alsace and already imagined a successful break-through toward Berlin. . . . On August 24 the death of Pope Pius X was, in the words of Albert de Mun, like the darkening at the height of the tempest, of the lighthouse battered by the storm. Almost at the same time the Germans entered Brussels. The next few days were all but unbearable. The invading tide swept on to northwestern Belgium. In Lorraine the French armies retreated along the Seille, a tributary of the Moselle, and along the Marne-Rhine canal. On August 24 the disaster of Charleroi gave rise to the most alarming rumors. Two days later the Viviani government was re-shuffled: Millerand took over the war ministry, and Delcassé the foreign office. And on August 28 an official communiqué revealed that, "from the Somme to the Vosges," the situation of the front remained unchanged. I was very young at the time, but I remember witnessing the shock, the consternation, the panic caused by this unexpected and indirect admission of the German advance.

Beside these national calamities Claudel was also deeply affected by various individual events. One of the most outstanding was the death of Renan's grandson, Ernest Psichari, who died like a saint on August 22, on the battlefield of Saint-Vincent-Rossignol.[10] Thirteen days later, on September 5, Charles Péguy was killed at Villeroy, near Meaux, while leading his men into combat.

But when Péguy fell, France was already beginning to recover. It was the first day of the battle of the Marne, the first harbinger of victory. The government had left Paris for Bordeaux at the very beginning of September, when the invaders reached Compiègne. Claudel followed the war ministry, where he was foreign office representative for the censorship of newspapers and telegrams. He took lodgings at 17 rue du Champ-de-Mars. His mother and his sister Louise had also left Paris, and were offered hospitality by André Berthelot (Philippe's brother) at his estate of Benest, near Champagne-Mouton and Confolens, in the Charente district.

The military operations developed rapidly. They were conducted by General Joffre, ably assisted by Galliéni, the Military Governor of Paris. On September 7 and 8 the French armies moved forward between the Grand and Petit Morin and Vitry-le-François. In the course of the three following days their left wing, including a British force, succeeded in throwing back the enemy between Château-Thierry and La Ferté-sous-Jouarre. By the evening of the 13th the Germans were in full retreat, while in Lorraine, Castelnau saved Nancy and dislodged the invaders from the lines of the Meurthe and of Mortagne.

[10] "What a mystery, what a parable, the story of that race of Renan. Yes, once again, *You are victorious, O Galilean.*" Letter to Henri Massis, Feb. 10, 1916. *Table Ronde,* April 1955.

Along with many other Frenchmen Claudel believed in an early and total victory, and expected it during that month of October, which was dedicated to the Rosary of the Blessed Virgin. But he felt very lonely in Bordeaux, since his wife and children were at Hostel-en-Varomey. The Mauriacs, the Calvets (a family of winegrowers), the Frizeaux and Jammes (whom he was able to see, all too briefly) helped him to bear this separation. In December his Ministry returned to Paris, and he expected to receive an assignment which would remove him from his temporary duties.

Now that the Germans were no longer quite as close to the capital the tension had relaxed. A fighting spirit prevailed, and all thoughts went to the men in the front lines, to the wounded, to the countless victims of the war. On March 27, 1915, Claudel gave a lecture at the *Annales*, the free university founded by Madame Yvonne Sarcey, better known under the name of "Cousin Yvonne." Accompanied by Eve Francis he presented poems on nature, faith and France, which the actress interpreted with burning fervor. The patriotic theme was in evidence in *La Nuit de Noel de 1914*, as flamboyant as a stained-glass window, a timely and episodic composition which owed much of its pathos to the wartime circumstances, and in which Claudel, on the occasion of the great national ordeal, proclaimed France's attachment to God; an attachment symbolized by two ravaged towers of his native Champagne: "Those two towers which still protect us, Rheims and that beautiful vessel from which the balm streamed over the whole breadth of the royal land [of France]."

II

THE ROMAN YEARS

PERHAPS CLAUDEL SENSED THAT HE WAS GOING TO BE SENT to Italy. Or his friend Philippe Berthelot may have already told him that he intended to entrust him with a mission in that country. In May and June he undertook a lecture tour through Switzerland and Italy. The dramatist in him was fortunate enough to meet Eleonora Duse, an artist "full of fire and life," who was then at the height of her career and had raised an exceptional talent to a rare degree of perfection. In 1917 she was to be Renée Claudel's godmother.

On the eve of Pentecost he was granted a twenty-minute audience by Benedict XV. And on Whitsunday he received communion from the very hands of the Supreme Pontiff. This Pope, whose reign was rather short, was not fully appreciated by the French, particularly on a national level. Yet he had demonstrated his thoughtfulness toward them by informing President Poincaré of his elevation, although at the time there were no official relations between Paris and the Vatican. The Italian government largely ignored the Holy See, and had just obtained from France, Britain and Russia a secret agreement excluding the Pope from any future peace negotiations. At a time when, more than ever, France needed to be duly represented at the Vatican, the French Ambassador to the Quirinal, Camille Barrère, did nothing to promote the resumption of diplomatic relations. The unofficial mission entrusted to Charles Loiseau was fruitful, but could not make up for the lack of an accredited envoy.

Early in November, Paul Claudel moved to Rome, at 19 Corso d'Italia. The National Foreign Trade Office had given him the mission of investigating the means by which France might "regain the field left . . . to German firms." Madame Claudel and two of their children went with him. His elder daughter had remained in Paris as a pupil at the Convent of the Assumption, and his elder son had been left with Madame Ferdinand de Massary, the child's aunt. Stability had returned to Claudel's life, which for so many months had been singularly unsettled, full of ups and downs. The atmosphere of Rome was a boon to his Catholic soul, painfully conscious of certain lapses and transgressions. On December 8 he wrote to the father of his friend Massignon: "What a wondrous city! St. Peter's alone is a world to be discovered at every hour of the day."

During these war years the French colony in Rome included several notabilities who awakened Claudel's amused curiosity, but whom he was unlikely to choose as his friends. Monsignor Duchesne, a Breton from Saint-Servan, was the director of the French School, and had written *Histoire ancienne de l'Eglise,* a scholarly book of doubtful orthodoxy. His quips and puns were delightful. His wit was of the same vintage as that of Flers and Caillavet; it drew on the humor of the Paris boulevards and also on a certain French tradition of ecclesiastical jocularity. But Claudel had never sought to be amusing in that particular way. . . .

Albert Besnard, a painter whose works were at the time held in high repute, was at the head of the Académie de France in Rome. Count Primoli, who was related to the Bonapartes, entertained lavishly in a palace filled with various art collections. Ambassador Barrère was highly respected, but did not enjoy the same esteem in the eyes of the poetic commercial attaché, who dealt with him very frequently. And it does not seem that the senior French representative properly valued the services of Paul Claudel.

During that period his literary activities sometimes proved damaging to his standing as a diplomat. He was already well-known as a poet, but his reputation—to the noninitiated, at least—suffered from the public's failure to understand such an esoteric form of expression. He had not yet reached full stature as a diplomat. F. Charles-Roux, Barrère's right-hand man, considered Claudel as an "outstanding commercial attaché," however, and admired in him a mind and a man with "the robust build of the farmers of our provinces":

> At that time [wrote F. Charles-Roux], since his career in government service had not yet made him prominent except among his fellow diplomats, the habit had not grown, outside a circle of initiates, of admiring in him two parallel activities. And since his fame as an author far outdistanced his progress in the Foreign Service, there existed, between that fame and his rank in our career, a lag which caused surprise and gave the impression of a contrast. For the public always finds it rather difficult to recognize that an outstanding mind can possess diverse faculties and can apply its intelligence to widely different objects.
>
> Whenever the diplomatic courier was due to leave for Paris, I would see Paul Claudel arriving in the embassy offices, carrying reports on technical subjects which were often arid, although sometimes agricultural. It might be a paper on citrus fruit . . . and on the means of finding a market in France for this crop, which is the main asset of Sicily and Campania; or plans for a railway to link Paris and Constantinople via the Simplon Pass, Milan and Belgrade, replacing the prewar Orient Express; or again a report on the importation into Italy of scrap iron, known in Italian as *rottami,* a raw material essential to the Italian metallurgical industry.[1]

F. Charles-Roux became a close friend to Claudel, of whom Berthelot had said to him: "There is in him something straightforward which you will like," a comment it took him some time to understand. Another reason why Charles-Roux

[1] *Souvenirs diplomatiques* (Fayard) pp. 181-183.

was drawn to Claudel is that he had seen few Frenchmen living in various foreign countries who, in the time-honored words, had kept "as much French soil stuck to the soles of their shoes." This fellow diplomat relates a few traits of character and actual anecdotes which provide valuable details for the Claudelian image. Claudel never spoke of the subject he was writing on. He did not flaunt his Catholicism, but neither did he hide it. At the home of M. Noblemaire (the managing director of the P.L.M. railway), he was seen "kneeling low" before Cardinal Amette, "striking the floor with a thud." When Hilaire Belloc (whom one could call a Franco-British writer), in an *osteria* of the Via Nomentana, the Pozzo di San Patrizio, spoke to him in praise of a certain talented young author, Claudel interrupted and asked: "Does he drink red wine?" Charles-Roux adds that Belloc was taken aback by this unexpected question, but quickly understood its meaning and answered, "Yes, yes, he drinks wine." And when he introduced another author's name into the conversation, he was careful to add to his words of tribute the statement, ". . . and he drinks wine!"

In the stronghold of Roman orthodoxy, Claudel suffered from being harshly judged. He complained to Henri Massis that the *Corriere d'Italia,* a Catholic newspaper, had unjustly accused him of lacking in respect for the Bible and other sacred writings, in *Corona benignitatis anni Dei.* He had already been attacked on diametrically opposite grounds by Paul Souday, an agnostic critic who, in *Le Temps* (issue of December 2, 1915), practically taxed him with childishness. But such wounds were negligible compared to the deep anguish with which he followed the development of the Battle of France, in the spring of 1916. "We must pay, for this is truly the hour of the Prince of this world. Yesterday I felt terribly sad, and went next to the basilica of St. John of Lateran to pray on the Scala Sancta."[2]

[2] Letter to Henri Massis, March 8, 1916.

Among Claudel's best friends in Rome, there was an admirable priest, Monsignor Wladimir Ghika, whom I myself have known and loved. Of royal birth, he was discretion personified, and would appear like some luminous presence just when one most needed the comfort of everything represented by this witness to the invisible. His gentle and very attentive gaze would rest on you and he would speak sparingly, in a low, almost confidential voice, but with a unique blend of fluent ease, striking figures of speech, insight and wit. He had studied extensively at Toulouse, had become a Catholic and later entered the priesthood. Francis Jammes said of him that he was a "Prince dispossessed by Christ." One sensed that he was capable of any self-denial, renunciation or sacrifice. Much later he settled in the Paris suburb of Villejuif, living in a hut among ragpickers. The Second World War found him in Rumania, where he died a few years ago in prison through faithfulness to his Christian consecration. He had had an opportunity to leave that country, but at the border, with no illusion on the fate awaiting him, he had chosen to give his place to a humble woman.

Monsignor Ghika has told me of his friendly relations with Claudel in Rome. During the agonizing siege of Verdun, he witnessed the diplomat's anguish caused by the perusal of the official communiqués. The prelate scolded Claudel gently but firmly when he found him passing harsh or unfair judgments on certain events, undertakings or persons. He knew how his friend struggled to fulfill all the demands of his Christian faith. I remember what the saintly priest told me about Claudel, "He can do much for others, but little for himself." The diplomat's trust in Monsignor Ghika showed itself when he chose him as sponsor for the confirmation of his son Pierre.

In Monsignor Ghika, Claudel also admired the artist, the painter who enjoyed discussing with him and Albert Besnard those realities inspired by the eternal Beauty, "which are also divine things." Claudel was careful to provide a frontispiece

for each of his more important works, and asked the prelate
to draw one for *Le Pain dur* (N.R.F., 1918).

With Monsignor Ghika and Father Fontaine, who was
passing through Rome, he made a Franciscan pilgrimage:

> ... Father Fontaine is at the moment in Rome. The Cardinal
> sent him to the Pope to settle certain matters relating to his
> former parish. . . . In his company, and in that of Prince
> Ghika, we went on that admirable pilgrimage to Subiaco,
> where all together we prayed for you. Prince Wladimir Ghika
> is a fascinating figure. A convert and a doctor of theology, he
> has remained in the laity although pronouncing vows, to
> obey the wishes of the Pope who felt that his action could
> thus be wider and easier. He brought to Bucharest the Sisters
> of St. Vincent de Paul, who were previously in Salonika,
> and has just settled the Assumptionists there. . . . Prince
> Ghika has also written a few small books of a high mysticism
> reminiscent of Father Faber's works, and among others one
> on suffering which made a deep impression on me. . . .[3]

An avid reader, it was then that Claudel made an important
discovery in the first two volumes of Father Brémond's
Histoire littéraire du sentiment religieux en France, a highly
original work which fascinated him through the light it
throws on some practically unknown writers, and also perhaps
through the somewhat whimsical freedom of the composition.
Brémond's purpose was not to erect a scholarly monument,
but only to transmit sparks of souls, spiritual rumors, echoes
of the sublime conversation between the creature and God.
Moreover, Brémond was a poet, a humanist who added to
Shakespeare's comment, "How beautiful is mankind!" the
inexhaustible afterthought: "Beautiful because the supernatural envelops it, gilds it on every side; because the weak-
est of the rays illuminating it issues from the Word, splendor
of the Father, living light of the world."[4]

---

[3] Letter to Louis Massignon, May 31, 1916.
[4] Henri Bordeaux, *Histoire d'une Vie* (Plon).

This major work, which changed all his ideas on French mysticism, fascinated, delighted and entertained him. He could not understand—I heard him say so most vehemently —why Brémond turned away from this subject and devoted his attention to pure poetry. Claudel saw in the priest's original field a great task which should have absorbed all the author's capacity for work and all of his time.

The war was not his only source of sorrow. His close friend Dumesnil, who had so generously received him at the *Amitié de France,* died brokenhearted over the national tragedy. This fearless Norman had defended Claudel against all comers. The diplomat lost another friend, the painter Odilon Redon, a Belgian who had enjoyed a great reputation in France during the symbolist era for his fantastic and haunting compositions.

Meanwhile, Claudel continued to perform his professional duties with scrupulous punctuality, and his fertile yet highly practical imagination succeeded in launching various concrete projects which required him to travel a great deal. Late in August, he returned to Paris and discussed his different undertakings with the Minister for Commerce, who entrusted him with a mission throughout the French provinces.

One may wonder how all these tasks, preoccupations, plans and tangible developments affected his literary activities. They were not neglected and he continued devoting an hour a day to them. There was no question of utilizing this time for anything else, for he had expressly set it aside for himself, once and for all.

While in Rome he wrote a Roman drama, *Le Père humilié,* inspired by the proximity of the Vatican, a play in which the main protagonist is the Pope, successor of Peter. The action takes place in 1870, when Pius IX suffers the humiliation of losing his temporal power and of being subjected to the will of the royal government. For a diplomat who was frequently called upon to deal with Italian political personalities, it must be admitted that this subject was inappropriate, to say the least . . . . But Claudel was a nonconformist, and did not worry about such considerations. Besides, the theme had forced itself upon him, so to speak. History merely served as a means by which he could express something which sprang from the deepest level of his being. At this particular time he felt the burden of an intolerable inner captivity from which he yearned to free himself, above all. The blind young girl he called Pensée de Coûfontaine represented his soul. Fate would not allow her to marry the man she loved, Orian, the Pope's nephew who was killed on the battlefield. But the child he gave her was to be cared for by Orso, who became her husband, and who symbolizes the Rome of Victor-Emmanuel. Being a fervent reader of the Bible, Claudel was attentive to the harmonies and dissonances of Church and synagague, and believed in the virtue of daring alliances. From evil, Rome drew good: "Liberation for the captive souls."

12

WAR AND PEACE:
BRAZIL AND DENMARK

ON JANUARY 1, 1917 PAUL CLAUDEL, NOW APPROACHING HIS fiftieth year, was named Minister Plenipotentiary in Rio de Janeiro. He was glad to leave Paris, where he felt that for the past month his life had been futile. The promotion naturally delighted him, and he soon learned that an enthusiastic welcome awaited the new envoy. The appointment came at a bad time, however. His wife was unable to travel, for she was expecting a fifth child, and Claudel hated the thought of the impending separation. Even though the American continent was not unknown to him, he had never been to Brazil, where tremendous difficulties were in store for him. The war had already spread to many countries of the world, and Brazil as a whole was favorable to the allied cause. But our sympathizers had to deal with adverse influences, with a powerful and determined opposition. Moreover, France had not always been wise or prudent in her investment and loan policies, and the new minister would have to work hard to repair the consequences of those mistakes.

On Saturday, January 10, he reached Lisbon. Submarine warfare being in full swing, detours, precautions and vigilance were the order of the day. On the 13th he sailed on a British steamer, the *Amazon*. His ship called at St. Vincent (one of the Cape Verde Islands) on the 21st and reached Rio by the end of the month. On February 1 Claudel took possession of his new post. The ocean, his daily companion for over two weeks, and one with which he would always feel in deep communion, had dispensed its blessings on him. His inner wounds —which in December, during a short trip to Lyons undertaken after his return from Italy, had led him to Notre-Dame-de-Fourvières—had seemed gradually to heal during the crossing, when the "professional absent" had only himself to worry about.

> Nothing but the sea on each side of us, nothing but the
> waves rising and falling!
> Enough of this constant thorn in my heart, enough of those
> days drop by drop!
> Nothing but the eternal sea forever and all at once! The sea,
> and we are in it.[1]

Claudel immediately settled in the Legation, a rather pleasant residence on the rua Paissandu. In the garden, palm trees nearly a hundred and fifty-feet high cast a cool shade, conducive to rest and meditation. When he considered the tide of world events, inevitably felt even on those distant shores, the new minister expected that the war would soon end. Like many other Frenchmen, in fact, he was of the opinion that peace would return before the year was out. These were the views of someone as well informed as Philippe Berthelot, for instance, who had great confidence in the Lyautey-Nivelle combination (the former was war minister at the time, and the latter commander in chief). But Lyautey ran into parliamentary opposition and was forced to resign; in April the Nivelle offensive failed on the Chemin des Dames, or at least its results fell far short of what had been expected. The government contemplated yet another change in the high command. The morale of the fighting units, target of a deliberate and concerted defeatist propaganda, was put to a severe test. While the Kaiser decided to intensify submarine warfare still further, the Russian revolution broke out in

[1] *Feuilles de Saints, Ballade.*

March, the Czar abdicated, and Lvov followed by Kerensky briefly headed a precarious provisional regime which was soon swept aside by Lenin and his Bolsheviks. In April the United States entered the war on the side of the Allies. "How many divine lessons," commented Claudel. "God's hand on the 'blackboard' is becoming increasingly clear."

The new envoy found it a major task to settle France's large financial interests. One of the most important of these was the Brazil Railway. Thanks to Claudel's skill as a negotiator, all the invested funds were recovered. In exchange, France was able to obtain the ships and raw materials sorely needed to prosecute the war. A *Convenio* allowed the purchase of thirty German ships. Changing "sacks of sugar and coffee into *milreis,*" the diplomat was amused to find that he had become a kind of glorified grocer. One day many years later he good-naturedly related these memories to me; it was unfortunate, he added, that his advice had not always been followed, which deprived the French treasury of substantial earnings. In a different field he signed with Nilo Peçanha a literary and artistic treaty negotiated several years earlier by Clémenceau. All this diplomatic activity was to lead to a formal alliance between France and Brazil.

Back at home, the brilliant way in which Claudel carried out his duties inspired a respectful admiration. In *L'Action Française* (April 28, 1917), Jacques Bainville echoed the unanimous feelings of all well-informed Frenchmen:

> The mission of representing France in Brazil, during this unprecedented crisis of humanity, has fallen to a poet. We must congratulate him and congratulate ourselves. Opinions on Claudel's literary merit may differ. But he is a representative of French letters and French thought to a people where ideas are in honor, and whose intellectual kinship with us is close. Moreover, Claudel is a realist. He knows business, and he knows trade. In Hamburg, where he was consul, he saw great [economic] ventures at close range . . . At the present

time, in Rio de Janeiro, he is in a good position to speak by turns the language of interest and that of Latin brotherhood.

Chance gave him as secretary the musician and composer Darius Milhaud, called up by the French consular authorities in Brazil. Claudel highly valued this typical and intensely French artist, who not without a kind of irony knew how to blend a renewed neo-classicism and his own original brand of impressionism. A native of Provence and a devoutly religious Jew, the composer was in Claudel's eyes something like a living presence of the Bible, which had remained dear to him ever since Sister Brigitte, in Bar-le-Duc, first showed him its holy pictures. And Milhaud admired in him the powerful lyricist, a continuator (in his own way) of King David's genius for adoration and penitence.

Darius Milhaud, one of the future glories of the *Ecole des Six,* was only nineteen in 1912—when Claudel had met him for the first time, through their mutual friend Jammes. The poet had taken the first step toward this young man, who was considerably his junior. Milhaud was extremely gracious and thoughtful, and years later at the boulevard de Clichy he kindly described for me the fruitful partnership between himself and the author of *L'Otage.* In a little book simply entitled *Etudes,* now out of print, he gave these amusing details: "The first I heard about Claudel was through Francis Jammes, whom I had gone to see at Orthez. [My friend] painted him as both a kind of saint and a frightful ogre, unable to stand the smell of vanilla, dressed in a Chinese robe and wearing a consul general's hat."

From their first meeting Claudel was impressed by the brilliant intelligence of the younger man and by his bold and highly original conception of music. The author realized that he had found a composer capable of providing an accompaniment of the type he had always wanted for the dialogues of his dramatic works. This musical support had appeared essential to Claudel when he read the Greek tragedies, particu-

larly those of Aeschylus, some of which he had translated
when he was consul in Foochow. It will be remembered that
Aeschylus, as well as Sophocles, made a deep and lasting
impression on him. He had immediately suggested to Milhaud
that they work together, and this plan of his had been enthusiastically accepted.

The co-operation between Claudel and Milhaud was to be a
source of great satisfaction to them both. In Brazil, they
discovered together magnificent landscapes which no European could possibly imagine. Sometimes they rode through
exuberant tropical forests during the night. Having seen
Nijinsky dance in Rio, Claudel conceived a plastic poem, an
enchanted ballet. The idea was carried out: the scenario
occupied only two pages, and Milhaud wrote the musical
score. The cast of characters in *L'homme et son destin* (such
was the title chosen) included the Hours, the Moon, a sleeping man and the ghost of a dead woman.

Claudel's major literary work during this period was *La
messe là-bas*. As in *Cinq grandes Odes,* the author laid his
soul bare. A few lines are enough to give an idea of the
tragic situation of this Christian and Frenchman, exiled once
again:

My only company here is this greater intensity of light.
. . . My mind knows no more rest than the sea, it is the same
mad agony.
. . . This chaos of leaves and ferns in the sun, this abode of
my fiftieth year.
It would be no more difficult, simply by closing my eyes, to
blot it out, than it was to forget the homeland where I was
born . . .
. . . Things are leaving me little by little, and I leave them
in my turn.
Only naked can one enter the counsels of love.   (*Introit*)
. . . There is a man who has never known how to protect
himself against the sea!

There is a man who is professionally outside everything, and
   his residence is to be nowhere at home.
No task is properly his, he is eternally the Amateur, and the
   Guest everywhere, and the precarious Gentleman:
Only exile teaches him the fatherland.
. . . O God, I offer You the absence of everything!
. . . These things in which all Appearance is summed up, I
   have what is required to destroy them rather well.
So that there may remain only You.   (*Offertory*)
. . . Friend of my guilty days, farewell! I forgo your thorn,
I no longer find the rose amid the divine breath.
                                          (*Communion*)
. . . You struggle in vain, you will not defend yourself
   eternally against my peace.
Do you sense it or not, that I am here, this table companion
   you were awaiting?   (*Communion*)

The time Claudel spent in Brazil helped him to see more
clearly within himself, to find his past gradually more explain-
able, and above all to gain a heightened awareness of his rejected vocation.

While in South America Claudel was fortunate enough to
meet several outstanding personalities. The best known was
Ruy Barboza, federal senator and economist, of whom Louis
Barthou said that there was in him the vigor of several men,
each of them first rate. A great admirer of French literature,
he had welcomed Anatole France to Brazil in 1909, and although he paid tribute to the perfection of the master's prose
he did not hesitate to denounce those of his ideas which
seemed harmful to him. A professor of law and a hero of
political liberty, Barboza had not waited for full maturity
before proving himself a man of exceptional caliber: at
eighteen, he had championed the abolition of slavery, and at
twenty-three had distinguished himself in Bahia as attorney
for a young woman of the lower classes, against one of the
richest men in town. In 1907 his speeches at the Peace Con-

ference of The Hague attracted considerable attention. As early as 1914, when the final issue of the war was still very much in doubt, he had taken a position in favor of the Allies. In July 1916 as Ambassador Extraordinary for the commemoration of the independence of the Argentine Republic, he unequivocally defined the duties of neutrality. Clémenceau called him "the humanitarian idealist, miraculously eloquent." His death in Rio at the age of seventy-four, on March 1, 1922, was a loss to the entire civilized world and affected Claudel very deeply.

The contacts between the French writer and the Brazilian intelligentsia left a lasting impression. One of the most pertinent tributes paid to Claudel after his death came from a member of the Brazilian Academy of Letters, Alceu Amoroso Lima (Tristan d'Althayde), who avoided the pitfalls of both extravagant eulogy and pedantic, fussy criticism:

> The eminent French poet treated the great subjects of Christian humanism in much the same way, twenty-five centuries later, as the Greek precursors treated the major themes of pagan mytholoy. "Mythology is search," said Chesterton. A search to which Christian revelation gives an answer.
>
> His works are not a farewell to a dying world, but rather the harbinger of the new times . . . Whereas Proust drew from his soul—delicate as a last flower of culture—everything which morbid states entail in the way of sensitivity and mental acuteness, Claudel—on the other hand—as the healthy man he was, gives us the red blood of his vigorous race. The former, at the beginning of this century, was the inspired reflection of the twilight of a civilization; the latter was the profound and mysterious voice of a spirit which transcends culture, civilization and time itself. . . . Claudel appears as the forerunner of a new era in which the desperate contest between good and evil is overshadowed by the idea of redemption.[2]

[2] "Paul Claudel vu par un écrivain brésilien," *La Croix*, 1959.

Among the friends of the French envoy, one should also mention, on both the social and artistic planes, Mrs. Andrey Parr, the Polish-born wife of a British diplomat. She had a beautiful home in Petropolis, and owned a miniature theater which could be placed on a table and had been constructed especially to help in the staging of *L'homme et son désir*. Over the weekends, Claudel and Milhaud would escape to this cooler haven from the torrid summer days in Rio. The composer related some of their occupations: "We would cut out of colored paper figures fifteen centimeters high, and this is how we planned our entire ballet."[3] Mrs. Parr was to prove a faithful friend. Later, she stayed on several occasions at Brangues, where she was known as Margotine.

As in all his posts, Claudel traveled very extensively throughout Brazil. He could not avoid various public demonstrations in his favor, and quite naturally found them flattering. But he knew how to distinguish between the compliment intended for the poet and thinker, and the homage paid to the diplomat as a kind of standard-bearer for France. He admitted that his attention was easily distracted. Once, for instance, as he delivered a speech in the refreshment room of a railway station, "a huge shelving-type dresser filled with bottles had seemed to topple slowly and feelingly toward him;" it was, he said, "the highest row, that of fancy liqueurs, which started first, with that rhythmic and musical shuffling called shimmy, if I am not mistaken."[4] Far from annoying him, such incidents satisfied his taste for the extravagant and the picturesque. They inspired the comic author he intended to remain, without however causing him to forget the serious lyricist and the austere dramatist.

The Bible fascinated Claudel, and he took notes in a thick copybook on the theme of Water, which had been on his mind

---

[3] Darius Milhaud: *Etudes* (Cl. Aveline, id.).
[4] *Paul Claudel interroge l'Apocalypse* (Gallimard), p. 67.

for some time: according to him, water symbolized the abode
of the elect, just as fire represented the element of damnation.
He was somewhat exasperated by the tedious analysis of so
much Biblical material; he felt that this fundamental task of
scholarship should have been undertaken long before, and
dreamed of a Biblical dictionary in which would be found,
with all appropriate references and quotations, words such
as Tree, Wood, Water, Spirit, Fire, Bread, Earth, etc.

Claudel missed his family terribly. On August 2, 1917 his
wife had given birth to a fifth child whom he had not yet
seen: Renée (later Madame Jacques Nantet), named after
one of her Sainte-Marie-Perrin uncles who died in the fighting around Ypres. A few days before Renée's birth, Claudel
received the news of the death of his father-in-law, the Four-
vières architect, "born [in the words of the poet] to that
better world whose reflection I saw on his face when I took
leave of him in Lyons last December."[5] Work and prayer
helped the diplomat to accept his bitter existence, and a few
devoted friends did everything they could to make it more
bearable. In this respect he could always count on one of his
aides, Henri Hoppenot, on the latter's wife and on the faithful
Darius Milhaud.

He would never forget Brazil. Though he was aware of certain shortcomings (no country is without some defects, and it
was mainly from the religious viewpoint that he showed himself hardest to please), the French envoy marveled at the
beauty of the landscape, was comforted by the warm and
disinterested friendships he found there, and believed in the
future of that land blessed with inexhaustible resources.
Moreover, his mission to Rio was a definite diplomatic success which brought concrete political and economic results,

[5] *Correspondance Claudel-Jammes-Frizeau,* p. 293. Letter to Francis
Jammes, Sept. 25, 1917.

and won for him, as his son Pierre humorously noted, "the gold medal of trade, Clémenceau's official congratulations and a silver coffeepot."

What Claudel liked most in Brazil was, as he declared to Jean Amrouche for his *Mémoires improvisés,* "a virgin land; a country where nature is untamed . . . [and] at the same time one which gives the idea of classicism, of classical antiquity; . . . the only country where the old royal civilization has left its mark." A whole area of his personality had found surprising affinities there.

The return from Brazil, in February 1919, turned out to be a perilous adventure. Claudel and Milhaud traveled together on one of the thirty German ships which had been purchased by France through her envoy. On the way to New York, during the first leg of the journey, the engines failed and the ship drifted along in the Amazon current. It took fifty-three days to reach New York, via the West Indies, where the passengers transferred to another steamer. Claudel described this unexpected Odyssey in a jocular vein:

> The war is over and, with my secretary Darius Milhaud, I am returning from Brazil where I covered myself with glory in the field of finance and in the grocery business, the worthiest of trades; one which since then I have never ceased to consider as my true vocation! The Atlantic Ocean is in fine fettle: this is February, the grand season, the liveliest season of the Herring Pond; and a relentless wind ravages without malice the amiable puddle, from the North Pole to the other (if it be true that there is one!). Hurrah! The war is over . . . ! To the unloosing of what the Newfoundland fishermen call a fresh breeze are joined all the bugles of Victory . . . ! Everything dances, jumps, capers and jostles on the happy ship . . . which dives down and offers a willing flank to the tremendous buffets administered from time to time by the ocean; in an orgy of spume and vociferation,

answered from the pantry by the crash of broken plates and dishes.[6]

Calm and unmoved, the poet translated the *Psalms*, entering deeply into the spirit and the thought of King David. This served as a prelude to one of his major undertakings, *Le Soulier de satin*, which would conclude a cycle in his literary work, and would also mark a temporary pause in his life.

When Claudel reached Copenhagen in September 1919, as Minister to Denmark, the French government was still headed by Clémenceau, and the country was getting ready for the November elections which were to produce the famous "Horizon-Blue" Chamber of Deputies. The Treaty of Versailles had been officially signed in June. Claudel remained for two years in this northern capital, a city proud of its weathered brick architecture; a bustling, cheerful and tidy metropolis full of reminders of King Christian IV and the seventeenth century. The diplomat liked the old quarters so rich in history, the busy commercial thoroughfares, the boulevards—in particular the Frederiksborggade—with their steady stream of bicycles, the canal embankments around the castle, dotted with little restaurants and stalls selling succulent eels considered a delicacy by Danish gourmets.

Another French author, Léon Bloy, who was nearly the same age as the envoy, had come to Denmark before him, and was to marry a Dane. Claudel admired Bloy and was fond of him, but had strong reservations concerning his temper. The two men did not see Denmark from quite the same viewpoint. Claudel was struck by the many conversions which were taking place. He lived alone, as in Brazil, but the war was over now. Paris and his family were within easy reach; he could be back home in a few hours. When winter came he enjoyed leaving in the wind and snow to attend seven o'clock mass, before tackling the heavy schedule of his days.

[6] "L'absent professionnel," *Le Figaro littéraire*, Feb. 12, 1938.

The peace treaty had made special stipulations for Schleswig, a former Danish province—at the base of the Jutland Peninsula—annexed by Prussia in 1864, at the same time as Holstein. An international commission had been formed to settle the fate of this area. Claudel represented France, and the other members were Messrs. von Sydow (Sweden), Heftge (Norway), Marbing (United Kingdom) and Bruce, who served as secretary. A plebiscite returned to Denmark the northern part of Schleswig, "a dismal land," said Claudel, "which is but moors and swamps."

Clémenceau having withdrawn from the race, Paul Deschanel remained the only candidate, and was elected President of the French Republic on January 17, 1920. A government in which Millerand served as both premier and foreign minister seemed to portend an era of relative political stability. Claudel rejoiced at the canonization of Joan of Arc. He spent the summer in Elsinore with his wife and children, who had finally joined him. In the Flagnatteri of Kronborg his imagination conjured up the first act of *Hamlet*, on the famous terrace. Before the citadel brooding over the Baltic, he saw in his mind's eye queen Caroline-Matilda, who was imprisoned at the age of twenty-one and was kept in captivity after the beheading of Count Struensee. Above all, Claudel found the imperishable memories of those great Shakespearean personages, Hamlet and Ophelia. The Church of St. Olav and the Convent of St. Mary also moved him deeply. He would always remember the enchantment of Elsinore, whose very name is heavy with dreams and nostalgic power.

Once more he had reached a turning point in his life. This return to Europe, at a time when he was at the height of his vitality, inspired him with mixed feelings; with both elation and sadness. He wrote to his friend Massignon on August 4, 1920: "I am at a moment in my life when the old separations change into a kind of organic disengagement, which does not take place without melancholy. There are times when the evening coolness seems delicious to me, and others when it makes me shiver." Dom Besse, his former spiritual director, died during that same year.

When he left Denmark in 1921 he was given a rousing farewell. In one of his last speeches he summed up the many impressions filling his mind: "This feeling of peaceful possession, this natural sincerity, this unanimity between the land and its inhabitants; these are traits which make the memory of Denmark hard to forget, whereas many noisy cities fade away in the smoke of the train or steamer."[7] He declared in all sincerity that he was leaving that country a richer man than on his arrival. Reviewing the friends he had made during his mission to Copenhagen, he took pleasure in mentioning artists (Roose, Paul Reimert), great poets (Sophus Michaelis, Christian Rimestadt) "equally familiar with our two literatures"; a philologist and ardent Francophile of the caliber of Nyrop, and also Gobinot, a Frenchman living in Denmark to serve our literature in that country. In addition, he took away with him from this northern land some preliminary ideas for an imaginary nautical festival, and these were to become the fourth day of *Le Soulier de satin*.

[7] Given on Feb. 28, 1921. Quoted in *Contacts et circonstances* under the title "Adieu au Danemark."

13

JAPAN

On January 11, 1921, Paul Claudel was named Ambassador to Japan, replacing M. Bapst, who had reached the retirement age. Taisho (Yoshihito) reigned over the Japanese Empire. Hirohito, the present Emperor, was to become Prince Regent after a tour of study through Europe. Since 1880 that great island country had moved far along the road to industrialization, with initial emphasis on textiles, chemical products and foodstuffs. Following the First World War, in which it had taken part on the side of the Allies, Japan emerged as a major power. Its highly efficient army and navy were forces to be reckoned with. Its merchant fleet was the third largest in the world. Formosa, Port-Arthur and Korea were under Japanese control, and could absorb the population overflow from the home islands. In short, Japan dominated the entire Far East.

For many years, Claudel had wished for an assignment to the land of the rising sun. The Nipponese mind, reputed to be inaccessible and inscrutable, was to become familiar and brotherly to him. Through his contact with Japan—and this cannot be overemphasized—his art, which was at times rough or harsh, took on a new-found polish, subtlety and transparency. As he one day said, in a mood both judicious and jocular, "Everything in Japan, from the shape of a mountain to the design of a hairpin or a saké cup, obeys the same style. . . . The specifically Japanese attitude toward life is what I shall call, for want of better words . . . reverence, respect, spontaneous acceptance of a [principle of] superiority inaccessible to intelligence; the humbling of our personal existence before the mystery surrounding us, the sensing of a presence around us which demands ceremony and precaution." The physical appearance of Japan delighted him: "Japan rests like a group of solidified clouds amid a boundless ocean. Its worn and fretted coast line, its inner basins, its mysterious passages, are for the navigator a never-ending surprise. . . . All nature is a temple already prepared and arranged for worship." Although the religion of most Japanese was not his own, and although he regretted that it was not "the worship of the transcendent Being," he noted with approval that it is "closely associated with the natural and social milieu in which it holds sway." He was amazed to see that, in Japan, "everyone is a poet."

On the way to his new post, he stopped on November 2, 1921 at Angkor, which had astonished Pierre Loti before him. But they were not struck by the same things. Claudel would remember mostly the fantastic temples, the "cellars where terrified flights of bats whirled amid a horrible stench."[1] Emerging from a forest and beholding the great palace crowned with its five tiaras, he exclaimed, "It looks like five pineapples on a dish."[2] As a matter of fact, Cambodia left him with a most unpleasant memory: during his short stay he came down with malaria which recurred some fifteen years later and nearly cost him his life.

The death of Father Fontaine, on November 10, 1920, had left him at a loss, spiritually speaking, and he doubted whether he could ever find another adviser who would be— like the good father—a "saint," or at least a priest combining piety and generosity of heart and knowing something of life: this is how, in a letter to Louis Massignon, he defined the

[1] *Connaissance de l'Est.*
[2] From a lecture by Roland Dorgelès.

qualities he expected from a spiritual director. At about the same time he told me about the great difficulty he had experienced, since his return to God, in obtaining spiritual help and guidance for the conduct of his soul; which had also been the case for St. Thérèse of Lisieux. It is not surprising to learn that he once asked a friend to find him a complete prayer book, in Latin if possible, and a compilation of meditations, preferably written for the clergy. He felt at home with such manuals intended for the use of clerics; perhaps they sometimes made him think of the priest he might have been.

In the diplomatic field various important developments were of immediate concern to him. Aristide Briand was then Premier and Foreign Affairs Minister. A stormy debate on the Banque d'Indochine, which filed a petition in bankruptcy on June 30, was to force Philippe Berthelot—whose brother André was a director of the bank—to submit his resignation as secretary general of the Quai d'Orsay. Claudel felt his friend's ordeal as keenly as a personal misfortune, all the more so since he knew that Philippe Berthelot lacked religious faith to sustain and comfort him. The Briand government fell on January 12, 1922, and Raymond Poincaré headed a new cabinet. During the same year other significant events included the triumph of Fascism in Italy, when Mussolini came to power, and the abolition of the Sultanate in Turkey.

Claudel fulfilled everything expected of him by his own government (which had selected him at a time when it was essential for France to be represented in Tokyo by an envoy familiar with the particular problems of the Orient) and by the Japanese themselves, who had welcomed him with the flattering name of "Shigin Taishi," which means ambassador-poet. But he continued to set aside for himself one hour every morning which he devoted entirely to his work as an author. In this literary field he was occupied almost entirely with *Le Soulier de satin,* the crowning achievement of his entire career as a dramatist; the conclusion, in renunciation and joy, of that agonizing *Partage de midi,* whose two main protagonists had met again in the radiance of those spiritual summits, where lasting peace and serenity are born.

As everyone knows, earthquakes are frequent in Japan, and everything is conditioned by a continual attention to danger. Claudel had hardly reached Tokyo before he and his family realized "of what Cyclops asleep under the leaves and flowers they were the guests." (*Terra tremuit . . .*) And in *Trois Figures saintes* (p. 66), he wrote: "I remember those heavy nights in Japan when you wake up with a start, [sensing that] there is going to be an earthquake. . . . A deep silence reigns, a kind of general catalepsy, and then suddenly an open door starts to rattle and bang . . ."

On Saturday September 1, 1923, shortly before noon, a few violent tremors shook the cities and villages of Japan, caused thousands of houses to collapse, destroyed countless homes, drove terrified multitudes into the streets and onto the highways. Fires and a tidal wave completed the work of destruction. Smothered, crushed, drowned or burned to death, entire populations were surprised in full activity, and lost their lives in the space of a few minutes. Among piles of rubble there arose here and there wall sections, skeletons of monuments, gaping fragments of buildings. Tokyo was laid waste, except for a few districts in the north and west. Yokohama, the great commercial port and capital of the silk industry, was also devastated, as well as Yokosuka, the naval base.

"Premonitory quivers" had already shaken and seriously damaged the miserable building of the embassy, which had been reinforced and propped up on the ambassador's order.

Paul Claudel's residence—that house near the Bridge of Pheasants, visited by a certain crow which the poet's children named Adhémar—was reduced to charred ruins. The ambassador and those of his family who had remained with him escaped with their lives, but the absence of Reine, his second daughter, caused him considerable anxiety for two days. She had gone away for the weekend to visit the family of the Belgian ambassador, M. de Bassompierre. After the catastrophe she found refuge on board the cruiser *Colmar*, flagship of the French naval detachment in the Far East, based in Port-Arthur. Her alarmed father had vainly searched for her, several times over, as far as Dzuski, about forty miles away from the Japanese capital.

He never forgot all the other victims, however, and worked actively to help and comfort them, subordinating his own anxieties to theirs. He made his headquarters aboard the *André-Lebon,* a Messageries Maritimes liner in port near Tokyo at the time, and sallied forth to discharge his various duties. A striking photograph published in *L'Illustration* shows him in shirtsleeves helping to clear away rubble. He had personally lost everything; all his books, letters and manuscripts, including the third part of *Le Soulier de satin.* The embassy staff was safe, but M. Déjardin, the French consul in Yokohama, was killed in his office. In the same city, a Frenchman named Fomberteaux, the agent for the Messageries Maritimes, had seen his family escape death as though by miracle though their house was destroyed: he distinguished himself by his devotion to the many victims.

Madame Claudel herself set a remarkable example of dedication and worked tirelessly to alleviate the sufferings of the population. On this occasion as always, she proved herself truly an ambassadress, both of France and of charity. She became ill with typhoid fever resulting from the unsanitary conditions brought about by the disaster. The Claudel children, who were too young to be subjected to the inevitable aftermaths of the national calamity, were sent back to France.

The following lines which appeared in Gustave Hervé's

newspaper, *La Victoire,* testify to the selflessness shown by
the ambassador:

> We already knew that diplomacy is not a career for men
> without financial means. Our Ambassador to Japan, M. Paul
> Claudel, the author of *Tête d'Or* and *L'Annonce faite à
> Marie,* has just experienced this, much to his disadvantage.
>
> His furniture, destroyed by the Tokyo earthquake, was
> worth at least 200,000 francs. M. Claudel, and this was most
> generous of him, did not want to be reimbursed in full by the
> government. He himself suggested reductions [in his claim],
> which his personal means allowed him to bear. Consequently
> this scrupulous civil servant presented a claim for 106,725
> francs.
>
> The government considered that the rich M. Claudel could
> deduct even more, and granted him 100,000 francs. . . .
>
> The total for the entire embassy was reduced from 692,275
> to 300,000 francs. . . .
>
> M. Claudel's subordinates, who had requested 150,000
> francs each, received 115,000. They were better treated than
> their superior. Obviously, even in regard to people who have
> almost lost their lives, the powers that be are awfully close-
> fisted!

The loss of his manuscript reminded the author that everything here below is but "ashes and dust," and for a time inspired in him a certain indifference toward literature, which
had already happened once when he was at Solesmes. But
soon he realized once again that he had definite duties to perform as God's witness.

In France, he was not forgotten. Lugné-Poë, Maurice Martin du Gard and several others planned a festival in the
Théâtre des Champs-Elysées, to show France's sympathy
and admiration for the poet and ambassador, and for the
benefit of the Japanese artists who were victims of the earthquake. Barrès was one of the first patrons. Although rather

unfamiliar with Claudel's works, he had thought of presenting his readers in *L'Echo de Paris* with what he knew of the
subject. He saw in the man a *baoué* (bauer) of Lorraine, that
is to say, a peasant. He told Maurice Martin du Gard that, in
his opinion, Claudel had just "missed his death": "It suited
him. Let him try to die, now!" Nevertheless, Barrès had been
deeply moved when he heard of the dangers his fellow author
had gone through, for he was not totally unaware of Claudel's
genius. On the following December 5 it was Barrès who died,
and his commonplace end was probably far different from the
one he would have wished for, from the one he deserved. But
great "committed" geniuses, such as Pascal, sometimes die in
their beds without losing stature in the memory of men.[3]

But the strong attachment of tried and true friends, and the
few expressions of sympathy he received, brought him no il-
lusions on his fame, nor on the influence of his thought and
works. There were times when he experienced an aching sen-
sation of utter isolation. *L'Annonce* and *L'Otage*—both of
which received high and pertinent critical praise—actually
reached a very limited public only, and were never made into
large-scale theatrical productions. Various books were written
about him: that of Georges Duhamel, so fervent; that of
Father Joseph de Tonquédec, so intelligent and perceptive,
but tinged with reservations; others too, lacking completely
in understanding or goodwill, like that of Pierre Lasserre
(*Les Chapelles littéraires*), written in the name of an uncompromising neo-classicism, or that of Raymond Hubert, blindly
and maliciously fanatical. The accolades he received from his
peers, such as Maeterlinck, Elémir Bourges, Léon Daudet
and Schwob, should have dissipated any doubts he might have
had. . . . Nevertheless he was downcast and confided in a
young teacher, Pierre Moreau (who is now a professor at the
Sorbonne), in a letter thanking him for an excellent study
published in the *Revue des Jeunes*.

[3] *Les Mémorables* (Flammarion) p. 350.

French Embassy to Japan
Tokyo, November 29, 1923

Dear Sir:

The *Revue des Jeunes* brings me the kind article which you have devoted to me, and I would be ungrateful indeed not to express all my thanks to you. For some time now I have been accustomed to spiteful words and insults rather than to compliments, and your warm and generous sympathy is to me an act of charity. I have now been writing for thirty years, and when I see works to which I have given my whole soul engulfed in a crushing silence, the feeling of being useless, of having served no purpose, of having spoken for no one, of having awakened not a single echo, is such as to rob me of all courage. I often wonder whether I will not stop publishing (my works), or at least whether I will not limit myself to the publication of a few copies which will reach only those to whom they can really be of interest. Thank you, therefore, from the bottom of my heart, for having kept me company during a few steps in this bitter solitude where I have the feeling that I am sinking more and more.

Your comments on the kind of verse I have chosen show me how necessary it would be for me to publish the work of justification which I have been preparing for a long time. Please believe that I have something to say. Do you really think that the prosody of Molière, Ronsard, Emile Augier, Voltaire, Alfred de Musset [whose name has been added between the lines], etc., which to me is the essence of platitude, resembles in any way the "breathing of a giant chest?" You are probably thinking of Victor Hugo, but if so, that respiration is more like a snore. Are you not struck by the fact that, in our literature, with a few exceptions, the most powerful, generous, imaginative and lyrical minds, from Rabelais to Michelet, all wrote in prose? And that poetry has been rather the [mode of] expression of dry, insubstantial, flimsy minds; or else of mere rhetoricians, of verse makers? Poetry is much less the expression of our need for an ideal than that of our need for the absolute. It always leads to an inscription, to a proverb. But true poetry is something else.

Please believe, dear sir, in my gratitude and in my most sincerely devoted feelings,

Paul Claudel

Claudel started writing *Le Soulier de satin* toward March of 1921. This was precisely the sixth centennial of Dante's death, and Claudel had just composed a jubilee ode in which Beatrice speaks these words, this advance explanation of his dramatic work:

> Though I am beautiful, for you I have wanted to become more beautiful still; and though I am young, I have wanted to pass into a greater youth.
> The joy I could have given you in this world would not have satisfied you any more than my youth,
> And I did not want to share being alive with those things you found so real!
> The first time I saw you, I took an oath to die no more.

The joyous love of Christian and human unity animates the four "days" of this drama. It is no longer Ulysses returning to Penelope. Nor the heroes of the Round Table leaving in search of the Holy Grail. Nor Don Quixote, tilting against formidable enemies. In *Le Soulier de satin*, the Renaissance —which was, according to Claudel, "one of the most glorious periods of Catholicism"—brings forth a cry of joy, as in the paintings of Rubens; and Spain occupies the dominant place. A Spaniard, Rodrigue, conducts and lives the drama. He has seen only once Dona Prouhèze, the young wife of the old Governor Don Pélage, and since then his heart has been filled with a desperate love. Prouhèze is committed to the care of Don Balthazar, to whom she confesses her own love for Rodrigue and her plan to meet him at the inn and to run away with him. Deep within herself, she does not want to yield to temptation and surrender to evil. More than a gift of self and a bond, the sacrament of marriage, in her eyes, is a consecration which can only end with death. Her guide will do everything to restrain her, "while she tries everything to elude him." Before a statue of the Virgin, she gives one of her satin slippers as a votive offering, and asks the Madonna to hold it against her heart.

As for Rodrigue, informed of Prouhèze's intentions, he fails to answer the summons of the king—who intended to appoint him as his representative, Viceroy of the Indies—and prepares to abduct the one he loves from the protection of Don Balthazar. A Chinese manservant accompanies him. On the road leading him toward Prouhèze, he is attacked by brigands, manages to fight them off, but is seriously wounded.

Rodrigue is cared for in the castle of his mother. Prouhèze, learning of this development, escapes from her guardian and arrives at the castle but is unable to see the man she loves. She knows only that he is struggling against death. Her husband, who also makes his appearance, tells her that, with the king's consent, she is to command personally the fortress of Mogador, which is threatened by the Moors, in the place and stead of Don Camille who is to become her lieutenant. She sets off against the wish of Rodrigue, and will be exposed to the love which Camille feels for her. Rodrigue recovers and tells the king that he will accept the viceroyalty under the condition that Prouhèze will return to Spain. The king consents to give the young woman this advice, which is backed by her husband's plea, but Rodrigue will have to convey the message. When he appears before her she refuses to speak to him, and lets him leave for America.

Ten years go by. Rodrigue has won fame in the new lands he has gloriously conquered. A letter reaches him from the woman he still loves. In a desperate mood she had written it when he reached the New World, but the missive was relayed from hand to hand and could not be delivered any sooner. In the meantime she has become a widow, she is free, so that they can join their destinies. Rodrigue quickly sets

sail for Mogador. On his arrival in Africa he finds that Camille and Prouhèze have been married. She asks Rodrigue to
show generosity: "Cast off everything, discard everything,
give everything away, so that you may receive everything!"
Prouhèze dies beneath the ruins of the fortress which has
been blown up at the instigation of her husband. Before dying
she places Doña Maria of the Seven-Swords, her child by
Don Camille, under the protection of Rodrigue, whose spirit
of self-sacrifice and abnegation matches her own.

Rodrigue loses favor with the king and sets off again, this
time as governor of the Philippine Islands. He takes part in
a war against the Japanese, loses a leg, and is taken prisoner.
Assisted by his adopted daughter and a Japanese manservant,
he lives miserably in an old vessel, selling pictures of saints
painted by himself.

His fate is to sink even lower. A new king ascends the
throne of Spain and offers him the command of the forces
against England. But Rodrigue behaves in such a way that
he is soon abondoned to the soldiers as a slave, then left
to a nun as a derelict, while his daughter—he is advised of this by the blast of a trumpet—manages to swim
to the ship of Don Juan of Austria, who was to defeat the
Turkish Fleet at Lepanto in 1571.

One cannot separate *Le Soulier de satin* from *Le Partage
de midi*. In the latter play, the only purpose of the guilty
lovers is the satisfaction of their mutual passion, which is
resolved only in death. This brings to mind the precedent of
Tristan and Isolde. God is not absent, but everything takes
place as though He were not an active participant, whereas
in such a case He is inevitably a party to the action. In *Le
Soulier de satin*, God is active, the beloved woman is like a
promise made to man; not of an actual happiness depending
only on her, but a promise she can neither accomplish nor
fulfill. Claudel's vision here is the same as that of Dante.
"Beatrice's eyes were turned to God, and mine were turned

to her." For Claudel, woman is not "divine," but she is a "bearer of God." She is the way which can lead to God. The goal of human wishes is happiness, but the kingdoms of this earth do not bring felicity. Madame de Staël has seen this clearly: the purpose of life is not happiness, but improvement. Happiness on earth resides in a progression toward that final unity with absolute Love, through an arduous ascent and a will to conquer all difficulties. Such is the Claudelian message.

Claudel thus throws on the vocation of woman a light reminiscent of great feminine authors like Sigrid Undset and Gertrud von Lefort. But he is the only one to project this light with such brilliance, one might even say with such violence. Through the Angel, he declares that God is not jealous of the love of creatures for one another, but that man in his human love must take care not to forget God—for man is nowhere "else but with Him" when he partakes in the "mystery of His creation." The Angel adds that woman, in awakening man's desire for her, acts as a guide leading him to God. In the words of Prouhèze, she gives man to God "for God to fill him, in a clap of thunder," and her happiness as a woman is to see man's joy, witnessed by God and herself; a joy which has no other cause but herself. Claudel, who believed that we were created to write the story and history of God, to ensure God's Joy and Glory, "gives woman the space and role necessary for her to exercise her vocation and her mission." Each human being thus posesses an instrumental value, thanks to which God can be discovered and can allow us to discover the world and the significance and symbolism of every creature.

Le Soulier de satin is a summation, it is Claudel's Odyssey. It will no doubt give theorists pleasure to show and explain how the great Catholic dramatist's earlier works are summed up and carried to their conclusion in this play. It has been pointed out, not without reason, that Rodrigue was already

prefigured in *Tête d'Or*, the conqueror whose ambition knew
no bounds. Without disowning the past, Claudel was turned
toward the future; he saw life as a magnificent adventure,
and the Catholic's condition as a wondrous risk in which
nothing is separated, and nature and the supernatural are
closely, deeply and harmoniously connected. His need of the
absolute and of total possession bursts forth throughout his
works.

In February 1925, returning from Indo-China to France,
Claudel sailed on the *Amazone*. At the railing of the first-
class deck he noticed two Carmelite nuns, and one day bowed
deeply to them. They too had been aware of him and of the
respect he showed for them. One of these nuns was Mother
Aimée de Marie, who had founded the Carmel of Hué, in
Annam. And the other was Sister Anne de l'Enfant Jésus,
whose future destiny will be described below. Both belonged
to the Carmel of Cholet. One morning Claudel came up to
them, bowed once again and introduced himself. He explained
that, having crossed in 1894 from Marseilles to Saigon on
board the *Jarra* with a Carmelite, he had remained very attached to their order. A first conversation was followed by
several more. Claudel's family had sailed before him, so that
he was alone and did not speak much with the passengers
chance placed in his path. At the suggestion of the nuns he
read a book entitled *La Science de la Prière*, which made a
deep impression on him. As we have seen, his friendly relations with many members of the Japanese elite had developed
in him a strong liking for Japan, and he felt that the Carmel
should open a branch there. The nuns were convinced by his
arguments and declared themselves ready to take the necessary steps. But the ambassador grew insistent. He wanted the
first Carmelite foundation to be for Japan.

The conversations took on an increasingly spiritual turn.

The subjects discussed included prayer, St. Theresa of Avila, St. Thérèse of the Child Jesus and the spirituality of the Carmel. Claudel felt that this meeting was providential, and believed that it would orient him—he said so—toward a life of closer union with God.

Mother (at that time Sister) Anne de l'Enfant Jésus, the companion of Mother Aimée de Marie (who was to found the Tokyo Carmel in 1933, before starting that of Guadeloupe), never forgot these talks, during which Claudel often confided in her, in the absence of the other nun who was in poor health and often remained in her cabin.

> M. Claudel appreciates the things of God, and ardently aspires after them. He always speaks with open heart, and does not fear to accuse and humble himself, to ask for advice. . . .
>
> He is seeking. . . . For several years he has been devoting an hour to prayer [every day] but, not having succeeded in "fastening" his mind in God, he occupies this hour with the Stations of the Cross. He attempts recollection and conversation with God, but is not as successful as he would wish, [for he is] beset by painful memories . . . images . . . reminiscences of nonreligious books he has read, etc. It is an hour of struggle, suffering and anguish. Will he give up? No, because his soul hungers for the living God. What should he do?
>
> . . . Carmelite spirituality will resolve his anxious question by opening to him the salutary path of "inner poverty." The words of the Psalmist, "I have become before You, O Lord, like a beast of burden . . ." (*ut jumentum ante Te,* but for the purpose of the *ego semper Tecum*), will be the beacon lighting his dark road toward entering into the powers of the Lord. He faces squarely the sacrifices which his literary vocation multiplies. He knows the words of the Psalm which his guide discreetly refers to, and which he himself bravely quotes: "Because I have not know literature, I shall enter into the

powers of the Lord." He consents to the choices and rejections required to defend and safeguard his soul. Identical precautions for his duties as an ambassador, and for that life so removed from the simplicity of the children of God. In all humility, everything is disclosed, examined, accepted.

But one question remains almost insoluble for him: what is the difference between the *nothingness* of St. John of the Cross and the Buddhist *nirvana*? He sees in both a diminution of being which seems to annihilate the gifts of God by destroying the personality. He will understand that the *nothingness* of St. John of the Cross does not annihilate the human being in a stilling of nature, but leads it to the full flowering of all its faculties in God.

But this undertaking is difficult for nature: first, to have the contemplative shed his own self, cast off that spirit of ownership which gives him the illusion of possession so as to make him cross over "to the other side of the lake whipped by the storm." True, the disciples did not appear in too favorable a light when they received the Master's injunction. . . . He had to prod them before they would accept the "risk" and understand that there, in pure Faith, they would be sorted out: those who accept and go beyond their reason and their own intelligence, on His word, to believe in Him and remain His; and those who back away, saying: "This precept is too hard. . . . Who can accept it?"—"To eat His Flesh": what a baffling and unprecedented proposition! And yet, in full trust and confidence, the beautiful cry of Faith answers: "Master, to whom would we go . . . ? You have the words of eternal life . . ."

The soul thus divested of itself "surrenders the keys of the citadel," in the striking words of Ste. Theresa, so that God may be the Master and may destroy it *usque ad fundamentum* —in the Hope that the Holy Ghost will become the soul's guide and will inform his whole being according to Christ and in "Charity." Paul Claudel understands, allows himself to be convinced . . . he is won over to the Evangelical message. "By Myself I can do *nothing*, but the Father works ceaselessly, and I am His working."

Claudel never again doubted the living reality of this doctrine. His daily conversations with the two Carmelite nuns were for him an effective proof that in souls thus surrendered to God all is pacified, enlightened, spiritualized; and that no sacrifice is too great if it prepares the fruitful union, which is a source of life and of graces for other souls.

The narrator of these conversations continued as follows:

The very setting of these meetings seemed chosen by Providence for the soul of the poet so sensitive to the beauties of Creation. Very early one morning he was on the deck where Sister Anne de l'Enfant Jésus was reciting her breviary. The disc of the full moon rested on the horizon line and covered a perfectly calm sea with silver. At the opposite side the rising sun ascended in a golden mist, and the sea itself participated in this riot of colors. Before these two heavenly bodies resting on the immensity of the waters, in the awe-inspiring peace, a silent solitude unspoiled by anything human, Paul Claudel was visibly moved and uttered these words: "It is like the Day of Creation."

In another letter, she related their farewell:

Two days before the arrival, returning the book "*La Science de la Prière*," he added, "I took the liberty of joining to it an envelope for the foundation of the Carmel of Jesus-Emmanuel, and would be very happy if your Mother would accept it. If you would occasionally write to me and keep me informed of the foundation, it would always be a joy for me to receive news from you." One would really have thought that to accept was to do him a favor, and I must admit that I was very touched by the tact with which the offering and the request were made. He asked for permission to return the next day to bid us farewell, a farewell he repeated on the very morning of the arrival, not knowing how to thank us enough for the spiritual benefit he had received.

On August 17, Mother Aimée de Marie, in a letter to the Carmel of Hué, related another instance of the ambassador's thoughtfulness:

Paul Claudel had continued to correspond with his traveling companions; while he was staying with friends near Tours, he took the trouble to come and see us at Cholet before returning to Lyons. We were very touched by this new demonstration of friendly interest from such an eminent personality. Well, around two o'clock a large car stopped at our door, once more causing great excitement in our small town whose inhabitants practically live on their thresholds. Monsieur Claudel got out, accompanied by his daughter Reine, a delightful child of sixteen. After a few moments of conversation in the parlor, M. Claudel accepted, with obvious pleasure, our invitation to visit the convent. The enclosure not having been canonically established as yet, we were very happy to grant this privilege to a man of such moral and spiritual stature, who has been so particularly kind to us. He saw everything with great interest, all the more so since he had spent some time in Spain as attaché to our embassy and had seen several Carmels established by our Holy Mother.[4] While speaking to us—always in a spirit of warm admiration for Carmelite spirituality, an admiration fed by close friendships with prominent personalities of the contemporary mystical school, such as Jacques Maritain, Father Henrion, Father Bremond—he kindly presented us with a very fine copy of the "Way of Perfection," in Spanish, a richly printed quarto volume which will be the first book and the finest ornament of our small library; still no more than a fond hope. We told him so in expressing our thanks; he was very touched, and offered us in addition the works of H. Brémond, *Histoire de la mystique en France,* which he will send us.

We spoke of Japan, of Annam, the beauty of which delighted him; as I showed him the pleasant view from the windows of the library, he remarked most aptly, "Ah! Reverend Mother, what is that beside the River of Perfumes in Hué!" You can imagine, my dear children of Annam, how much my heart agreed with those words!—When he left us, he seemed as moved as on board the *Amazone,* and his little Reine kissed us very prettily.

[4] Claudel actually visited Spain on his own, and not as a diplomat.

In the Far East, Claudel acquired a taste for popular poetry, particularly for the sort Chinese poems of the *Tang* period (Eighth Century A.D.), and for those Japanese songs called *dodoitsu,* "which last only the time of a glance, a smile, or a ray bringing out an answering flash at the bottom of the leaf-shadowed spring, or in the soul of the maiden." And he added: "It is always a matter of a shaft issuing from the heart and reaching our own heart, of a finger placed so accurately on the string that the note answers by itself: just one note, it is enough."[5] It is interesting to notice the contrast between such poems, which Claudel understood and admired, and his own tendency toward long lyrical developments as evidenced in the vast outpourings and transports of the *Cinq grandes Odes.* Many Europeans were introduced to this peculiarly Oriental art form for the first time when Radio Luxembourg, during the Spring of 1938, broadcast a number of these short poems, recited by Mlle. Maria Scibor and set to music by Mlle. Louise Vetch.

This poem by the Chinese Cheng Jo Soo, for instance, seems positively pre-Verlainian in its inspiration:

> One single cloud in the sky,
> My boat alone on the river.
> Here is the moon rising
> In the sky and on the river.
> It is less dark in the sky,
> There is less sadness in my heart.

And some Japanese songs, many centuries in advance, appear to foreshadow Francis Jammes.

In 1925 Claudel finally saw France again. On March 31 he was back in his quai de Passy apartment, but reached Paris too late to assist Jacques Rivière, carried away by illness on February 14. He and his family needed rest. They

[5] *Nouvelles Littéraires,* coll. 1938.

had been sorely tried by the disastrous earthquake, by sickness and by overwork. The ambassador looked for a suitable place where they could all spend the summer and finally chose an estate in the Loir-et-Cher: the château of Lutaine, in the township of Cellettes.

This village, lying in the forest of Russy, near the Loire and near Blois, was a very old feudal holding where there lived, about 1150, one Garin de Luctane or Lutaine. According to an article I have before me, the castle boasted a private chapel which was still standing in 1778. The present owner, the Marquis de Chevigné, is the grandson of Count de Forbin des Issarts, to whom the château belonged at the close of the nineteenth century. Claudel found a haven of peace there, for himself and his family. The local people were very impressed—I know this from an eyewitness—by the religious convictions and practices of these summer residents. The author followed his usual work schedule and was very soon on visiting terms with a few notabilities of the district, including a physician in Cour-Cheverny. Claudel enjoyed calling on the farmers, and one of his daughters, Renée, then eight years old, liked to spend part of her time with the wife of the farmer who lived on the estate.

During that summer Claudel wrote *Les conversations dans le Loir-et-Cher,* a typically and exuberantly imaginative book. In the first "days," he introduces four men (Acer, Civilis, Flaminius and Furius) and two women (Florence the musician, and Palmyre the actress and dancer): they are as many representations of various facets of the author's own personality. This work includes considerations on social co-operation, federalism, town planning, justice, sin, death, hell, sequestered souls, cathedrals (Chartres, Soissons, Le Mans), works of art like Monet's Nymphéas, the Eucharist, the fullness of the personality, war, the novel, the communion of saints, the configuration of France, American skyscrapers, reinforced concrete, markets, the art of living together, motor cars, jazz, motion pictures, etc.

In June he left Cellettes for a trip through Spain. It was his first contact with that great country which he carried deep within himself like a sunny presence. In his eyes Spain was the epitome of the Renaissance—a period of history particularly dear to him—and of a radiantly conquering Catholicism in keeping with his own religious conceptions. He visited Madrid, the Escorial, Segovia, Toledo and Burgos; but Avila moved him, it seems, more deeply than any other sight. In a letter to Louis Massignon on July 11, 1925 he wrote: "What impressed me most, by far, is Avila, where I spent a most rewarding and beautiful hour in that golden furnace, the oratory of the Saint with whom I feel a deep tie." Returning to France, he stopped at Saint-Benoît-sur-Loire to meet Max Jacob.

In September, under the auspices of the Alliance Française, he went to England on a lecture tour. First he spoke at the French Institute in London, under the presidency of M. de Fleuriau, the French Ambassador, and before an audience including Chesterton, the English Claudel. Referring to himself by the initials P.C., he related his life and his development as a writer. Deploring the divorce which has taken place between literature and religion, he quoted Chesterton: "The Christian knows that, at each season, nature tirelessly repeats the same rose and the same crocus," which he felt was an example to be followed by every author. Claudel then lectured in Oxford, Liverpool, Cambridge and Manchester. At the end of the year he also spoke in Switzerland, at the Zurich Polytechnicum. Toward the middle of January he had to return to Japan.

Few if any of the memorable sights he had been fortunate enough to behold throughout his life can have matched in

beauty and colorful pageantry the Shintoist funeral ceremonies of Emperor Yoshihito, who died on Christmas day
of 1926. From all over the Empire, some six hundred thousand men had gathered, lining the route of an interminable
procession. The old and the new were strangly mingled. The
members of the clergy carried symbolic banners waving from
bamboo poles. Generals and admirals, their uniforms studded
with decorations, accompanied the hearse, which was followed by the diplomatic corps and the members of parliament. Fifteen thousand soldiers, marching in slow and solemn
cadence, accompanied the Emperor's mortal remains.

In Japan, Claudel had the pleasure of seeing again his great
friend Admiral Yamamoto, who lived in Tokyo, at 143 Nishi-
Okubo. A former aide-de-camp to the famous Admiral
Heihachiro Togo, who defeated the Russians, he had served
as Naval Attaché in Rome (where Claudel met him in 1915),
and then in Paris. Yoshihito had chosen him as tutor to the
crown prince. He had been a member of the Japanese delegation to the Conference of Versailles. An ardent Catholic
since the age of sixteen, he was a leader of the missionary
movement in his country, and was one of the greatest figures
of modern Japan. He was to die in 1942.

One of Claudel's most important official achievements
during this period was without a doubt the foundation of
the "Maison de France" in Tokyo, later known as the "Maison Franco-Japonaise," an institution which greatly facili-
tated and multiplied the cultural exchanges between the two
countries. (This was one of the many grounds upon which the
ambassador was raised, in 1924, to the rank of commander
in the Legion of Honor). He supported all French educators
and missionaries in Japan, among them the Jesuits and their
University, and "the good Alsatian Fathers whose discipline
is at once so firm and so gentle." Moreover, he kept well

informed of Japanese literature and art, and took a great
interest in all their manifestations. He was full of exuberant
vitality, and took an ardent interest in everything around
him. He even followed with deep interest wrestling bouts in
the Ryukyu circus, on the far side of the Samida. He admired
the Japanese form of this sport, because it "consists less in
fighting than in looking at each other." With his daughter
Reine, he visited the Bunraku Marionette Theater, in Osaka,
where each puppet is controlled by several "conspirers," who
become something like its collective soul.

He was also filled with enthusiasm for the Nō, a kind of
lyric drama in which motion is reduced to a bare minimum,
with a prosody based on the alternation of long and short
verses. The Nō is typified by the effort—as in the traditional
tea ceremony—to attain perfection, to reach the ultimate in
refinement. The Hai-Kai, a poetic flower unfolding in three
quintessential stanzas, also inspired him, and Wladimir
d'Ormesson quotes this Hai-Kai which Claudel composed on
the occasion of the death of Emperor Taisho, and which the
Japanese considered as a kind of national epitaph:

> Taking advantage of this gaping tomb,
> The Japan of the living on one side
> And the Japan of the dead on the other
> Communicate.

I could hardly end this chapter more fittingly than by
quoting the tribute paid on the poet's tomb by Tetsuro
Furukaki, Japanese Ambassador to France, on February 24,
1957. This is a twin expression of homage, that of a nation
and of poetry, springing from the deepest layers of a discriminating intelligence and a delicate heart:

February 24, 1957

My dear Master, Paul Claudel!
Can you hear me? If you hear me well, answer me in
silence!

Humbly I am here to pay homage to the memory of my revered Master, Paul Claudel, that illustrious and immortal man who established indissoluble bonds between France and Japan.

Before this silent grave I seek the inspiration of that great Ambassador, who has set an example for those whose duty it is to cement friendship between the different nations.

In my country the name of Paul Claudel is forever etched in the heart of the Japanese. All my compatriots faithfully preserve the precious and affectionate memory of that representative of France, who had the capacity to bring them the soul of France and the knowledge of her civilization.

That great poet and writer of our time has left permanent traces in the Japanese soul, as in the souls of the people of the whole world.

I therefore salute you, dear Master, Paul Claudel, in the name of all my compatriots, and I beg you to remember that there exists, at the other end of the world, a nation which loves and admires you.

On this occasion, and with all the humility befitting one who, although modestly, follows in your path, allow me to read a few lines written in short stanzas and dedicated to your memory; lines which describe my feelings, upon recently arriving in Paris.

PARIS UNDER THE JANUARY SUN

Here is the January sun, pale disc
Blending to infinity in an enlarged sky,
And the sleeping roofs turn iridescent.
Here is my Paris barely awake. . . .
Dear languid Paris of Bernard Buffet.

O sweet Paris, with the clear river Seine,
Devout Paris beneath the Sacré Coeur,
Stately Paris of the Place Vendôme,
Paris of suffering—O cruel Bastille,
But Paris so touching to the maternal heart.

Bois de Boulogne, Saint-Cloud, tender foliage,
Delightful Parc Monceau with its verdant arbors,
Welcoming me graciously with the singing of birds,
Luxembourg gardens and their host of memories,
Place de la Concorde, crystal-like fountains!

Friendship of Paris, fervent and eternal,
Ancient city, always tender and ever beautiful,
How I love your trees standing guard,
Dripping raindrops in confidential tears,
Land of liberty and of faithful love!

14

AMBASSADOR IN WASHINGTON

DURING THE SPRING OF 1926, THE FRENCH GOVERNMENT seriously considered the possibility of appointing Paul Claudel Ambassador to Berlin, replacing Jacques de Margerie. The 1927 edition of the *Almanach catholique français* even shows this title opposite his name. At that time the German Chancellor was a relatively young statesman, Dr. Hans Luther, the former mayor of Essen; although somewhat of a reactionary, he seemed eager to promote a deeper reconciliation with France. This wish coincided with the policy of Aristide Briand, who was then French Foreign Minister. Claudel carried a high reputation in Germany. It was there that he had found his most receptive and enthusiastic audiences, and he was fond of saying that the man who had best understood *L'Otage* was a Jewish banker he had met in Frankfurt. On April 10, 1926, Claudel was interviewed by *Germania,* the paper of the Catholic Center Party, and his words are all the more striking since they preceded by several months Cardinal Andrieu's letter on the *Action française:*

> Any sincere Catholic must be opposed to nationalist fanaticism, which is the negation of culture. One should consider it as a monstrosity for a nation, whatever its excellence, to claim to be self-sufficient. I am deeply patriotic, but I am no less deeply convinced that the idolatrous love of the fatherland constitutes a real crime against human thought. No Catholic should think otherwise on this subject. For

Catholicism is the brotherhood of all men in Christian equality. It unites us, over and above national bonds. . . . Europe in its present form is suffocating. Present means of communication and technical advances have revolutionized our way of life. Europe is like a very small boat overcrowded with passengers. It is time to establish harmony on board, if we do not want to waste our few chances of salvation. For this little ship of Europe carries with it the destiny of the world. The world was born of Europe. The world's brain and heart are there.

For the building of the United States of Europe the main point is the reconciliation between France and Germany. It is not now the idealist in me speaking, but the realist. Franco-German understanding, in the vast field of realities, is not only desirable; it is normal and logical.[1]

Opposition to Claudel's appointment arose, however, and probably came from Germany. German national pride had been stung by his harshness toward Goethe, who appeared to Claudel mainly as a pagan genius, although in many respects he was a deeply spiritual and religious man. It is not even certain that Claudel acknowledged his genius, judging from certain comments, which should perhaps not be taken too literally. Although the diplomat was filled with admiration for Beethoven, and even for Wagner, he considered Goethe, with Luther and Kant, as "one of the three scourges, one of the three evil genii of Germany."[2] He probably never forgave Goethe because of having had to study and explain *Hermann und Dorothea* for eight long years, at the lycée.

By the time this interview was published in *Germania*, Claudel was back in Japan. He was in a melancholy mood and, although remaining as always deeply attentive to his professional occupations, he sought spiritual comfort from certain Christian groups which recalled the life of the primitive church. This led him to approach Violette Sussimann, a

[1] From the *Bulletin catholique international*.
[2] *Figures et paraboles*, p. 193.

strange mystic who dwelt in a shanty and who, while living in Paris on the rue Boulard, had been miraculously cured of Pott's disease which had immobilized her for twenty years. With two priests, Father Iwacita and Father Totsuka (who was also a surgeon, and headed a nursing-home in Shinagawa, a Tokyo suburb), she taught catechism to young Japanese women yearning for the contemplative life. The ambassador-poet also tried to locate the body of a certain Father Sidotti, who had come to Japan as a lone missionary in the middle of the eighteenth century, at the peril of his life; and who had left behind him a reputation for holiness.

On December 1 the Paris newspapers reported Claudel's appointment as Ambassador to the United States, replacing Henry Bérenger, who had declined an extension of his term. Claudel was very attached to Japan, that great country which had won him over at his first visit and where he had so much wanted to live. But he was delighted to receive this new assignment, for several personal reasons: the separation from his family, the difficult living conditions in a land which had just been struck by calamity, and mostly the tormented state of soul he found himself in as he approached his sixtieth year.

> I am reaching the end of my life: how I regret having dragged along at my heels that curse of paltry literature! How much better it would have been to give myself fully and simply [to God], as I once tried to do.[3]

When Claudel left Asia and when he had completed *Le Soulier de satin*, he found himself in a state of complete detachment. Nothing held him any longer, nothing seemed important. Life and the world had become alien to him. He experienced near-apocalyptic days, and faced at close range the abyss of the human predicament. He was fond of saying to those around him: "All that's left for me is buffoonery." On February 17, after his last official duties were fulfilled,

---

[3] Letter to the future Sister Agnès du Sarment, Dec. 10, 1926.

he sailed on the *Korea-Maru* with his daughter Reine, directly for the United States. After a few days spent in Hawaii, he passed through the Golden Gate and landed in San Francisco. Upon his arrival he was greeted by Paul Morand, who later wrote that the new French envoy had imediately "wished to size up the huge country, to visit those scattered French populations which no ambassador before him had [ever] thought of comforting."[4]

Faithful to his established custom, and although he had already lived in the United States at the beginning of his career and had returned once more since that time, he was anxious to enrich his experience; he wanted to know the West as well as he knew the East. In this way he carried out his childhood dream, his early wish to "gather the earth," to close the loop. With Madame Morand, Paul Morand showed him Hollywood, then the Grand Canyon in Colorado, and painted this living portrait of the ambassador:

With enthusiasm, Claudel
pointed out, on the far side of the abyss,
entire cities engulfed,
circuses,
ocean liners,
an Acropolis.
—"One senses," he said, "something like the determination
   of an architect always to repeat the same pattern."
—"One is faced with something very important, among the
   most important things in the world . . ."
—"In France, only the sunsets dare such colors and such
   shapes . . ."

Suddenly, the French Ambassador to the United States spoke
   of Bach, then of Beethoven's last quartets, which surely
   have an undiscovered meaning.
He pulled his small hat down on his head and, filled with

[4] Un grand serviteur de l'état," *Figaro littéraire*, March 30, 1955.

silent excitement, Napoleon-like, optimistic and natural,
he left us to walk off alone in the snow.[5]

Arriving via Chicago in Washington, where he was to stay
for six weeks, Claudel met with a certain amount of preju-
dice. Some American officials felt that the French government
had been ill-advised in entrusting such a key diplomatic post
to a poet—and a highly controversial poet at that.

President Coolidge, a true Yankee, taciturn and Puritani-
cal, particularly mistrusted poets. Thanks to the loans made
to the Western European countries, America was experienc-
ing a period of exceptional prosperity. The President strongly
favored wide international agreements.

When the new French Ambassador presented his creden-
tials, on March 27, 1928, President Coolidge was remarkably
cordial. Serious financial problems were outstanding between
the United States and France. To start with, Claudel had to
negotiate the provisional settlement of an initial annuity on
the French debt. His knowledge of the English language—
which was less thorough, he recognized, than that of Jules
Jusserand, one of his predecessors—faciliated his task considerably. The common sense he showed, his old peasant common sense, the experience he had of business circles, his
character and reliability, soon won him the recognition,
esteem and friendship of government circles in Washington.
Thanks to the wisdom of the views he had the courage to
uphold against a certain fanatical segment of French official-
dom and public opinion, the explosive question of the French
war debts was, if not solved, then at least made less critical:
it had been enough for the ambassador to show the goodwill
of the French government by suggesting a down payment. He
soon became one of the most respected members of the foreign diplomatic corps in Washington, which included several
outstanding personalities, and in particular the young and
distinguished German envoy, Prittwitz von Gaffon, who

[5] *Nouvelles littéraires,* U.S.A. 1927. Issue of Feb. 11, 1928.

was assisted by an eminent economist. Claudel's many speeches in various parts of the country won over the American public through their good-natured simplicity and loftiness of thought.

One handicap which he found most humiliating was the inadequacy of the embassy building, a rented residence almost completely lacking in representative works of art worthy of France. St. Paul's Church stood some two hundred yards away. Claudel could be seen there twice a day, every morning for mass and every evening for a meditation. He would take walks in Rock Creek Park, which he reached by skirting the walls of the embassies, and during the hot summer months he did not hesitate to take off his coat and carry it over his arm.

He visited New York, Pittsburg, Cleveland and Chicago, Louisiana and Georgia, and sometimes appeared in areas where no French representative had set foot since the days of La Fayette. In Washington he was soon drawn into all kinds of activities, many of them extremely worth-while. For instance Max Reinhardt, the famous German impresario, who had just achieved a real triumph in the United States with a play entitled *The Miracle,* urged Claudel to write a similar and corresponding work: this was to be *Christophe Colomb*.

At the end of April he returned to France with Robert Lacour-Gayet, his financial attaché, who for the past two years had established a highly effective co-ordination between the French and American treasuries. In Paris Claudel was fortunate enough to count on the friendly co-operation of a man of stature, Myron T. Herrick, an ambassador France will never forget. The negotiations, often critical, gradually led to the Briand-Kellogg pact which was signed on August 27, 1928, a few months before Herbert Hoover replaced Calvin Coolidge as president.

During this stay in France Claudel kept a busy schedule

and had little opportunity for rest. In Paris at the rue Huysmans Conférence Saint-Michel, before the female students of the Grandes Écoles, he gave a lecture interspersed with quotations from his own poems. Gaétan Bernoville's Catholic periodical, *Les Lettres,* which had recognized him long before he had achieved wide fame,[6] and the Cardinal Ferrari Italian Association jointly organized a reception in his honor. The Paris American Club invited him to one of its weekly luncheons, together with Jules Cambon (the greatest name in French diplomacy during that period, who always followed the ambassador-poet's career with warm interest), Myron T. Herrick and Henry Bérenger. Reticent on the subject of America, a country still rather unfamiliar to him, he took pleasure in acknowledging his debt of gratitude toward Ambassador Cambon, saluted the achievements of his predecessor Henry Bérenger and emphasized the reasons for Franco-American friendship. *Devant l'obstacle,* by André Tardieu, a book he heartily approved of, had just explained that this friendship was not necessarily natural or spontaneous, but that it was based on reason and had for a century and a half stood the test of time.

The American Legion had just organized a pilgrimage to the battlefields of France where the soldiers of both countries had together shed their blood for the same cause. On landing in America, Claudel was deeply moved to receive an invitation from the Massachusetts Legion, and to have revisited after an interval of thirty-three years, the city of Boston, one of the first assignments of his diplomatic career: "I was very young, and America was younger still. Younger? This is inaccurate, for America grows younger day by day. I mean only that she was a little too new, a little too restless for her timid and slightly bewildered admirer."

During this stay in France, he purchased—as will be seen

[6] Cf. René Johannet, May 1, 1921, and *Plaidoyer pour l'air libre,* Feb. and Sept. 1926.

in a later chapter—the estate of Brangues, in the province of Dauphiné. But we know him too well to imagine for a moment that in the future, during his periods of leave, he would retire exclusively into the haven of the past. Although approaching the age of sixty, he was a man of new beginnings and fresh departures. America was in keeping with his daring conception of the future. On the literary plane, having in the main completed his dramatic cycle with *Le Soulier de satin*, he intended henceforth to devote his time mainly to the study of the Bible. It was in the United States that he started to comment on the Book of Books.

Claudel's leave was drawing to an end. On August 24, 1927, he had a long meeting with Raymond Poincaré, who was then premier. The ambassador did not yet realize how popular Poincaré was in America, in spite of the memory of the occupation of the Ruhr.

On Saturday, September 29, 1928, Claudel was to sail back to his post accompanied by one of his daughters, on board the cruiser *Duquesne*. An incident occurred which deserves to be related. An honor guard awaited him at the Saint-Nazaire station, but the train which was to bring him from Paris arrived and he did not appear. He reached the port of embarkation exactly twenty-four hours later by the same express, and was greeted by the Mayor's assistant who, in spite of the unforeseen delay, read a warm address of welcome. It was on this occasion that Claudel met an astonishing person, whose identity he did not reveal and whom he attempted to rescue from the clutches of despair; in vain, since shortly later the unfortunate man committed suicide.[7]

Before resuming his duties in the United States, Claudel was entrusted with a different kind of assignment. The French West Indies had just been struck by a cyclone which

[7] According to Claudel's unpublished Diary, the man he met on the train to Saint-Nazaire was Professor Aurousseau, a specialist in the Far East.

had left many victims and caused considerable material losses. In his own words, he was called upon to be the ambassador to misfortune. He fulfilled this mission with charity and compassion as a Frenchman, as a Christian and as one who had himself suffered, in Japan, through a comparable natural calamity.

The *Duquesne* then carried him back to Washington. A week later he was off to Chicago to attend the unveiling of a monument raised in memory of Louis Pasteur. These ceremonies bore witness to America's admiration for the noblest examples of French science and charity.

In Chicago, Claudel was received by the French consul who, with his English-born wife, had prepared a welcome which delighted and touched the ambassador: his name was Charles de Ferry de Fontnouvelle. He belonged to an old family of the nobility of Provence, and brought to America, in a climate of friendship, the most engaging aspects of French life. He later served as consul general in New York, from 1931 to 1940. He was cultured and young in heart, loved music and life, and Claudel was immediately drawn to him. For his part, the consul soon became one of the most fervent admirers of the ambassador and poet.

In Chicago, Claudel was greatly impressed by the hugeness of the city, the enlightened vitality of the inhabitants and the large number of active Francophiles in society. He was entertained lavishly, and in particular by Colonel McCormick, owner of the *Chicago Herald Tribune*, Mrs. Potter Palmer, Mrs. Walter Borden, Mrs. Bertha Bower and Edward Bennett, a well-known architect who had studied at the Beaux-Arts and was president of the local Alliance Française.

Claudel's works received considerable attention in America. A leading periodical opened a contest for the best translation of *L'enfant Jésus de Prague*. In New York, Virginia

Gildersleeve, the Dean of Foreign Languages at Hunter College, (later Dean of Barnard) organized a performance of *L'Annonce faite à Marie,* in French, by the Hunter students. Claudel was the guest of honor and, according to an eyewitness, admired the ability and diction of the young actresses.[8]

Claudel's professional duties were soon to bring him back to Paris and to Brangues. Before leaving the American continent, he undertook an extensive tour through the South of the United States:

> It has been an extremely moving trip: people came to meet us, gave me medals. It was a great joy for them [the Americans] to see the representative of France, which they have never ceased to love and whose language they speak very well, particularly in Louisiana . . . . This faithfulness to France is due to the French priests: their achievements deserve the highest praise. As a matter of fact this whole area, which is so often ravaged by the floods of the Mississippi, has a very pronounced French flavor: I shall not forget the Angelus ringing from the huge French steeples of Louisiana . . . . In Charleston too, there was once a whole French settlement, from which came a certain Captain Cotidé, one of John Paul Jones' key officers aboard the *Bonhomme Richard;* and in Savannah, in Carolina, in Florida where I attended the unveiling of a monument to the Frenchman who was the first European to visit these parts. During my stay the daughter of our innkeeper found on the beach, while digging in the sand, a gold Huguenot ring, like a symbolic token of friendship between France and America . . . .[9]

The Dawes Plan, drawn up in 1923 to allow Germany to pay her debts without ruining her economy, was followed

[8] In 1946 Charles de Fontnouvelle, who was then President of the Lycée francais de New York, organized a New York performance of *L'Annonce faite à Marie,* with Ludmilla Pitoëff and her children filling the main roles.

[9] Paul Claudel, "Malles et valises. Retour d'Amérique." *Nouvelles littéraires,* 1928 collection.

in 1929 by the Young Plan which set down new procedures for the discharge of the same obligations. But one of the last official actions of President Coolidge—who in 1929 was to be replaced by Herbert Hoover—was to sign the Briand-Kellogg Pact with the representatives of sixty other nations. The initiative had come from Frank Kellogg, the American Secretary of State, and the pact's purpose was to outlaw war except in cases of self-defense. Briand had become interested in the idea, hoping that it would lead the United States back into the current of international co-operation. Claudel was the French negotiator of this plan for perpetual peace, and we may be sure that he brought to this work both idealism and realism, in equal parts. At first the French proposal met with some opposition. It embodied the ambiguous term of "aggressive war," which frightened the American government, and might reduce the United States' freedom of action in certain cases where American interests were at stake, particularly in South America. Briand did not wish to go beyond the commitments he had made in Geneva. A compromise between the opposing views was gradually worked out through long and patient negotiations. The signature of the Briand-Kellogg Pact, on August 27, was one of the highlights of diplomatic activity between the First and Second World Wars. Claudel had also signed, with Robert Olds, a Franco-American arbitration treaty.

Other hours had struck, or were about to strike, on the clock of history. In Soviet Russia, Stalin had seized the upper hand in January 1928, and Trotsky had been forced into exile. In France, 1929 would see Briand form a new cabinet to replace the Poincaré government, of which he had been a member. In Great Britain, the Laborite Ramsay MacDonald returned to power. In Germany, Stresemann died. In the United States, on October 29, the Stock Market crash ushered in a catastrophic depression. In the words of André Maurois, "An excessive rise in prices had prepared an excessive drop." President Hoover, who was not responsible, was nevertheless blamed: the crash cost him his second term.

Claudel had foreseen this great economic crisis in the course of which unemployment reached an all-time high of thirteen million. The fantastic and continuous rise in market prices had seemed most dangerous to him. In various reports he emphasized its alarming artificiality. The inevitable economic collapse was to have far-reaching consequences throughout the world, particularly in countries dependent on American credit. The depression confirmed his predictions. He knew that American energy, tenacity and optimism would eventually overcome this incalculable misfortune. But until that time, how far would the shock-waves spread?

During this trying period he experienced the grief of losing his mother. She had been living in Villeneuve-sur-Fère, and died on June 19 at the age of ninety. "By God's grace," he wrote to one of his correspondents, "my prayers of forty years have been answered, and I prevailed upon her to receive Extreme Unction and the Viaticum. I feel that her salvation is assured and that all is well."[10] On this occasion the most important consideration to him was precisely the return to God's friendship of this woman who had gradually drifted away from it. He was to call his mother "an honest soul, but too long blinded."[11] He stood by her side at the end, and her Christian death, which followed eighteen months of suffering caused by a tumor, softened the bitterness of his grief.

One of Claudel's greatest American friends was Mrs. Agnes E. Meyer, the wife of Eugue Meyer, owner of the *Washington Post*. This friendship had started rather stormily in 1926, with a heated discussion on Goethe, whom the ambassador, with flagrant unfairness, called an "imbecile."

[10] Letter to Sister Agnès du Sarment, *Lettres inedites* . . . , p. 40.
[11] Letter to Gabriel Frizeau, *Correspondance* . . . , p. 327.

Mrs. Meyer, to whom Catholicism was something completely alien, inevitably appeared as a challenge to Claudel, that highly militant lay missionary. She was subjected to his proselytizing efforts and parried his arguments with skill, for she was determined not to budge from her position. This offensive and defensive skirmishing did not affect their mutual friendship, which grew with the years and gave rise to a voluminous correspondence between them. On the very day of his death the poet had the joy of receiving a letter from his American friend.

They were sometimes most outspoken with each other. Mrs. Meyer once sent Claudel a copy of *Standards and Values*, by Thomas Mann, which she had translated. The Catholic poet's answer was sharp: "What is this Christianity without Christ, this religion without dogma, this gravy without a roast? I know but one standard: the Cross. I know but one value: the blood of Christ."

But Claudel's jocularity, I was about to say his playfulness, was often in evidence either in the letters he sent his friend or in the course of their conversations:

> We were driving one day in New York state [relates Mrs. Meyer], when suddenly he took my arm and exclaimed, "Look! Look! What is that?" He pointed at a signpost bearing the word *Sodom*. I explained to him that in America various religious sects had given their cities Biblical names, and that the village we were driving through was Sodom.— "Then let us stop! I absolutely must send a card to my friend Gide."[12]

Claudel was deeply gratified when the French Parliament ratified the Young Plan on March 29, 1930. This represented the happy conclusion of his persevering efforts. In France one heard a great deal about European Union, an ideal whose apostle and propagandist was Aristide Briand. Certain ominous signs had already started to worry the most vigilant

[12] Cf. *Figaro littéraire*, March 5, 1955.

observers, however. On the following September 14th for instance, it was learned that one hundred and seven Nazi deputies had been elected to the German Reichstag.

That same year, during his stay in France, Claudel saw Eve Francis in *L'Otage* at the studio des Champs-Elysées, while the Berlin Staatsoper played *Christophe Colomb*. On July 27 his predilection for cloisters led him to visit Notre-Dame-des-Dombes, in Burgundy, and in September he journeyed to Bruges to attend the solemn profession of Sister Agnès du Sarment, whose sponsor he was. For many years he had wanted to go on a pilgrimage to La Salette; on August 11, with one of his daughters, he fulfilled this wish. He did not see this shrine with the same eye as Léon Bloy, but he sought, like the latter, to define the symbolism of the holy mountain where the Blessed Virgin wept.

At that time, he was asked to take part in a special retreat for writers. This did not suit him in the least! His answer to the Jesuit Father who had approached him was rather rough. He was fond of his fellow authors, and enjoyed seeing them individually. On the religious plane, however, I believe he felt closer to the monks whose life he would gladly have shared, than to men of letters who might wish to discuss literature at the very time when he wanted to forget it. Besides, he liked the company of simple and humble people. He once wrote the following lines to his friend Louis Massignon:

> I was deeply conscious between us of that link of fraternal charity which unites Christians, on the day of our meeting at Paul Petit's, all coming from different points, *Arabes et Parthi, Medi et Alamitae*. . . . They are samples of every kind which the divine Economist brings together in that purse of the Omega, whose strings He holds.
>
> But I feel those ties no less strongly each morning in my village church, where I receive Holy Communion from an old priest who resembles Berlioz and the Saint of Ars, next to

two old sisters and to a stout-shoed girl of twelve, as calm as a lamb. How close I feel to these humble souls, and how kind is God thus to have given us brothers and sisters everywhere.[13]

During this period, the ambassador-poet was extremely active as a lecturer. Never was he so much sought after, and never did he respond with more cordiality. He spoke before all kinds of audiences: actors and members of the clergy, business men and society women, bishops and students. Paradoxically enough, he was both awkward and at ease whatever the occasion or the public. Communication was not always easy although he tried to speak simply: as a lecturer he generally sought to abandon the manner of *Les Cinq grandes Odes* and *L'art poétique*.

I cannot relate all the trips Claudel made, all the conventions he attended, all the speeches he delivered during this time. I will merely select a few scenes.

At the Alliance Française, in 1927, he opened a lecture with striking formulas which went straight to the heart of everyone present, "The more one is American, the more one is a friend of France. The more one is American, the more one is French, in the sense of an attribute, a tendency, a shared preference."

Throughout the United States the Saint-Jean-Baptiste Society is dedicated to the preservation of Catholicism and of the French language. In 1928 Claudel was invited to the Society's Congress held in Burlington, the Vermont university town, and took this opportunity to speak in heartfelt praise of the Franco-Americans:

Fifty years ago in these New England states, two of which still bear French names, however, you were still but a handful, with faith and courage the only elements in your favor. Today you are more than a million. You owe much to

[13] Brangues, June 13, 1930.

America, and I know, as a matter of fact, that the Star-Spangled Banner shelters under its folds no more determined and more convinced patriots than you. But you love your new country all the more since, being on its soil, you know that you are at home, that you were the first in this vast land. . . .

To the Catholic actors of New York, before whom he had spoken a few months earlier, on May 11, his approach was professional and he chose words which they could well accept and understand:

All the skill of a dramatic author and of his interpreters resides in the art of questioning, of finding the word, the formula, the tone, the modulation which elicits the desired response from the deepest level of the spectator's soul. When a young girl sees the entrancing features of Novarro or Valentino appearing on the screen, when she beholds that imperious gaze gradually taking shape, all kinds of favorable and unexpected thoughts arise from her flustered heart. I will not compare this feeling to that of a foreign minister studying a well-prepared report. And yet, there is no statesman who does not recognize the importance, the authority of a well-phrased formulation which throws light on the whole of an obscure discussion and catalyzes the latent decisions.

On November 4, 1932, Franklin Delano Roosevelt was elected to the presidency of the United States. He would raise his country to unprecedented power. The ailing Aristide Briand had been successively replaced as French Foreign Minister on January 13 by Pierre Laval (who became premier), on February 20 by André Tardieu (who also headed a new government), and on June 1 by Edouard Herriot. On June 11 an agreement on payment to the United States of the debts for which a moratorium had been granted was signed by Claudel. It had been decided that reimbursement would take place in ten annuities, starting on July 1, 1933.

French public opinion was angered by this settlement, however, and in the chamber of deputies, during a heated debate which extended through the night, many of Herriot's supporters joined ranks with the opposition. The premier stood firm, arguing that France had a long tradition of honoring her commitments. But he was outvoted, and had to hand in his resignation on December 14. A new cabinet was assembled under the premiership of Paul-Boncour.

Claudel knew and liked Herriot, whom he held in high esteem in spite of the deep religious and intellectual differences between them. He had first met the eminent statesman during the First World War, and had set before him a plan for the construction of a railway roughly following the forty-fifth degree of latitude. This had given Claudel an early opportunity to appreciate Herriot's high intellectual humanism.

> I spoke to the mayor of Lyons about Rome and its marbles, and suddenly, advancing his thick arm and large fist over the table cluttered with maps and files, he quoted a line from Ovid (was it from *Les Fastes* or *L'art d'aimer*?) where the delightful poet compares the glow of a young girl's cheek to the reflection of a purple velum on a polished column. . . . I raised my eyes to his craggy face, I looked at him, I really saw him for the first time and I heard a voice inwardly saying to me, "This man will always be my friend."[14]

Since that time, they had often met again. Claudel had read *La forêt normande, La porte océane, Beethoven.* . . . He felt that Herriot could be the most effective intermediary between the policy of the Quai d'Orsay and that of the White House.

Franklin D. Roosevelt was inaugurated as president early in 1933. Adolf Hitler had been chancellor of Germany since January 30, and the Reichstag had just been destroyed by fire. Depressed and ill, Philippe Berthelot had retired and had been replaced as secretary general of the foreign office by Alexis Léger (the poet St. John Perse). For Claudel this

[14] "Souvenirs diplomatiques," *Nouvelles littéraires,* May 23, 1936.

was a crucial year, and it is said that, returning from France after his summer leave, he had entrusted his embassy to the Blessed Virgin, Queen of Wisdom, who alone could carry its difficulties and help him to resolve them.

Claudel found President Roosevelt both affable and open-minded. A meeting between them on February 21 marked the resumption of Franco-American negotiations on the grievous problem of outstanding debts. Roosevelt was anxious to "talk" with Western Europe. He invited the British Prime Minister to Washington, and also wished to see a responsible French statesman. Claudel reported:

> He wanted France not to be absent either: in cordial and moving words, he asked my help in obtaining a representative personality to confer with him. One to whom he could unreservedly explain his way of thinking. Who was better qualified than President Herriot? It is therefore to him that America sent its official invitation, which was accepted. Herriot reached Washington as preparations were under way for the London Economic Conference, at a time when the President was definitively getting ready to orient his world policies.[15]

Claudel's mission to the United States was drawing to a close. On March 8, 1933 he was appointed Ambassador to Belgium (to replace Charles Corbin, who was being sent to London). It is true that, in America, he experienced particularly difficult circumstances. But the memory of so many privileged days outweighed that of his tribulations. He had become attached to the artists and writers of this friendly country. Its businessmen interested him. The heroic proportions, the noble and exalted quality of this young country, were attuned to the most generous elements in himself. Finally, he would not forget that he had shared with the Americans the bitter bread of affliction. And he was happy to have seen gradually rising a great hope, which would soon unfold into a renewal of prosperity.

[15] "Souvenirs diplomatiques," *Nouvelles littéraires*, May 23, 1936.

15

THE LAST EMBASSY

PAUL CLAUDEL LEFT THE UNITED STATES ON APRIL 18 AND lost no time before taking up his new duties in Brussels.

Over the years some of the warmest expressions of praise received by Claudel had come from Belgium. Maeterlinck had sent him this tribute: "You suddenly appear to me as the greatest poet on earth. You have entered my house like a horrible storm." The psychologist Dwelshauvers, an unbeliever, literally worshiped the inspired Catholic writer. The critic Edmond Joly, who shared something of Claudel's victorious optimism, was grateful to him for his synthesis on Notre Dame. The authors of the younger generation—whose voice was heard through *Jeune Belgique,* Father Moeller's *Durendal, La Wallonie, Synthèse, L'Art moderne, Antée,* and *La Vie Nouvelle*—had enthusiastically received his various works. Eve Francis, one of his best interpreters, was a Belgian and so was Emile Francqui, one of his closest friends.

On June 30, a few weeks after his arrival, a literary celebration was organized in his honor. It was held in the ballroom of the Maison d'Art (the former Russian legation) on the Avenue Louise, where Chinese sculpture and Khmer art are represented by outstanding masterpieces. Most Belgian writers of any importance were present. The first tribute was presented by a Fleming, Toussaint van Boelaere, who pointed out that the truculent *Protée* and several other Claudelian works had been translated and played in Flemish. Thomas

Braun spoke for the Catholic authors. And after an address by Professor de Reni, Louis Piérard, President of the Belgian Pen Club, recalled an earlier gathering (around 1925, in the heart of the old Brussels), congratulated the ambassador—an itinerant poet who had never broken the ties to his native soil—and finally echoed the words of Charles-Louis Philippe: "Do you know that we have a great genius, equal to Dante? It is Claudel." The French envoy then answered and thanked the various orators, let his heart speak, and defined for his Walloon and Flemish friends his conjugate role as a diplomat and a lyricist.

He felt very much at home in Brussels and would often say so to those around him. To be sure, his many contacts with distant lands had been invaluable to him, had brought about countless instances of fruitful exchange and even communion during which he had both given and received superabundantly. But the time had now come when he found it restful and beneficial to hear his own language spoken in the streets, to be among a people so close to his own in their way of thinking and feeling. In Brussels he was to all intents and purposes in France, yet with the advantage of finding himself for a time at a crossroads between Flanders and the French-speaking world.

Besides, although it had been instructive and enriching for him to come in touch with Buddhism and Confucianism in the Far East and with Judaism in Central Europe, he breathed more freely in a country where Catholicism was the dominant religion.

"It is a joy for me to find myself once again in a Catholic and French environment. . . . It is comforting to kneel every evening in a dark church, and to realize that the end is no longer very far away."[1]

He loved to take long walks along the streets, avenues and boulevards of Brussels, and to stop by in the many churches

[1] Letter to Gabriel Frizeau, Dec. 3, 1933.

and oratories of the city: Sainte-Gudule, probably, where the dazzling irradiation of the stained-glass windows respected the intimacy of small chapels bathed in dense shadows; Notre-Dame-du-Sablon, where he could see an inscription concerning the French poet Jean-Baptiste Rousseau, who died in exile and never counted among Claudel's masters; the church of the Finistère, with the revered statue of Notre-Dame-du-Bon-Succès;   Notre-Dame-de-la-Chapelle; the church of the Béguinage; Saint-Joseph, in the Leopold district; and several others.

His life remained as disciplined as ever. Raymond Brugère, his counselor at the embassy, has described the "zeal, almost that of a neophyte, which he devoted to the exacting and at times tedious work which fell to him."

His days were organized and scheduled in such a way that his literary activities were never allowed to interfere with the performance of his official duties. "He was never late, neither for a meal, nor for a reception, nor for appointments with visitors or cabinet ministers. No matter, no task was below him. He devoted to his vocation as an author only the small hours of the day. At ten he put on a stiff collar, entered his ambassador's office and occupations, and did not leave them for the whole day."[2]

As he had done in all his previous assignments, Claudel made it a point to travel throughout the country where he represented France. He revisited Liége, where in 1905 he had seen the *Exposition universelle* with his old friend Francqui, and where, upon his return from Japan in 1925, he had had occasion to deliver a lecture. Liége, a "necessary city," "one of those strategic positions which the race has always clung to with invincible tenacity." He inspected Antwerp's port in detail, and even more so its museums, tirelessly admiring *Le Christ à la paille,* one of the masterpieces of Rubens, a native son of the Flemish metropolis in whom

[2] *Nouvelles littéraires,* March 1955.

Claudel recognized a kindred spirit. The ambassador welcomed the opportunity to see some dear friends again such
as Thomas Braun, the Belgian Jammes; Albert Mockel, who
was associated with his memories of Mallarmé; and Louis
Piérard, a highly creative poet.

I have just mentioned Rubens, whose pervasive presence
greeted Claudel in Flanders. Anyone who has read *Le Soulier
de satin* can understand what the great painter meant to the
French envoy. Heir to diverse strains of humanism, having
reinterpreted Titian, Tintoretto, Veronese and Michelangelo,
as well as the Flemish naturalists, and even the masters of
Baroque art, haunted by grandeur, power and plenitude;
capable of embracing the breadth of the two worlds; sensitive
to the joys of home and the delights of childish innocence;
devout Christian starting his days with one or several
masses; truly Catholic artist who painted above all the glory
of God, the Passion of Christ and the Triumph of the
Eucharist; who depicted so many lives of saints; ambassador
with a taste for magnificent residences and parks, Pieter Paul
Rubens offers us, three centuries back, Claudel's counterpart
in the realm of painting, with the same joyous and optimistic
feeling for life as the French contemporary poet. On June 20,
1933, before the notables of Antwerp welcoming him to their
city, the French envoy in his distinctive and sumptuous style
proclaimed his great admiration for Rubens:

> At the conclusion of my long sojourns among the sun-baked
> and swarthy populations of inclement latitudes, I enjoyed
> taking [visual] refreshment, cooling my eyes amid the
> Rubenses of your museum. There is in particular a painting
> called, I believe, *Le Christ à la paille,* which I always remem-
> bered with love and predilection. Before this wonderful
> canvas one has the feeling that flesh is truly the flowering of
> blood, and blood the vehicle of the soul. Whether it be the
> body of a child, the breast of a young woman, or those sacred

drops which trickle from the brow of a God, one senses that
the great native of Antwerp, in order to fashion from these
elements the luminous inhabitants of his garden of delights,
has borrowed from the entire ambient nature; from that
breath of azure, honey and milk which, on these beautiful
June days, wafts over your full-blown countryside the most
efficacious and most suave products of the creative sap, of
the divine ray of inspiration. I know a certain number of
paintings of which it can be said that they live, but I do not
know whether one could say of works other than those of your
Rubens that they "breathe."[3]

And Claudel protested against this line by Baudelaire:
"Rubens, stream of oblivion, garden of indolence," melodious
though it may be. In the "magnificent creatures" of that imperial artist, the prevailing mood is certainly not one of
oblivion; "it is a feeling of power and plenitude." Far from
inspiring indolence, they make one think of the "captains and
administrators" who created an empire in the heart of Africa.

From Belgium, Claudel must surely have made a number
of incursions into Holland, for the remarkable Dutch museums no doubt exerted an irresistible fascination for him.
Actually, all forms of art were a subject of deep interest to
him, and he had always been eager to understand or experience every one of them.

How did he ever find time to study dancing? Writing about
Wagner, he referred incidentally to rhythmic lessons which
he took, probably during his early years in Paris.

He never separated the various art forms from the main-
stream of life. He liked to observe them in the setting where
they were born and where they developed, like living beings.
His visits to the Dutch museums prompted him to formulate
a kind of geography of Holland, which is summed up in the
following remarks:

[3] *Salut à la Belgique* (Thône).

The idea of understanding the Netherlands must be abandoned if, immediately after entering really and fully into that country one does not feel that secret elasticity underfoot; if one does not somehow participate in that kind of cosmic rhythm like a chest alternately rising and falling.

Holland is a breathing body, and that vast pocket of the Zuider Zee, what is it but a kind of lung?

On an important point, Claudel disagreed with Fromentin, whom he admired, as a matter of fact, and whose eye *listened* before his own to the secret of the *Maîtres d'autrefois*. Fromentin saw only a fortuitous accident in the appearance of a grain of warmer sensitivity "which makes thinkers and even poets of the Dutch painters." As for Claudel, he recognized in all these painters and in the canvases of the entire Dutch school, the secret flavor of that sensitivity. With the enjoyment of a gourmet, he listed Gérard Dou, Mieris, Ter Borch, Metzu and also Van Ostade and Steen, with their "riots of gnomes and goblins," their "clusters of congested faces and sagging paunches"; as well as Vermeer of Delft, whose "celestial blue and limpid yellow" show a harmony "as pure as Arabia." Claudel pointed out "the strange attraction of Dutch landscapes and interiors." Before the portraits by Frans Hals, and some of those by Becker and Van der Hest, he expressed what he called "a kind of intake of air or intake of soul, a spiritual invitation, a word emanation." To make his thought or his feeling clearer, he reached this highly original formulation:

> Just as Holland, all around us, is a kind of reparation to the sea, a smoothing out of all reliefs, a maximum generalization of the surface view, an anticipation of water by pastures, in the same way one would not have to press me much for me to advance that the undertaking of Dutch art is, so to speak, a liquidation of reality.[4]

[4] *L'oeil écoute,* passim.

Claudel chose April 1935 for one of his art tours, which took him to Rotterdam, where strangely enough he recognized certain forgotten perfumes of Asia; to Delft, where "all Vermeer has remained dissolved in a damp and clear atmosphere"; and to Utrecht, where he was pained to see former Catholic churches "eviscerated by Protestantism . . ." He nevertheless savored an hour poised between winter and springtime; the deep and meditative silence was barely interrupted by the carillon of an invisible belfry.

In 1934 at the end of Holy Week, Claudel went to the abbey of Clervaux in Luxembourg, for a short retreat. He wrote *Nuit de Pâques* during his stay at the monastery, which for many years he had been anxious to visit.

In Mons and Brussels he came across the trail of Paul Verlaine, "son of the Ardennes and of Slate," whom he had once met during his student days in Paris, on the sidewalk of the rue Gay-Lussac. With his friend Louis Piérard, the French ambassador entered the prison where, in his words, "divine grace awaited the child of anger."

The Belgian Exposition Internationale offered Claudel an occasion to make a speech in praise of wine. Nor was this merely a formal tribute; it sprang from an intelligent predilection, in full accord with the Bible, for the stimulant of human personality, "the liberator of the spirit," the generous agent of social communion.

He visited Ghent and the cathedral of Saint-Bavon, where Eve Francis—who twenty years earlier had been entrusted with the role of Sygne de Coûfontaine—had experienced the first hazy revelation of the character she was to portray. (The full impact and insight came to her later at Loochristi, in a small chapel, when she understood with a shock "the horrible and sweet moment when Sygne chooses the sacrifice which frees her from the conflict between the duty of her race and her Christian soul.") He stopped at the *Béguinage* of Bruges to see his godchild, Sister Agnès du Sarment. (I

remember my own surprise, in 1945, when he introduced me
to her in the visiting room of the convent, and I thus learned
of the presence of this admirer and spiritual kinswoman of
Paul Claudel.) Besides artistic masterpieces and monuments,
a town or locality often brought to his mind the soul of a
man or woman to whom he had fulfilled his mission as ambassador of the supernatural. Henri Massis relates that one
day near Tournai, during a trip, Claudel asked him to wait
for a while and went off alone; upon returning he made some
reference to a young man he had been to see. "He remained
abstracted, wrapped in a silence inhabited, I sensed, by
haunting memories . . . ! And I dared not say a word, when
suddenly as though speaking to himself, he muttered, 'I believe he has the vocation.' "[5]

Claudel experienced many memorable moments in Belgium, when he felt the communion of an entire people around
his voice and thought. It seems that one of those privileged
occasions was the day when, in the heart of the capital, he
spoke of the French poet he understood best, the only one
standing in some respects on his own level, Victor Hugo. A
distinguished eyewitness, the novelist Franz Hellens, has described the scene:

> I shall not forget that afternoon on the Grand' Place of
> Brussels, all its gilt [adornments] aglitter, when I heard
> Paul Claudel speak before the façade of the house, next to the
> *Maison du Roi,* where Victory Hugo stayed during his exile
> from France, and wrote a few chapters of *Les Misérables.* I
> can still hear the poet of the *Odes,* who read his speech in a
> voice lacking outer sonority, a harsh and heavily articulated
> voice, extoll the genius—not of the poet of *Les Contempla-
> tions*—but of the novelist of *Les travailleurs de la mer* and
> *Notre-Dame de Paris,* and take the opportunity to praise a
> few serial novelists of whom France, he said, had the duty
> to be proud.

[5] Henri Massis, *De l'homme à Dieu* (Nouvelles Editions Latines),
p. 126.

I do not believe that the great man meant to be facetious or paradoxical. First I rebelled, then I agreed. This opinion, professed by a man whose glory was mostly in the field of poetry, tallied too well with an idea, or rather a taste which I had myself formed rather recently for Claudel's works. In the last analysis, it is this author's prose that I prefer.[6]

A curious meeting and a strange contrast: in Belgium, Hugo had tasted exile, and Claudel felt at home for the first time.

At a time when Claudel's diplomatic career was drawing to a close, it was found improper . . . for an ambassador to be connected with the theater! And this realization occurred precisely when L'Otage was about to be added to the repertoire of the Comédie Française, twenty years after it was first produced at the Théâtre de l'Oeuvre. A man's detractors must indeed have interchangeable motives for their disparagement. Claudel did not take the matter too seriously. He had already discussed this subject in one of his lectures, and returned to it in a newspaper interview (L'Excelsior, October 27, 1934), pointing out that diplomacy, like dramatic art, is "the art of weighing men and facts." And he added:

> Besides, I have illustrious references, for instance—without mentioning Richelieu himself—Mussolini, who wrote several Napoleonic plays. I myself discovered along the embankments a play by Delcassé, which I gave my friend Berthelot and which is now included, I believe, in the famous library Louis Barthou loved so much.

L'Otage, as offered by the Théâtre Français, had been revised, not only in its staging but also in the actual dialogue. The play had been given a new ending. Madame Renaud Thévenet, a Brussels actress, allowed Claudel to make use of a technique she had acquired from the Japanese theater:

[6] "Claudel en Belgique," La Nouvelle Revue Française, Sept. 1, 1955.

the introduction, between music and dialogue, of the excla-
mation, a field which opens interesting possibilities. The
first and third acts were transformed by spoken choruses and
the result was felicitous in the extreme. On December 15
Claudel had the joy of seeing *L'Otage* given in the Belgian
capital, at the Théâtre des Beaux-Arts, in the presence of
King Albert.

On February 17, 1935, at four o'clock in the morning,
Claudel received news of the king's death. At seven, accompanied by Raymond Brugère, he hurried to the Palace
of Laeken.

> We entered a scene of disruption, all inner doors open.
> Toneless voices guided us to a vestibule where we ran into the
> Marshal of the Royal Household who, in spite of the early
> hour and although we had come only to sign our names to
> the register, asked us whether we wished to pay our respects
> to the mortal remains of the king, who had just been laid out,
> with a bandage covering the head-wound he had sustained
> during his fall. The Marshal showed us into a small and very
> simple room, and all my life I shall remember Claudel, his
> eyes filled with tears, kneeling and reciting the Rosary at the
> side of the sovereign held by France in such affectionate
> admiration. Never was a more moving tribute paid more
> spontaneously by an official representative heeding only the
> man and the believer in him. Without pomp or public, there
> was greatness here. And no subsequent press release garbled
> or debased this gesture worthy of the noblest scenes from
> the past.[7]

In Brussels the king and queen went out of their way to
show their regard for Claudel, not only as the envoy of a
nation bound to Belgium by ties of friendship and kindred,
but also as an individual. He was deeply conscious of their
warm kindness toward him, and this was one of the great

[7] *Nouvelles littéraires*, March, 1955.

joys and major honors of his life. He proved it at the time of King Albert's fatal accident. After the tragedy, Queen Elizabeth's gracious solicitude became even more marked, if anything, as though she wished to express the esteem of the late sovereign, as well as her own.

> I have known King Albert well. He was a great soul, and his extreme nobility and almost rustic simplicity impressed me from the first day. His death was a cruel blow to me. At his side, I saw Queen Elizabeth, so engaging and so interested in new ideas. They were good enough to attend performances of *L'Otage* and *L'Annonce faite à Marie*. I do not believe that I ever met anyone who understood my works better and with more insight than the king and queen. Here, intelligence is fortunately at the top, as well as everywhere else. . . . Belgium can play a capital role in the world of thought and art.[8]

The death of his sister, Madame Ferdinand de Massary, in 1935, did not cause Claudel as much spiritual anguish as that of certain other members of his family. She lived in seclusion at Villeneuve-sur-Fère, and died like a Christian. Her daughter-in-law, née Moreau-Nélaton (whose father was an authority on the history of art), and her two grandsons, Philippe and François, surrounded her with affection. In God she would rejoin an admirable son, Dr. Jacques de Massary, who had been deeply devoted to his uncle. Thirty years ago, thanks to him, I was able to accomplish two Claudelian pilgrimages to Villeneuve-sur-Fère.

Also in 1935 Claudel retired as French Ambassador to Belgium, thus ending a diplomatic career spanning forty-six years, nearly half a century.

[8] Richard Dupierreux, "M. P. Claudel, ambassadeur a Bruxelles, égrène ses intéressants souvenirs," *Le Petit Parisien*, Feb. 11, 1935.

16

BRANGUES

THE CHÂTEAU OF BRANGUES, WHERE CLAUDEL WAS TO SPEND the greater part of his last years, stands on the left bank of the Rhone, a river matching the poet's powerful genius, in the township of Morestel (Isère), exactly opposite Groslée and the mountains of Saint-Benoit and Tantainet, which rise above the other bank. From his first visit to Hostel, he had become attached to Bugey, a province in keeping with his love for light, satisfied by the subtle shadings of an ever-changing sky; in keeping also with his taste for the violence of nature, suited by the torrential flow of the mighty river; with his attachment to the past, gratified by the wealth of history of that ancient district; and with his optimistic vision of the future, which made him marvel at an achievement like the Génissiat dam. The Grande Chartreuse, a place of abyssal solitude, was not far, and La Salette could be reached in a few hours by car.

After the first World War, this sixteenth-century château belonged to the Marquis de Virieu, who also owned two other estates. The marquis found that the financial burden became excessive for him, and mentioned these difficulties to his architect, Antoine Sainte-Marie-Perrin, who in turn spoke to his brother-in-law Paul Claudel. The poet was anxious to buy a suitable estate where he could live with his family and where he would later rest in the peace of the Lord. Brangues immediately took his fancy. He was drawn to this spacious country residence whose medieval towers contrasted with the classical lines of the solidly constructed seventeenth-century main building, adorned with a graceful flight of steps. He loved the linden and plane trees in the park, which promised long hours of meditation. As he approached his sixtieth year a new life opened before him.

The village church, built in 1847, had no architectural merit, but was adequate to fill the needs of the one hundred and fifty inhabitants, not all of them practicing Catholics. Claudel at once felt at home there, and was delighted by a statue of the Virgin, "fresh and pure as a glacier," before which he would often kneel in prayer.

A century earlier, Brangues[1] had been the scene of a horrible tragedy, and the author of *Cinq grandes Odes* gave it considerable thought. This tragic event had inspired *Le Rouge et le Noir,* the famous novel by Stendahl, Claudel's most intimate enemy. One day a reporter asked the poet for his opinion of the great nineteenth century novelist, and he answered disgustedly: "I do not read Stendahl!" Of course he had read his works, and probably more than just once, but everything about this denier sickened and shocked him.

Be that as it may, here are the facts. Antoine Berthet, the twenty-year-old son of a local craftsman, although physically and morally ill, was endowed with an uncommon intelligence. He had been noticed by his parish priest and sent to a seminary, but poor health forced him to interrupt his studies. The mayor of Brangues, M. Michoud de la Tour, took the young man as tutor for his children. Berthet asserted that he had become the lover of the mayor's wife, although there was never any indication or proof that this was so. (On the contrary, Mme. Michoud had an excellent reputation.) This unstable individual then went to Grenoble to study for the priesthood, but did not remain there for long either. He next

[1] Not the château purchased by Claudel. A different one, at the other end of the township.

served as tutor in another family and was dismissed when a
scandalous intrigue he became involved in came to light.
Furious against a society which kept him in a subordinate and
humiliating position, the unbalanced youth resolved to com-
mit a spectacular crime. On July 22, 1827, during a mass
celebrated by the priest who had tried to help him, he shot
Mme. Michoud. He was tried, sentenced to death, and guillo-
tined on February 23, 1828.

This sordid episode, used as a theme by Stendahl, interested Claudel from a very personal standpoint. It led him to
an illuminating self-examination. He knew that in certain
instances the wish to become a priest could be motivated by
inferior and merely human considerations. He also knew
from personal experience that this wish could arise from
generous and purely spiritual motives. This is how he considered the case of the "village Hamlet," in a light totally
foreign, in every way, to Stendahl's very limited viewpoint:

> Berthet's idea—his constantly affirmed obsession, present-
> ing all the earmarks of a vocation . . . and the frustration of
> which was the deep cause of the bitter resentment he
> nourished against the two families he brought trouble to, per-
> haps unintentionally—was to enter the seminary. Of course,
> not for one moment does the thought that the wretched youth
> might have been sincere, or might have been guided by
> motives other than the basest, enter what I must call the
> "mind" of the pachyderm to whom we owe one of our alleged
> national masterpieces. And yet, what if this were the case? If
> the idea of being a priest—of becoming in his way a leader
> of men, a specialist of human passions, and (who knows?)
> the repairer of an obscure misfortune—had been in the head
> of that dreamer, an idea nurtured by the long hours of
> solitude and meditation afforded a cowherd, the essential
> and deliberate ambition, the axial orientation whose failure
> brought about the loss of reason and life in a weakened con-
> stitution? On the steps of that very altar where he had been

forbidden to ascend, he immolated the cause reponsible [in his eyes] for his misfortune.[2]

During Claudel's daily visits to the church of his new parish, one can be sure that his thoughts often dwelt on the criminally deluded seminarist who had known the honor and the burden of being called by Grace.

On July 14, 1927, Claudel moved into Brangues: "This makes a strange impression on me, the eternal exile, at last to feel over my head a roof which I can call my own. It seems to me that only on this day did I truly found my family, for there is no family without a house. I have bought an estate, not so much for myself, for I will probably not enjoy it for long, but for my children."

But it was mainly after his retirement, when his last ambassadorial mission ended in June 1935, that he really grew to know and love Brangues, where a blessed solitude—even with his children and grandchildren all around him—drew him into those depths of contentment and nostalgia in which a tenuous veil barely separates man from his eternity.

A few weeks before this move, during the spring of 1935 and against the advice of a few discerning friends like Paul Petit, he presented his candidacy to the Académie française, but the novelist Claude Farrère was elected instead of him . . . which came as a surprise to French literary circles. Yet, Monsignor Baudrillart, Abel Bonnard, Jules Cambon, Georges Goyau, François Mauriac, Maurice Paléologue, Marshal Pétain, Paul Valéry and General Weygand had voted for Claudel.[3] This disappointment was followed by a great family sorrow, the death of his sister Louise.

Toward the end of the year, on November 27, at the Catholic Institute of Paris, he was enthusiastically received by

---

[2] *Seigneur, apprenez-nous à prier,* pp. 111-112.

[3] Claude Farrère was elected by 15 votes, against 10 to Paul Claudel, 1 to Alfred Poizat, and 1 invalid vote. The absence of two of Claudel's supporters, Henri de Régnier and André Chaumeix, was a determining factor in his defeat.

the faculty and the entire student body. He found in the
warmth of this greeting a partial compensation for his failure to enter the Académie. The occasion was the diamond
anniversary of the foundation of that great independent university. Claudel paid tribute to the rector, who had been his
spiritual guide and faithful friend, and described his "gaze
free of illusion" and his "heart overflowing with charity." He
reminded the audience that the spirit of Catholicism is "a
spirit of freedom, courage, daring and initiative," at the
same time as a spirit of order and discipline; and emphasized
that the Catholic Institute represented all these elements.
Cum grano salis, he ascribed to that spirit of freedom the fact
that he had been chosen to deliver the keynote address for
the commemoration ceremonies:

> What other educational institution would have had the
> idea of selecting as bard and speaker for its celebration, not
> a laureate of the official art, but a kind of freak whose torso
> is garbed in an ambassador's uniform, and whose hind-
> quarters, according to his enemies, end in sinuous coils? A
> poet in whom the solemn vistas of classical Alexandrine verse
> have inspired but boredom, and who, deaf to the song of the
> secular sirens, has listened with rapture to the bells of his vil-
> lage, the chant of vespers and the modulations of Dumont's
> royal mass.

The following year added to the blessings and graces which
followed Claudel's failure to enter the Académie. The world
scene was undergoing deep changes. The French elections
were to lead to the formation of a Popular Front. The German
army reoccupied the Rhineland. Edward VIII ascended the
British throne in January and abdicated in December. In
Italy, Victor Emmanuel was proclaimed Emperor of Ethiopia.
The Spanish Civil War broke out in July. And Franklin D.
Roosevelt was re-elected to the presidency of the United
States.

Among those blessings was the benefit Claudel derived

from a springtime retreat to Solesmes. So many years had
passed since his first visit to that abbey! He relived in memory those days of intense dedication to God, when he had
made the sacrifice of his own person and of his literary career.
The magic of Gregorian chant affected him like a presence of
the invisible world; but perhaps he realized nevertheless how
difficult it would have been for him to become reconciled
to a completely secluded existence. So many deeply ingrained
habits had conditioned him to investigate and experience,
with tireless curiosity, the innumerable facets of the world
and of life!

During Holy Week, he journeyed to the shrine of La Sainte-
Baume, in Provence. (The idea may have come to him at
Solesmes, before the statue of the Magdalen, one of the admirable series of saints adorning that abbey.) He was greatly
moved by the grotto, to which—according to tradition—the
sister of Lazarus and Martha had withdrawn to live a life of
penance. He gazed into a reliquary at "that brow which,
nineteen hundred years ago, touched the feet of Christ, and
which, in its sepulchral elegance, still radiates grace and
light."[4] He also attended the services at Le Thoronet, the
neighboring Cistercian monastery, and savored the life of contemplation which might have been his forever.

At the end of the summer, however—and according to
him even this was a blessing in disguise—he was confined to
bed in his Paris apartment, at 11bis rue Jean-Goujon, by an
attack of pernicious anemia contracted in the tropics; an
illness which first troubled him at the time of his visit to
Angkor. Two blood transfusions saved his life, but he had to
remain immobilized in his room for nine weeks. And when
eventually it seemed to him that he had "regained a new
youth," he was still weak and vulnerable.

In 1937, at Easter, Paul Claudel went on a pilgrimage to
Chartres, but ill health forced him to return to Brangues.

[4] *Contacts et circonstances*, p. 185.

Every morning he was taken out in a wheel chair and placed in the shade of his dear chestnut trees. When he had fully recovered he visited Le Puy, and prayed before the marvelous Black Virgin adorning the main altar of the cathedral. He also stopped at La Chaise-Dieu, one of the most astonishing places in France, whose history has been written by the great folklorist-author Henri Pourrat, a friend of Claudel.

On October 26 he was in Paris, on the stage of the Théâtre des Champs-Elysées with François Mauriac, for the triumphal appearance of Francis Jammes, who had traveled up from the Pyrenees especially for this occasion. Jammes ran briskly toward them, with all the ease of a hunter, and addressed the public with the whimsey and volubility of a poet on a vacation from home.

French Catholic opinion was bitterly divided on the Spanish Civil War. Maritain and Mauriac, later joined by Bernanos (who originally favored Franco), were strongly opposed to the Nationalists.[5] Claudel saluted the victims of the revolution, in which he saw a demonic undertaking. Moreover, he originated a pro-Nationalist manifesto, which was circulated among intellectuals. He plunged headlong into the controversy, through faithfulness to his Catholic conception of Spain; a conception which emerges clearly from *Le Soulier de satin*.

These were days when he felt alone and isolated. The death of his dear friend Frizeau, on January 11, 1938, came as a great blow to him. The following month his grandson Charles-Henry Paris was carried away by acetonimia, in the space of a few days. "At that time, I wanted to die," he wrote later, "I asked to die; it still hurts me. . . . He was dead when I arrived."[6] In March I visited him at the rue Jean-Goujon (he was again very weak, and found it difficult to leave his bed)

---

[5] Maritain's position was subtly differentiated. For instance, he wrote: "Not to take Salamanca's side does not [necessarily] mean that one supports Valencia."

[6] Henri Guillemin, *Le Figaro Littéraire*, March 5, 1955.

and spoke to him of a similar loss I myself had suffered. He lifted his arms and exclaimed, "How horrible that we cannot even imagine those little ones . . . any longer!" Nothing was more important in his eyes than the integrity of childhood. These words written by Péguy might have been his own: "It is the children who know everything, for they know the primal innocence which is everything." And Claudel himself said that "what is sweetest in the world is [to have] a child's head resting against your own." A little later, he moved to a new address, 4 avenue Hoche, in the parish of Saint-Pierre de Chaillot.[7]

The year 1938 saw the Anschluss and Munich. Aghast, the ambassador-poet followed the slow but steady deterioration of the international situation, the unmistakable approach of a global tragedy. Sorrow struck at him once again: Francis Jammes was the next of his close friends to die, on November 1, at Hasparren. Shortly before the end he murmured these words, no doubt inspired by the thought of one of his daughters who had taken the veil in the desert, "I have sowed my finest grain in the sand." This death, following that of Frizeau, was a warning. And Claudel knew, better than anyone, how to decipher certain signs.

Nevertheless, Claudel gladly gave of his time and energy to commemorate the dear friend, indeed the brother, he had just lost. On February 26, 1939, accompanied by his daughter Marie, he gave a lecture in Caen, devoted to Jammes and organized by Madame Marie-Jeanne Durry, before the *Amis de l'Université*. March saw him in Alsace, where he had so many faithful admirers, among them Pierre Bücher, always a champion of French thought. He spoke in Sélestat, Strasbourg and Haguenau, with the authority of an old friend.

Soon he left for Rome to attend the coronation of Pius XII, who had just succeeded Pius XI on the throne of St. Peter.

[7] Around this time he had many meetings with Paul-Louis Weiller, the great French industrialist, who induced him to become a director of the Compagnie Gnôme et Rhône.

Claudel was a member of the French delegation led by Champetier de Ribes, a cabinet minister. Only Nazi Germany and Soviet Russia were absent. On this memorable occasion, Paul Claudel felt intensely everything which bound him to the rock of Rome:

> I think of the whole Catholic universe, of that Cenacle made of four hundred million brothers of all races, believers and unbelievers, of the sick, the little children, the destitute, the persecuted of every kind; of that whole Church made of millions of beings who suffer and hope; of that tidal wave beneath us; of all the dead raised by the Eucharistic star; of that terrible sobbing summed up so simply by that lonely voice which rises in the overwhelming silence, *"Pater noster,* Father, Father, Our Father!"[8]

These various trips and lectures never seemed to interfere with his literary activities, however. The oratorio entitled *Jeanne d'Arc au Bûcher,* which he wrote for Madame Ida Rubinstein, with music by Honegger, was presented at the municipal theater of Orleans for the feast day of the national heroine. And *Christophe Colomb,* which he had written in Washington, was given at the Salle Pleyel.

Another distinction was added to all the other tributes Paul Claudel had already received. In June 1939 the University of Cambridge bestowed upon him a degree of doctor *honoris causa.* In his own words, he donned the "honorific plumage, that toga of scarlet moiré and that mortarboard of black velvet which one sees on the figures painted by Clouet and Holbein."

> Then Baldwin, holding my hand, declared . . . that he admitted me into the illustrious University of Cambridge, . . . in the name of the Father, of the Son and of the Holy Ghost.
>
> I could not prevent myself from murmuring, "Amen."[9]

[8] *Contacts et Circonstances* (Gallimard), p. 202.
[9] Ibid., p. 232.

This was an occasion for Claudel to publicly recognize his debt toward English literature. In the first place, toward Shakespeare, "that magic window opening on a vast horizon of dreams and action." And also toward Milton, Keats, Coleridge, Tennyson, Coventry Patmore, Francis Thompson and Blake, Shelley, Rossetti and Browning. Among the novelists, he singled out Thomas Hardy, "whose bittersweet quality," he said, "had for me a fortifying virtue."

We have already seen how Claudel spent the summer of 1939. In September, the Second World War broke out.

17

FROM THE UNIVERSAL
CONFLAGRATION TO THE l
YEARS

BORN TWO YEARS BEFORE 1870, CLAUDEL LIVED LONG EN
to witness three wars. The one which started in Septe
1939 with the twin aggression against Poland, did not con
a surprise to him for he had anxiously and attentively
lowed the premonitory signs of the global catastrophe wh
was to shake the world.

When war broke out he was at Brangues, and the vario
members of his family were scattered all over France. Praye
the reading of the Bible and his daily work represented hi
main recourse. He wrote to Louis Gillet, the art critic, who
was one of his closest friends during those times of trial:
"Prayer is my great resource, and I have the feeling, in praying, of doing something effective and efficacious. Without
prayer, I think that I would die."[1]

At the time of the armistice Claudel favored the policies of
Marshal Pétain. After the temporary defeat of the French
armies, he had seen the magnitude of the disaster which then
seemed irreparable. In a poem he wrote on the Marshal, he
described:

[1] *Claudel présent*, Louis Gillet (L.U.F.)

Those crowds on all the roads, like a river becoming a torrent
Of women, children and men, like a herd of panic-stricken
    animals,
And that cry of despair mingling with our decimated troops.

Moreover, he recognized in the Messages of the old soldier, who had been one of his supporters at the Académie française, something of his own peasant instincts and attachment to the land; the same deep roots which he had always preserved in spite of his many trips and long absences. Claudel wrote that Pierre Laval's dismissal, in December 1940, prompted him to write his *Paroles au Maréchal*. And on May 9, 1941, *L'Annonce faite à Marie* was played in Vichy, in the presence of the Chief of State.

And yet, as early as June 20, 1940, the former diplomat had gone to Algiers so as to offer his services to French authorities there. He sailed from Toulon on June 20 aboard the aircraft-carrier *Commandant Teste*, landed in Algiers on June 23, and told Governor-General Le Beau that he had come to place himself at the disposal of the authorities, in response to Winston Churchill's broadcast appeal to all Frenchmen. Everything depended on General Noguès, whom he was unable to reach. On June 25, the Italian armistice was signed. Claudel conferred with the head of the Governor-General's personal staff, and also with General Cornilion-Moniglier. On June 26, a meeting at Military Headquarters left him deeply discouraged. During the next few days, he also met Monsignor Leynaud (Archbishop of Algiers), Vice-Admiral Richard, and Antoine de Saint-Exupéry. Seeing that all his efforts were in vain, he finally returned to France, reached Marseilles on July 2, and was back home in Brangues on July 4. The next day, he wrote this brief entry in his diary: "Gloom, despair." The district had been occupied by the Germans two weeks earlier.

In 1942, he joined the Gaullist movement, and henceforth put his trust in General de Gaulle, with whom he was on

excellent terms. Claudel raised his voice in protest against the persecutions suffered by the Jews. His book entitled *Une voix en Israël* was to testify to his interest in Judaism, just as *Le Pain dur* had done years before.

Engrossed in his interpretation and commentaries of Holy Scripture, and also working on *Présence et prophétie* and his *Apocalypse,* he was officially most reticent, as a writer, on the trend of events which, however, inspired his daily meditations. He rose in spirit from the ominous reality around him to the surprisingly pertinent vistas of the Bible. The sufferings of his fellow men were close to his heart, and he consigned his thoughts of spiritual communion to loose leaflets which piled up on his desk gradually, to form his very personal exegesis:

> It is autumn, and I stand on this woeful and slumbering shore, while afar are heard the repeated blows of that hammer striking the earth! London is in flames, and from everywhere, from Bristol, Liverpool, Calais, Hamburg, Amsterdam, Bremen, Frankfurt and Berlin, smoke mixed with fire rises over and over again.
>
> There are terrified children howling and sobbing on the body of their mother, there are old people shaking with a terrible tremor, there are women in mourning clutching one another beneath the arch of a shell-struck church! Does He now exist, would He perchance finally start to exist, that Avenger we had forgotten?[2]

The year 1941 was dark indeed, and heavy with anguish. Yet hope flickered on and its small flame refused to die, even though the tide of events had not yet started to turn. The poet continued working on his *Apocalypse,* and *Présence et prophétie* was published in Switzerland. His two sons were in the United States, and his son-in-law was entrusted with a special mission by the Red Cross. To all those who had not lost courage, Claudel's works represented one of those spiritual assets which deserved to be preserved at all costs; an

[2] Sept. 30, 1940.

asset as precious as the very soil of France. French youth was well aware of this. *L'Annonce faite à Marie* appeared as the tidings of French faith in brighter days. In May, as we have already seen, it was played in Vichy. Five months later in Paris, *Le Rideau des Jeunes* staged *L'Annonce* in full, at the Théâtre de l'Oeuvre, then at the Théâtre de Saint-Georges. The necessary authorizations had been granted by Jean-Louis Vaudoyer, and the rue Daru choir consented to sing for the occasion. Louise Vetch had written the music and directed the play. After one of the performances the actress portraying Violaine was carried by the students in triumph along the Boulevard Saint-Michel.

Among so many causes for alarm and tears, another welcome consolation came to him from his old comrade and friend Romain Rolland. They had met as pupils at the lycée Louis-le-Grand, and had studied under the same masters, Bernage and Gaspard in particular. Rolland failed to pass the entrance tests for the Ecole Normale Supérieure. Claudel "flunked' his baccalaureate examination. They often walked together, "talking tirelessly," according to Rolland, "about Wagner and Aeschylus . . . or about Paul de Saint-Victor."

A little later, they had seen each other again at the Conservatoire, and had shared the same admiration for Beethoven's *Mass in D*. Life had then drawn them apart, and their ideas had developed in completely opposite directions. But Claudel had not forgotten those noble features illuminated by blue eyes as deep as the sea. He never completely lost touch with the compassionate Rolland, who always remained closely attentive to all the miseries of his fellow-men and deeply appreciative of beauty in all its manifestations. Claudel was to write these significant lines to his friend:

> Certainly, we have never been really far apart. We have both kept our eyes turned upward. . . . I am surprised at the foolishness which caused me to misjudge you for so long.

But it is precisely the admiration, esteem and affection I now feel for you that make some sections on which I stumble in your works so painful and wounding to me. A mind such as yours is not meant to be immerged or submerged in anything created, even nature or music. "Nature is not our mother, but our sister."[3]

They met again, first in Paris, then at Vézelay in April 1940, on those hills of Burgundy where there rises a twelfth century basilica dedicated to St. Magdalen, and where St. Bernard had preached the second crusade.

This was one of the places where, according to Barrès, "the spirit blows." In Vézelay, the author of *Jean Christophe* had bought, in 1937, a house overlooking a wide and wonderful landscape. In spite of appearances, or at least of those appearances which superficial minds are incapable of interpreting correctly, Rolland at heart had remained deeply religious. In a kind of hazy pantheism, he had promised his mother, many years earlier, that every evening he would recite the *Pater;* the prayer which causes man to recognize a higher love, a love indulgent, tireless, never discouraged. Out of faithfulness he had always kept this promise, and soon added the *Ave Maria* to the fundamental orison. The Bible and prayer book became his favorite reading material. But he never returned to the faith. While his heart was ready to surrender, his reason continued to raise objections and obstacles. He was helped and comforted to an extraordinary degree by the prayers of his friends, however. These were indeed three uncommon destinies: Rolland, drawn toward God and practicing the prayers, although unable to believe; Péguy, converted and having recourse to prayer, but stopping short of the sacraments; Claudel, who was privileged since he could join faith and practice, but who felt profoundly unworthy of so many gifts!

[3] Letters dated March 20, April 10 and June 6, 1942, quoted by Bertrand Barrère in *Romain Rolland par lui-même* (Editions du Seuil), p. 177.

Romain Rolland was to die on December 30, 1944. Nearly two years earlier, in January and February 1943, he already knew that he was doomed, and wrote these lines, transcribed by Claudel, who thus received the beginning of an answer to his ardent implorations:

> I was going to die, I knew that I stood at the extreme edge of the abyss. At that moment I felt sustained and comforted by the prayers of all those friends, especially of my Catholic friends, which rose up to God for me. I felt that ardent communion of the Christian souls, coming to the help of one among them who was in danger; and the links with which they surround God, Who Himself aspires after this reciprocity of love. All this penetrated the fever's parched solitude, it was like the affectionate pressure of a friendly hand. Sublime idea of a God Who became a man and Who offers Himself in sacrifice at every moment, through love for each and for all; and of the community of the faithful who associate with this sacrifice, and who, as far as their strength permits, participate in it! What a relief for the heart which, during those hours of anguish, finds nothing to comfort it in the frozen pantheism which was adequate during the days of health. Moral poverty of pantheism! A Being in Whom all beings are absorbed. Of what interest is this if He and they are impersonal? This does not in any way explain the real problem, which is the *I*, the *I*'s [in the plural], that infinity of *I*'s.[4]

Meanwhile, before the loss of his friend Rolland, another death, far crueler still, overwhelmed him with grief. In October 1943, as he was writing a commentary on the *Song of Songs*, he was called to Montfavet, near Avignon, where his sister Camille was dying in the Mont-de-Vergues nursing home. She was eighty years old and had lived there since she lost her reason, thirty years earlier, in a kind of night barely interrupted by a few brief flashes of lucidity. She had not forgotten her brother, however, and had asked that he be sent

[4] *Le Figaro littéraire,* 1945 collection.

for, so as to assist her at the moment of death, when she would recover her full reason, in the endless contemplation of an eternal God. She said only four words to him, words which emerged from the faraway days of their childhood and youth, *"Tiens, mon petit Paul!"*

> I kiss that face, which is awesome, and yet—how can I express it?—illuminated! That powerful brow, whose majesty has been enhanced by age, and from which neither tragedy nor illness could erase the stamp of genius. She is happy to see me, but yet I disturb her; she is anxious to return to those important matters which engage her. Returning home through the mountains, through all the fructification of vineyards and walnut trees, along that long road like a golden ribbon. . . . I sorrowfully brood over the whole past. I see again, emerging from [the mist of] childhood, that young and triumphant face, those beautiful dark-blue eyes, the most beautiful I ever saw, resting mockingly on that clumsy brother.[5]

A month later, on November 27—the date was not of his choosing, and he had to overcome the heart-rending memory of that death—the Comédie Française presented *Le Soulier de satin* for the first time. This wartime performance, carried out under German occupation, was a sign of the undiminished vitality of the French national spirit.

Jean-Louis Barrault had approached him early in 1939, when Claudel still lived on the rue Jean-Goujon. Accompanied by his wife, Madeleine Renaud, he had then been to Brangues, in June 1939. Encouraged by the warm welcome he received from the poet and his family, the inspired actor "offered him (Claudel) his services," as he put it. Barrault asked for no less than three plays: *Tête d'Or, Le Partage de midi,* and *Le Soulier de satin,* which can be considered respectively as Claudel's creative "sap," his "ordeal," and his "synthesis." The playwright would not agree to the produc-

[5] *Le Cantique des Cantiques* (Gallimard), p. 141.

tion of the first two of these works: *"Tête d'Or* has become unreadable to me. It is senseless gibberish which would make the public laugh." And he had personal reasons, at the time, to be opposed to the staging of *Le Partage*. As for *Le Soulier de satin,* he insisted on a complete and unabridged rendition. At the most, he might have accepted a separate performance of *Sous le vent des Iles Baléares,* the fourth "day" of the play, which he had written before the other parts.

Then had come war, defeat and the division of France into two zones. In 1941, Jean-Louis Barrault renewed his request. Their contacts—mostly by letter—became frequent. The young actor felt an increasing admiration for Claudel on whom he wrote these remarkably perceptive and profound comments: "To understand him one must not see in Claudel the great man, the celebrity full of years, the inspired poet, the patriarch presiding over a large and noble family; but a young horse, headstrong, neighing, kicking, bolting, frisking about, rolling in the meadow and sometimes hanging its rope at the foot of the altar . . . so as to calm down."[6]

Jean-Louis Vaudoyer, who was then general manager of the Comédie Française, gave Barrault's plans his complete backing. "It is thanks to his tenacity," testified the actor, "that *Le Soulier* was staged."[7] The excessively long play was cut down to four hours, which was an absolute necessity, but nevertheless pained the author considerably. Toward 1925 when he had nearly finished writing *Le Soulier,* I had heard him say that he would never consent to its being given in an abridged version, and that Wagner's works, after all, were played in full at Bayreuth.

The opening, held on November 27, 1943, was a real triumph, and gave living proof, under the heel of enemy occupation, that the spirit of France refused to die. Honegger had composed the music, and the stage settings were by Lucien

[6] *Paul Claudel et Christophe Colomb,* "Les Cahiers de la Compagnie Madeleine Renaud—Jean-Louis Barrault." (Julliard, 1953), p. 53.
[7] Ibid.

Coutaud. Not only had Jean-Louis Barrault adapted *Le Soulier,* in close partnership and agreement with Claudel, but also he played the part of Rodrigue with a faith and a flair which filled the audience with enthusiasm. Marie Bell filled the role of Prouhèze with proud dignity. Madeleine Renaud and Jeanne Sully, although they did not have the major parts, also demonstrated their superb acting abilities. Aimé Clariond was a brilliant Spanish lieutenant. And Pierre Dux, as the Announcer, gave a dazzling performance.

> "Rodrigue," she said. "Prouhèze,"
> Said he. Each hearkened and waited.
> Nothing but the moon high in the sky, glittering on the ocean.
> Nothing but that lonely red light, shining through the Stygian night.[8]

In a Claudel chronology I have before me there are no entries under the year 1944. He was busy studying and commenting on the Bible, and followed fervently, with the entire French nation, the world-shaking events which were to decide France's destiny: on June 6 the Allied invasion forces swarmed ashore between Caen and the Cherbourg peninsula; on August 15 a French army, under the command of General de Lattre de Tassigny, landed between Toulon and Cannes; General Leclerc's armored division drove into Paris on August 25, and General de Gaulle entered the French capital a few hours later. The day before the liberation of Paris, Claudel's friend Paul Petit was shot in Cologne, after three years in prison; he had been arrested in France for writing an anti-German leaflet. Years earlier, hearing of the Tokyo earthquake, the young diplomat had spontaneously written to Claudel, without knowing him. They had met in Rome, in 1925, when Petit was attached to the French Embassy to the Quirinal. Two years later, Claudel became godfather to his son André. Petit was a frank, loyal and straightforward soul

[8] Paul Claudel, *Visages radieux* (L.U.F.) p. 114.

and adhered to the highest moral standards. At the same time, his heart was filled with true Christian generosity. He deeply admired Claudel, and understood his works to a degree matched by only a few others. "A staunch Catholic, and a true son [of the Church], in the full strength of the word," as Claudel put it, he was instrumental in drawing Bergson closer to the Thomist viewpoint of his master. Two conversations I had with Petit before the Second World War enabled me to gauge the strength of character and warm heart of that husband and father who made the supreme sacrifice for a just and noble cause.

Gabriel Frizeau had also been one of Petit's friends, and had one day written these lines to him: "How right you are: our great Claudel is irresistible each time I read him. That naive outburst of admiration of a heart which is attracted toward everything beautiful and joyous: this defines all Claudel, and [also] what is best in man."

As for Claudel, he had freely confided in Paul Petit and had told him, quite simply but not without whimsy, of his plans for the future: "From Washington, March 4, 1932. The other day I spent some time daydreaming of what I would do after retiring, and pictured myself writing unassisted a kind of monthly compilation I would call *Les Veillées du Château*,[9] and which I would not find it difficult to compose."

In four lines, Claudel had left Petit a kind of testamentary message, without foreseeing that the younger man would return to God before him: "The only memory you must keep of me is that of a man who attaches importance to but one thing: total commitment and faithfulness to God and to His Church. The rest is nothing."

On March 14, 1945, Henry Bordeaux, dean of the Académie française, and François Mauriac, who was a friend of

[9] An allusion to *Les Veillées des Chaumières*, a popular and widely read periodical.

Claudel's, took it upon themselves with the approval of several other members, to ask the author of *L'Otage* whether he would accept an invitation to join the ranks of the Immortals; it being understood that the various "visits" customarily required would be waived in his case. Claudel's answer, written from Brangues on March 16, 1946, declared that he valued fully "the exceptional and highly honorable nature" of this offer. Louis Gillet's seat was selected for him, and Maurice Genevoix graciously withdrew his candidacy to it. The election took place on April 4, and Claudel received twenty-four out of twenty-five votes cast. Since good things generally come in pairs, the poet, who at the time had no dwelling in Paris and in whose favor Mauriac had made a discreet appeal in the *Figaro*, was offered an apartment at 11 Boulevard Lannes opposite the Bois de Boulogne, by a young Jewess converted to Catholicism. Her parents, who had previously occupied it, had been the victims of Nazi persecution.

Belgium claimed the honor of presenting the new member with the traditional sword. It was wrought by Marcel Wolfers, a Belgian artist, following a public subscription opened under the patronage of the Queen Mother Elizabeth of Belgium and of Cardinal van Roey.

Claudel was officially received into the Académie on Thursday, March 13, 1947, in an atmosphere of rare fervor. He was assisted by his sponsors, Monsignor (later Cardinal) Grente and Ambassador de Chambrun. After paying tribute to the memory of his friend Louis Gillet, that fearless champion of the intellect, he painted a faithful picture of the opening decade of this century, which all too often is considered merely a period of frivolity and worldliness conjured up by the very mention of the name of Marcel Proust:

> I know that in the minds of many young people, the mention of those remote years summons up only the idea of a frivolous era. They see this period only through the chronicle of Marcel Proust. Nevertheless, there was something else

during those honorable years when France subordinated all her temporal interests to the duty of correcting an intolerable injustice; something else, indeed, beside the chatter of Madame Verdurin and the amorous intrigues of Monsieur de Charlus. That very crisis is but the outward manifestation of a general and deep spiritual movement, illustrated by the career of Charles Péguy. The positivist conviction which had sustained and inspired the nineteenth century showed clear signs of fatigue and decline. The new forces awakening to life saw around them nothing but stagnation and suffocation. Nauseated by the familiar foods which for so long had flattered the palate, the stomachs were no longer fed. At the time of the Dreyfus affair remorse, with the bite of a cancer, had awakened slumbering consciences. In the best of men this remorse had turned into a fundamental grievance against the present.

Through the rotting partitions of an elementary materialism, through the cowardly suggestions of a decadent pessimism, the irresistible call of hope once again made itself heard. Far away to the East, the great voice of the Russian novelists had started to break up that spiritual darkness . . . which Dante wrote about. And in France that voice was answered by a general uplifting of souls and of weapons, by that *tumultus gallicus* which occasionally struck fear into the hearts of the ancient Romans. Why should I not recall with sadness and emotion those names of men, now all departed, who in the last analysis fought for the same cause, although under opposing banners: Péguy, Psichari and Léon Bloy, as well as Jaurès and Lucien Herr, Bourget and Maurice Barrès and also Huysmans and Francis Jammes? There had risen over the world a certain attention to music, a certain longing for the answer, a certain intolerance of fate—be it scientific or legal—a certain irrepressible feeling of our inner right, a certain call of our moral consciousness for outer confirmation. It was as though the ancient salt of the fatherland had grown restless under the feet of an entire youth; a youth chosen to receive this warning. All that younger generation asking to fashion with its heart a new countenance for itself, asking for a face, so as to go forth and seek the face of God.

François Mauriac answered in his own name and in that of the whole Académie, but also for the sacrificed generation of the First World War, of Péguy, Psichari and Paul Drouot. In his wounded and impassioned voice he expressed the deep gratitude which went to Claudel as to a giver of Light.

This memorable session of the Académie française was truly a high point of French intellectual life.

But the greatest joy of all, by Claudel's own admission, came to him on April 29, 1950. On that day, at six in the evening, in the Consistory Hall of the Vatican, that great Roman and eminently Catholic poet was honored by Pope Pius XII. All customs and traditions were broken in his favor. Never before had such a ceremony taken place in the pontifical Rome.

At the very spot where the Holy Father assembles the members of the Sacred College in solemn circumstances, or proclaims the new cardinals he has been pleased to select, six actors of the Compagnie Hébertot (three men and three women) appeared on a platform. Opposite them, wearing the Grand Cordon of the order of St. Gregory over his academician's uniform, sat Paul Claudel, visibly moved and happy. In the first row of the audience were Alcide de Gasperi (the Italian Premier), Wladimir d'Ormesson (French Ambassador to the Vatican), and Jacques Fouques-Duparc (French Ambassador to the Quirinal).

Pius XII entered the hall in all simplicity, followed by his private attendant and a chamberlain, and quickly strode to the pontifical throne. Alain Dhurtal then recited Claudel's poem dedicated to St. Peter: "Christ is the head, but Peter is the base and movement of the Catholic religion—Jesus has planted the Cross on the ground, but Peter secures it in the sky." Pius XII, who had crossed his fingers in an attitude of prayer, opened the applause, which was somewhat restrained by the majesty of the setting. Other poems were then read by Eve Francis, Jean Vernier, Hélène Sauvaneix, Michel Herbault and Carmen Duparc. The *Chant de marche de Noel,* sung by all six actors, concluded this well-chosen and admirably balanced program.

The Holy Father, clearly touched by the performance, expressed his thanks in a brief but warm speech. He then approached the kneeling Claudel, asked him to stand and presented him with a Rosary. "Now I can die," said the old poet, who had just lived an hour of incomparable fullness. According to a distinguished eyewitness, Wladimir d'Ormesson, it had been "an exceptional event granted to an exceptional writer by an exceptional Pope."[10]

Later, there occurred an incident which has embarrassed many of Claudel's friends and which must be related. Charles Maurras had died on November 16, 1952, in Tours. The old agnostic thinker had, at the last, turned to a Christian frame of mind. On his deathbed he spoke these words, which take on their full significance when it is known that he had been incurably deaf since youth: "For the first time, I hear Someone coming." Claudelians would be tempted to add this qualification, drawn from the writings of their Master: "Someone Who is in me more myself than I am." François Mauriac did not hesitate to write that the words spoken by the dying Maurras justified this addition.[11]

On the following Thursday (November 20) at the Académie, Jules Romains, who was presiding at the meeting, pronounced a tactful and inspired eulogy of the deceased writer

---

[10] This account is based on an article sent from Rome Feb. 28, 1955 to *Le Figaro,* by its correspondent Maurice Montabré. Ambassador d'Ormesson's words are taken from the speech welcoming Paul Claudel into the Académie française (*Documentation catholique,* April 28, 1957.)

[11] *Mémoires intérieurs,* 1959.

who had been excluded from the illustrious company in 1945. All the members stood, except Claudel, who declared when the address was ended, "I fail to understand the tribute which has just been paid to Maurras. Maurras was no longer a member of the Académie. Our rules excluded him from it, in pursuance of the law. . . . The words which have just been pronounced should have been spoken at that time. . . . No, I do not understand and I want my protest to be entered in the minutes of this meeting."[12]

Part of French public opinion saw in this attitude an expression of hostility toward a deceased colleague and judged it severely, for death demanded that the past be forgotten. Some observers made a different assumption: perhaps Claudel felt that if Maurras really possessed all the qualities described by Jules Romains he should never have been expelled in the first place, and that this belated tribute was highly illogical. Claudel never clarified the reasons behind his stand.

Starting in 1947, Claudel was brought back in a curious way to his Greek studies and particularly to Homer. One of his classmates at Louis-le-Grand, Gabriel de Roton (who is now almost a hundred years old) had not forgotten him, and in fact had followed with pride the development of his twin career as a writer and a diplomat. In his château of Rayne-Vigneau, near Sauternes, he treasured an old album containing sketches of various students of the top classical form, among them an excellent likeness of young Paul Claudel. He sent the poet a photographic copy of this portrait, then presented him with the original. Since Louis-le-Grand, Gabriel de Roton had devoted his time to the sciences—speleology, mineralogy, and paleontology. He had also published a book on the role of woman in Greek antiquity, and another on the *Iliad* as pictured through Greek ceramics. He was working on a more complete study, covering both the *Iliad* and the

[12] Cf. H. Bordeaux: *Ch. Maurras et l'Académie française*, 1955, p. 157.

Odyssey, with reproductions in black and in color—like the preceding ones—of his own drawings, which were inspired by paintings on Greek vases exhibited in the great museums of the world. He asked his former classmate to write appropriate commentaries for this volume. Claudel painstakingly prepared the required material and acknowledged that he would be happy to accept payment in bottles of Sauterne wine. By courtesy of Vicomte de Roton I am able to quote a few fragments from the amusing letters he received from the poet:

April 24, 1947

Does my memory serve me right? At the end of Canto XIX, in the *Iliad,* does Achilles not stand on the bank of the moat, and does he not give a shout which terrifies the whole enemy army? I am ashamed to admit that I have never reread the *Iliad* since the *lycée,* and that I do not even own a copy of it.

It is important for me to know this.

June 5, 1947

Here is the introduction you requested of me for your *Iliad.* I would also like to receive a dozen bottles of your excellent wine. . . .

July 1, 1947

I am continuing to read the *Odyssey.* Alas, the enchantment did not hold! I prefer by far the heroic youth of the *Iliad.* All these adventures of Ulysses are awfully childish, and the Bible has accustomed me to a more substantial fare. I have now reached the return to Ithaca, which is, I feel, the best part of the poem. A charming friend who is an invalid, and who has taken advantage of her illness to learn Greek like a scholar, finds all this ravishing, on the contrary, and her letters tell me so in the most delightful terms.

Alas, I must say that I do not in the least agree with you on the translation by our friend Bérard.[13] When I read I find it intolerable, instead of meeting Homer, to run into

[13] Victor Bérard, a schoolmate of Paul Claudel and Gabriel de Roton at Louis-le-Grand.

that pretentious individual. It is impertinent indeed to have tampered with that venerable text as he has done! The ancient documents are what they are, but the moderns have no more right to meddle with them than to alter an architectural monument. Moreover, the Alexandrine verse has nothing in common with the Doric hexameter, and the systematic anachronisms in the translation make me want to scream. Mazon's translation of the *Iliad* is far superior. The "poetic" ideas of M. Bérard are absolutely of no interest to me.

July 27, 1947

. . . Your wine, like a triumphant sun, illuminates our family table which is well provided at the moment. I hope that my *Odyssey* will earn me a few more cases when I return to Paris in October. If you have occasion to be there yourself remember my address, 11 Boulevard Lannes. We will reminisce together.

September 15, 1947

Well, *I was right* after all, and my old memories were not deceiving me. Open your *Iliad*, Canto XVIII, lines 100 to 260, and you will see Achilles on the edge of the moat, amid supernatural flames, thrice uttering a cry which puts to flight the victorious Trojans. The episode is magnificent, as indeed it must be to have left such a deep impression on me!

October 1, 1947

My discovery gave me the idea of rereading the *Iliad* from beginning to end, which I did with the greatest enthusiasm. It is far superior to the *Odyssey*. I was therefor impelled to write a second draft, which is much longer than the first. I hold it at your disposal, if you wish to have it.

November 7, 1951

I have just received your magnificent present[14] and have already had time to glance over it with wonder. A new world opens up to me, thanks to your admirable diligence

[14] *Homère: L'Iliade, l'Odyssée, illustrées par la céramique grecque.* Drawings by Vicomte de Roton (Delmas).

and miraculous pencil. Until now Greek art was to me something static, but from the fragile clay you have brought forth
a host of living human beings, in a prodigious accuracy of
invariably noble movements. It is a real treasure.

What a pity that Homer wrote only those two poems,
magnificent though they may be!

Greece did not cause Claudel to neglect his Biblical
studies. Between 1949 and 1954, as a matter of fact, he
pursued them more actively than ever, as evidenced by his
voluminous correspondence with Father Paroissin, another
defender of "that lost Paradise, overflowing with milk and
honey, which horrible pedants had turned into a museum
and a cemetery."[15]

[15] From a letter to Father Paroissin (August 17, 1949) in *Lettres de
P. Claudel sur la Bible* (Debresse, 1955). Father Paroissin wrote a
remarkable book entitled *Art et humanisme biblique avec Claudel*
(Debresse, 1955).

18

THE CLOSING YEARS

CLAUDEL'S OLD FRIEND ANDRE SUARÈS DIED ON SEPTEMBER 7, 1948. He was a noble writer, dedicated to art as to an exclusive religion, full of pride, and not ashamed to be proud. The death of a brother had brought him to the edge of despair, and Claudel had helped him to overcome his sorrow, which at times refused all solace. For many years, until just before the Second World War, they had exchanged inspiring letters. On the artistic plane, they esteemed each other highly, although their esthetic ideas were far from coinciding. At times it seemed that Suarès envied his friend's dynamic faith, and Claudel, who was a born missionary, did his utmost to convert him. In 1925, speaking precisely of Suarès, the great Catholic poet said to me, "There are letters I write that remain without effect on those they are intended for; but they help others, who seem to have read them over the shoulders of my correspondents." In his foreword to the letters between the two authors, Robert Mallet, who has a deep understanding of Claudel's thought, explains with remarkable fairness and objectivity the respective positions of each.

The death of Suarès had greatly affected Claudel. That of André Gide on February 19, 1951 was an even greater blow to him. A thick volume of letters testifies to their warm friendship between 1899 and 1926. Their attitudes toward life could hardly have been more different: Gide was essentially a relativist, while Claudel held absolute positions. Yet on sev-

267

eral occasions there existed a real closeness between the two men: Claudel was filled with pity by the disheartening state of mind of the author of *L'Immoraliste*, and the latter showed himself capable of rising to a more positive spiritual attitude. *Numquid et tu*, that little book in which Gide acknowledged the divinity of Christ and admitted that he sometimes prayed, awakened great hopes in his friend, but these hopes were soon destroyed by almost incredible aberrations. What neither Claudel nor Charles du Bos could accept was the attempt to justify a vice by an actual falsification or misrepresentation of the scriptures. "How many letters have I not received," Claudel declared to a journalist,[1] "from erring young men? At the start of their path toward evil, there is always Gide."

Gide died far from God and frozen in a complacent attitude. This probably did not surprise Claudel but it nevertheless pained him deeply. In his mind's eye he no doubt still saw the amiable features of a remarkably gifted man, he remembered the great kindness of a friend who for many years sought only to oblige him, and who had seemed to seek the living truth, loyally and painstakingly.

The warnings of destiny became more frequent. During the year 1953 his son-in-law Jacques Paris, the husband of his daughter Reine and the father of Philippe, Reine, Marie, Camille and little Charles-Henri (who died twenty years earlier), secretary general of the Council of Europe and one of France's best diplomats, was killed with his mother, in an automobile accident as they were on their way to the pilgrimage of Nôtre-Dame-de-Verdelais, in the Gironde district. Shortly after, and probably as a consequence of this family tragedy—added to so many other causes—Paul Claudel started to suffer from the first symptoms of a heart disease which would eventually prove fatal. He was kept busy travel-

---

[1] Dominique Arban, Combat, March 28, 1947. Cf. *Correspondance Claudel-Gide*, pp. 248-249.

ing and attending various performances of his plays, but these activities did not heal the wounds which had opened in his heart. He journeyed to Hamburg where *Tobie et Sara* was given at the Municipal Theater, and where everyone tried to make him forget his painful memories of the year 1914. He returned to Brussels where his *Cantique de l'espérance* was presented at the Palais des Beaux-Arts, then spent two days in Zurich. The following year he was honored mainly in the French capital: the Palais de Chaillot offered his *Cantique de l'espérance,* and the Théâtre Marigny revived *Le Partage de midi,* while at the Opera *Jeanne au Bûcher* was a veritable triumph, with Ingrid Bergman in the title role.

In September 1954 an attack of sciatica forced him to spend some time in an Aix-les-Bains nursing home. He took the occasion to reread the works of Racine, whose seat he occupied at the Académie française, and on whom Jean-Louis Barrault had asked him to write an essay. Formerly he had been highly critical of the author of *Britannicus* and *Athalie.* This "exploration," at his age and under such circumstances, was to bring him to a fairer and more favorable assessment. Daniel-Rops came to see him from his house in Tresserve, as a neighbor and a friend, and relates one of their conversations:

—I see that you are rereading Racine!
—Rereading, rereading, he muttered with a smile; you are too polite, you should say that I am reading him. During my school days I had not read everything, and even what I studied for the *bachot* is far away. I am reading everything. This rids me of feelings of remorse. You know, I have been occupying Racine's seat at the Académie for ten years. I am his unworthy successor. I had to make up my mind to give him the credit which is his due.
—And what is your impression?
. . . .
—You are lying in wait for me, aren't you? Well, I shall

tell you. I still find the Alexandrine verse tedious, unbearable; it reminds me of a fence with an alternation of pickets and spaces intolerable to the eye. And yet, not only do I accept the Alexandrine in Racine's works, I applaud with both hands. It was the medium which he needed.[2]

On the following October 7th, Racine formed the subject of a conversation between Claudel and Arcas (pseudonym of Jean-Louis Barrault), as related in the *Cahiers de la compagnie Madeleine Renaud—Jean-Louis Barrault*.[3] The old poet expressed himself in a wealth of unusual, concise and striking formulas:

> Lady Macbeth represents the human soul deprived of that sacred light which illumines every man coming into the world, and for which that smoky little candle flickering in her hand is a poor substitute; night has fallen. . . . Shakespeare is an unfolding spectacle, a story we are told. Racine is the realm of causation, a presentation logically satisfying to the intellect. . . . Racine's powerful hold resides in that intimate harmony between thought and sentiment, each heightening the other to the point of ecstasy. . . . The human drama remains incomplete, so long as a superhuman component is not added to it. . . . What makes *Phèdre*'s tragic predicament so deeply moving, because it is not only *Phèdre*'s but also that of Racine, is the question he places before the conscience of every inspired human being; both victim and accomplice of an unknown, ambivalent and questionable power.

He had also set his heart on another rehabilitation: that of Pascal. On December 18, 1954, receiving Jacques Chevalier, he thanked him for the gift of the first copy of Pascal's works in a new edition brought out as part of the *Collection de la Pléiade,* of which Chevalier was the publisher. And this was

[2] Daniel-Rops, *Claudel tel que je l'ai connu* (F.X. Le Roux) pp. 38ff. Through this compilation of particularly valuable memoirs a most lifelike portrait of Claudel emerges.

[3] (Julliard, 1955.)

GWENN MALESON

mixed media on paper

OPENING RECEPTION
Sunday, November 8
Noon until 5:00

Exhibition continues until November 29

ROSENFELD GALLERY
113 Arch Street, Phila., PA 19106
(215) 922-1376
therosenfeldgallery.com
Hours: Wed. - Sat. 10 until 5
Sun. noon until 5

an occasion for them to return to earlier conversations they had had concerning the author of the *Pensées*. In the past, as we have already seen, Claudel had disagreed with Pascal on a number of points, although he had drawn inspiration from his works at the time of his own conversion. On the previous March 15th, in the presence of Jacques Chevalier, Claudel specified his fundamental objections. In the first place, the Blessed Virgin seemed to be absent from the great thinker's preoccupations, according to the elderly poet. To which Chevalier answered that, although Pascal had not dwelt at any length on the mother of Christ, he nevertheless refers to her in *Le mystère de Jésus*, and that if this criticism were justified it could also be leveled at St. John of the Cross. Claudel had also been concerned about Pascal's ultimate spiritual attitude, until he read the testimony of Father Beurrier, pastor of Saint-Etienne-du-Mont, who had assisted the former Jansenist on his deathbed, and who declared that he had definitely turned his back on Port-Royal.

On this December 18th he made his position clear: "I now hold only two small things against Pascal." The first was this sentence in *Le mystère de Jésus*: "I have shed these particular drops of My blood for you." Brémond had seen in this a Jansenist conception of grace, and had said so to Claudel who took the matter very much to heart. Jacques Chevalier protested against this interpretation, "No at all! Pascal means that no man is excluded. These words are addressed to each and every man." The other remaining objection concerned the well-known sentence in *Les Pensées* criticizing those who leave their room: "All the misfortune of men. . . ." Claudel, that indefatigable traveler, could not accept this viewpoint. But these objections were not really important. They did not deal with essentials. "I want to review the matter," he concluded, "so as to show that Pascal is admirable beyond all expression. Some people seek to tear him away from us, and question the unquestionable."

After the tribute of the Church, given in the Vatican, which carried more weight with him than anything else, Claudel was to receive a national tribute whose value he fully realized, and which would make up for the lack of understanding he had all too often encountered in the course of his long career. After *L'Otage,* the Comédie Française added *L'Annonce faite à Marie* to its repertoire, and on February 18, 1955, gave a very special and particularly brilliant gala performance. It was honored by the presence of President René Coty who attended the occasion not only in his official capacity, but also as a man of taste and culture who knew and admired the works of the former ambassador.

Two days later, in his boulevard Lannes apartment, Claudel gave a reception for the actors who had interpreted *L'Annonce.*

His life was drawing to a close. During the difficult rehearsals of his play Professor Soulié, an eminent cardiologist, hardly left his side, standing by in case his heart should weaken. It was almost a miracle that the old poet stood such an effort so well.

On February 22, at midday, he had fallen asleep in his armchair. (France was in the throes of a political crisis, and awaited a new government, which was to be formed by Edgar Faure twenty days after the overthrow of the previous cabinet.) A quarter of an hour later Jean de Wenger, a young author, came to pay a call. Claudel received him kindly, and his last words were to deplore the "floods of idiocy and filth of the young literature, which dishonor us."

At four in the afternoon he was reading a book on Valéry by Professor Mondor, near his desk (on which rested his old and worn Bible, open at Isaiah), when he was seized with a fit of suffocation so violent that his family feared the end had come. But a window was thrown open, and he revived.

Doctors were called. Madame Claudel, his daughter Marie

and his son Pierre were by his side. A little calm returned. Then, at eight, he suffered a new attack of choking, accompanied by intolerable pain. An hour later Canon Sédillère, pastor of Saint-Honoré-d'Eylay, arrived at the boulevard Lannes apartment to find Claudel still sitting in his armchair, wrapped in a crimson dressing gown, and greeting him with a smile, "Oh! I was expecting you. . . ." And he added, "I am not afraid. . . . I have no fear." He confessed with exemplary humility and simplicity, then received Holy Communion so devoutly that the canon, remembering that day, said to me recently, "I envied such piety."

An injection of morphine dulled the pain, but he was clearly dying. Toward midnight he came out of a semicoma to say that he was perfectly lucid, "Leave me, let me die in peace. . . . I am not afraid." At two-forty he breathed his last.

The news was known in Paris during the early hours of a cold and foggy Ash Wednesday, and spread very quickly. It awakened in those who had known Claudel personally a feeling very different from sadness; for they knew how impatiently he had waited for the moment when he would penetrate the mystery, when the veils hiding the truth would be dissolved forever.

On the following day I saw him in his salon, lying on a very low bed, dressed in black, and holding between his hands a rosary which had been presented to him by Pius XII. On his chest had been placed a crucifix given to him by a missionary to China. It was a scene of utter simplicity, devoid of funereal pomp out of respect for that Christian joy which, in Claudel, dominated everything. He would not have tolerated sadness at the time when he saw God face to face. Mademoiselle Claudel said to me, "See how happy he is."

The rites took place at government expense (surprisingly enough, it was not strictly speaking a "state funeral") in the cathedral of Notre-Dame, the scene of his conversion, on Monday, February 28. (On the preceding day the poet's body had been brought to the basilica, and rested in the Sainte-Madeleine chapel, not far from the pillar where he had been struck by Grace.) The winter sun cast a pale light over Paris, and the weather was bitterly cold. A detachment of the Garde républicaine stood outside. In the chancel of the cathedral a huge French flag hung from the vault down to the catafalque. While Canon Sédillère celebrated mass in the presence of Monsignor Marella, the Papal Nuncio, Bach's choral—*La Faute d'Eve*—mingled its tender and repentant effusions to the ancient implorations of the liturgy. Before the prayers of intercession for the deceased, pronounced by Monsignor Marella, the same *Magnificat* Claudel had heard as the very call of the supernatural, on December 25, 1886, was sung by the children of the same choir. Ever since that date he had liked to hear this choir—almost every Sunday whenever he was in Paris—alternating with the singing of the faithful to which he would join his gruff peasant voice.

After the ceremony the procession leaving the cathedral was preceded by halberd-bearers in full regalia. First came Daniel Halévy (who had known Péguy, Claudel and so many others), then François Mauriac (who had welcomed the deceased into the Académie, and represented a slightly younger generation), Georges Lecomte, Robert d'Harcourt, Marshal Juin, Pierre Benoît, Marcel Pagnol, Maurice Garçon, Pasteur Valléry-Radot, Robert Schumann, Albert Sarraut, Pierre Pflimlin and a host of other notables. The entire Claudel family was present, with the grandchildren accompanying their parents.

While the coffin was carried to the cenotaph the strains of the funeral march from Beethoven's *Eroica*, played by the band of the Garde républicaine, rose into the frosty air. A piercing wind whistled through the stands. The first eulogy was delivered in the name of Belgium, by Luc Hommel, who proclaimed his compatriots' admiration and affection for

Claudel, that universal genius. Robert d'Harcourt then spoke for the Académie française and defined in inimitable terms everything which the deceased represented:

> A man of the soil who remained faithful to his land . . . a rough and simple nature, disliking subtleties, complexities and vain human quarrels . . . a gruff and straightforward being whose whole life was filled with the punctual accomplishment of his daily tasks, carried out with the reliability of the sun traveling along its trajectory . . . a hard stone statue amid the contemporary confusion . . . on our course, lookout of the spirit and of faith.

Finally the Minister of National Education, Jean Berthoin, expressed the sentiments of the government and of France, and concluded as follows:

> Between Earth and Heaven, he built a kind of cathedral with unshakable buttresses whose spires, although soaring out of sight, always remain accessible to a movement of the heart. As long as there are men who suffer and hope, they will all meet, be they believers or not, in this sanctuary of invigorating poetry, there to meditate on this eternal truth: every soul which rises, raises the world with it.

On the following September 3, Claudel was buried at Brangues, after a service in the church where the poet had so often come to pray. Cardinal Gerlier (the Primate of France) officiated, assisted by two bishops. In an inspiring address he emphasized the essential unity between the author and the believer for whom the Bible had been the beacon of life. The mayor of Brangues, Marc Mailler, speaking on the church square, called the day an important one in history; a day which would be followed over the years by countless pilgrimages to the grave of the poet. Edouard Herriot, a man of exceptional culture and a friend of the deceased, likened him to another *Aeschylus*, spoke of a lifework comparable to the cathedral of Chartres—with all its stained-glass windows —and expressed his affectionate admiration in this final flight of eloquence:

> Sleep, dear Paul Claudel, in your serene greatness, near this dwelling where you once commented the Apocalypse for me; among those beings created by your mind. Sleep in the bosom of the France you have served so well. Sleep, wrapped in your works, which are truly a Summation. Sleep, you who have broadened human life and thought to match the distant horizons of supernatural Life.

Accompanied by the slow chant of the *De Profundis,* and in the radiant light of the full summer, the procession then started off toward the château and toward that place in the park where the poet had wished to rest. "In Brangues," he had written, "at the end of the park, in the farthest corner of my garden, there is a long poplar slender as a candle; like an act of faith, like an act of love. It is there, in the shadow of an old wall covered with moss and ferns, that I have marked my place. It is there, barely separated from the countryside and its labors, that I shall rest." The grave bears this epitaph:

ICI

REPOSENT LES RESTES

ET LA SEMENCE

DE PAVL CLAVDEL

There was only one oration, that of Jean-Louis Barrault. His words were deeply moving and expressed his sincere fervor and almost filial reverence. Barrault spoke for the world of the theater and for himself:

> [In Claudel], there was never a break between earthly reality and the mystery of God. . . . God and the little grain of sand are closely connected, they hold one another by the hand. . . . Your works are a deep nest in which already three generations have found a haven. . . . Priest and poet have

comparable vocations, since they bring forth the life-giving sap out of the sterility of materialism. . . . Your work is that of a young man. You enlisted in the army of your church without losing any of your lucidity, of your innovating and indeed revolutionary nature. . . . Like a very unhappy little child, I thank you for the real life which you gave me. . . .

Such was the conclusion, the unfolding and the consummation of Claudel's earthly peregrinations. Another life, even here below, was about to begin. But his real existence, which cannot be related, belongs to the secret of souls, and must forever remain largely unknown.

Works of PAUL CLAUDEL

I. THEATER

Tête d'Or; La Ville; La Jeune Fille Violaine, l'Echange; Le Repos du septième jour, l'Agamemnon d'Eschyle (Mercure de France, 4 vol., 1911–1912)
L'Annonce faite à Marie (Nouvelle Revue Française, 1912)
L'Otage (Nouvelle Revue Française, 1911)
Le Pain dur (Gallimard, 1918)
L'Ours et la Lune (Gallimard, 1919)
Le Père humilié (Gallimard, 1920)
Les Choéphores d'Eschyle (Gallimard, 1920)
Les Euménides d'Eschyle (Gallimard, 1920)
Protée, drame satirique (Gallimard, 1920)
Le Soulier de satin (Gallimard, 1920)
Le Livre de Christophe Colomb (Gallimard, 1933)
Jeanne au bûcher (Gallimard, 1939)
La Sagesse ou la Parabole du festin (Gallimard, 1939)
L'Histoire de Tobie et de Sara (Gallimard, 1942)
Le Partage de midi (Mercure de France, 1948)

II. POEMS

Cinq grandes Odes (Nouvelle Revue Française, 1913)
La Cantate à trois voix (Nouvelle Revue Française, 1913)
Corona benignitatis anni Dei (Nouvelle Revue Française, 1915)
La Messe là-bas (Nouvelle Revue Française, 1919)
Ode jubilaire pour le sixième centenaire de la mort de Dante (Art Catholique, 1919)
Poèmes de guerre (Gallimard, 1922)
Feuilles de Saints (Gallimard, 1925)
Cent phrases pour éventails (Gallimard, 1942)
Poèmes et paroles durant la guerre de Trente-Ans (Gallimard, 1945)
Les Sept Psaumes de la Pénitence (Editions de Seuil, 1945)
Visages radieux (Fribourg, Librarie de l'Université de Fribourg, 1947)

III. PROSE

Connaissance de l'Est (Mercure de France, 1900)
Art poétique (Mercure de France, 1907)

L'Oiseau noir dans le soleil levant (Gallimard, 1929)
Conversations dans le Loir-et-Cher (Gallimard, 1929)
Positions et Propositions, 2 vols. (Gallimard, 1928–1934)
Introduction à la peinture hollandaise (Gallimard, 1935)
Figures et Paraboles (Gallimard, 1936)
Contacts et Circonstances (Gallimard, 1940)
L'Œil écoute (Gallimard, 1946)
Du côté de chez Ramuz (Neuchâtel. Ides et Calendes, 1947)
Discours et Remerciements (Gallimard, 1947)
Sous le signe du dragon (Editions de la Table Ronde, 1948)
Accompagnements (Gallimard, 1949)

IV. RELIGIOUS PROSE AND WRITINGS ON THE BIBLE

Le Chemin de la Croix (Art Catholique, 1915)
Ecoute, ma fille (Gallimard, 1934)
Toi, qui es-tu? (Gallimard, 1937)
Introduction au livre de Ruth (Desclée, 1938)
Un Poète regarde la Croix (Gallimard, 1938)
L'Epée et le Miroir (Gallimard, 1939)
Présence et Prophétie (Fribourg, Librairie de l'Université de Fribourg, 1942)
Seigneur, apprenez-nous à prier (Gallimard, 1942)
Introduction à l'Apocalypse (Egloff, 1946)
La Rose et le Rosaire (Egloff, 1946)
Le Livre de Job (Plon, 1946)
Les Révélations de la Salette (Editions de la Table Ronde, 1946)
Paul Claudel interroge le Cantique des Cantiques (Fribourg, 1948)
Emmaüs (Gallimard, 1949)
Une Voix sur Israël (Gallimard, 1950)
L'Evangile d'Isaïe (Gallimard, 1951)
Paul Claudel interroge l'Apocalypse (Gallimard, 1952)